COSMIC
MUSIC

COSMIC
MUSIC

*Musical Keys to the
Interpretation of Reality*

essays by
Marius Schneider
Rudolf Haase
Hans Erhard Lauer

edited, with an Introduction, by
JOSCELYN GODWIN
(Professor of Music, Colgate University)

translated by
MARTON RADKAI
and JOSCELYN GODWIN

INNER TRADITIONS
Rochester, Vermont

Inner Traditions International
One Park Street
Rochester, Vermont 05767

Library of Congress Cataloging-in-Publication Data
Schneider, Marius, 1903–
Cosmic music : musical keys to the interpretation of reality : essays / by
Marius Schneider, Rudolf Haase, Hans Erhard Lauer; edited with an
introduction by Joscelyn Godwin; translated by Marton Radkai and
Joscelyn Godwin.
p. cm.
Includes bibliographies and index.
ISBN 0-89281-070-X
1. Music—Philosophy and aesthetics. 2. Harmony of the spheres.
I. Haase, Rudolph. II. Lauer, Hans Erhard.
III. Godwin, Joscelyn. IV. Title
ML3800.S2588 1987
780'.1—dc19 88-9605
CIP

7/95

This book contains translations of *Die Natur des Lobgesangs,
Klangsymbolik in Fremden Kulturen* © Marius Schneider
*Harmonik und Heile Überlieferung, Fortsetzungen der
Keplerischen Weltharmonik, Keplers Weltharmonik und Ihre
Bedeutung Für Die Gegenwart* © Rudolf Haase
*Mozart und Beethoven im Entwicklungsgang der
Abendländischen Kultur, Die Entwicklung der Musik im
Wandel der Tonsysteme* © Hans Erhard Lauer

Design by Judith Lerner

Printed and bound in the United States

10 9 8 7 6 5 4 3 2

Distributed to the book trade in the United States by American
International Distribution Corporation (AIDC)

Distributed to the book trade in Canada by Publishers Group West
(PGW), Montreal West, Quebec

Distributed to the book trade in the United Kingdom by
Deep Books, London

Distributed to the book trade in Australia by Millennium Books,
Newtown, N. S. W.

CONTENTS

INTRODUCTION

WHAT is the cosmos? Perhaps the word summons up before the mind's eye a vision of dark and terrifying spaces, of dimensions and times surpassing understanding, apparitions of unearthly beauty: cold white galaxies, warmly colored planets, suns without number. It is a place of supreme mystery, where the relative security of earth is left behind, the climate is hostile to every form of life as we know it, and even matter ceases to behave predictably. On its fringes lurk the bizarre imaginings of science fiction, apparently to be gradually realized like a bad dream coming true.

This picture of the cosmos which so many people share today reflects the aspirations and fears of modern humanity at the very end of a world cycle; and like every other epoch, this one has formed its worldview largely in its own image: not in the image of its physical body, but in an image that reflects what it has made of the human mind. Where once gateways opened to the heavens, now there gape black holes, ready to swallow everything into oblivion. Such is the view many people hold of death: a doorway to the extinction of consciousness. Where once the planetary angels guided their astral chariots, now mindless forces propel stars and planets inexorably to their doom. And the creative song or word of God is reduced pitifully to a "big bang."

To the Greeks, the word *kosmos* originally suggested none of these facts or fancies, but rather something orderly, decorative, and neatly arranged. Like many ancient root words, it opens a window onto a very different view of the cosmos: one that revealed it as a divine ornament. The heavens appeared to ancient civilizations as artistically arranged, regular and predictable, pleasing to eye and mind. In Latin the corresponding word *mundus* also carries overtones of cleanliness and elegance, suggesting a state of affairs far different from that of our dirty and disorderly planet. Not only is the universe exactly as it is designed to be, but so beautiful and ingenious a phenomenon can only be the handiwork of a supreme artist. If the cosmos seems hostile to mankind, that is only through special circumstances known to the science of astrology. That it should be hostile to life—as *they* knew it—is absurd. For where could life be more lively, intelligence more keen, than in the rarefied and unconstricting atmosphere of the heavens? Where could one hear music more beautiful than that of the spheres and their guiding angels, the Sirens?

What our difficult and threatening times need, more than anything else, is a revolution in cosmology: a complete revision of the way in which educated people have been trained to regard their cosmic environment. Only after this can those other changes take place on earth for which every responsible person longs. The authors of this book are well aware of this. Each in his own way has made that cosmological revolution, and they invite us to do likewise. But the revolution they propose is even more radical than that of Copernicus, Kepler, and Galileo, which only exchanged one picture for another—the sun-centered for the earth-centered. What is now demanded is that the ear again be given precedence over the usurping eye: that tone, not diagrams or words, be acknowledged again as the truest reflection of reality, and hearing honored as the sense through which we can best learn of its nature.

Every music lover knows intuitively that music embodies a certain truth, but few go so far as to obey this intuition and search for truth by way of music. Most people accept that truth belongs by rights to science, religion, or philosophy, while the arts, vital as they are to a fully human life, are still only matters of opinion and taste. We propose on the contrary to take literally Beethoven's dictum that *"Music is a higher revelation than all wisdom or philosophy."* Accordingly, to penetrate the mysteries of music is to prepare for initiation into those fathomless mysteries of man and cosmos. One's discoveries will be pregnant with implications for every department of life: that much will be plain to anyone who reads these essays.

Our three principal authors are concerned with reviving the ancient discipline of *Musica Speculativa*, of music as a mirror (Latin: *speculum*) held up to reality. Marius Schneider's approach is through re-creating the musical cosmogony of archaic civilizations. Rudolf Haase demonstrates that harmonic principles are empirically present throughout the universe. Hans Erhard Lauer uses music to illuminate and explain the changes that have taken place in the evolution of human consciousness. "Cosmic Music" is their theme, but it can mean different things. For Schneider it is the song with which the gods and primordial man greet the emergence of a new world: a song that resounds through all of creation, planets, animals, plants, and stones, and forms the musical instruments with which individual man responds to it. For Haase, cosmic music is the law of harmonics that prints its signature on all things, recognized in the past by philosopher-scientists such as Pythagoras and Kepler, but needing a veritable new science to recast it for the modern mind. (To supplement Haase's essays, we include the extracts from Johannes Kepler on which they build.) For Lauer, it is the song of the gods in their starry spheres, heard there by archaic man before his descent into the physical body: it is the wellspring of all human music, its expression varying as man journeys through the cycles of world history.

Why should such a book consist entirely of translations from German-speaking authors? One can only answer this question with another: Why do German-speaking composers predominate on classical concert programs? It is simply the case that most current work in speculative music appears in German, whether from Switzerland (Lauer and other anthroposophists), Austria (Haase and his pupils), or Germany itself. Perhaps it is their rich heritage of *musica instrumentalis* that inclines Germans and Austrians to think more musically than other peoples. Perhaps it is the memory of Germanic idealist philosophy that makes their musical Platonism or Pythagoreanism an acceptable stance. Haase can trace his philosophic ancestry through his teacher Hans Kayser to the Pythagorean philologist Albert von Thimus on the one hand, and on the other to the Romantic writers (Novalis, Tieck, Kleist, etc.) and the mystics of the German Renaissance (Paracelsus, Boehme, and Kepler himself). Lauer's leads back through Rudolf Steiner (1861–1925), the founder of Anthroposophy, to Nietzsche, Hegel, and above all to Goethe, within a view of history that regards Central Europe as the current nerve center of human evolution.

Evolutionary nerve center or not, the German background subjected each of these authors to painful personal experience of the crises of the twentieth century. The bare biographical facts are given at the head of each one's essays: here I try to give those bones a more human form.

Lauer, the oldest of the three, suffered directly from both world wars. He tells in his autobiography how he spent most of his military service in the hospital, at first ill from epidemics, then with a shattered femur caused by shrapnel. His father, who had patriotically volunteered for a few months, was mobilized for four and a half years and lost his job, while his mother worked in an office to support her three sons. The Second World War saw Lauer exiled from his home and wife in Vienna, always fearful that his Swiss residence permit would be denied, forcing him to return to a Germany where, as a prominent anthroposophist, he could scarcely expect to survive. Lauer's natal horoscope is in bowl formation, its limits marked by a 2° opposition of Saturn to Pluto, with Mars square to both, the Mars-Saturn square being within 6'. One could scarcely find a more difficult configuration, yet Lauer succeeded in channeling these potentially destructive energies into a life's work that can well be described as a triumph.

Schneider's biography is less fully documented. A native of

Alsace, that disputed territory that is neither French nor German, and, through his comparative studies, a spiritual citizen of the whole world, he must have been appalled by the compulsory patriotism of the Third Reich. One can only imagine his feelings on learning that his doctoral thesis was unacceptable, this judgment being passed by Alfred Rosenberg's ideological headquarters and by Schneider's own Nazi students. (Karl Jaspers was at least gentlemanly in his rejection of Lauer's too anthroposophical thesis). No chance of a university post remained for Schneider under this regime. Then came military service in North Africa, in the same campaign that was to leave Rudolf Haase stranded for three years as a prisoner-of-war. And suddenly, through the good offices of the great scholar-priest, Higinio Anglés, came the summons to Spain, a land where Schneider would find not only support for his researches but also the mute and living survivals of an archaic worldview that was to become peculiarly his own. As a result, his major speculative work (*El Origen musical*...) was published only in Spanish. Probably few of his German colleagues ever explored this vast cosmogonic vision which sustained him until his death, surfacing only fragmentarily in the scholarly writings on which his exoteric reputation was based.

Schneider's horoscope is dominated by a Y-formation: Jupiter square to Uranus within 2', both aspected within a degree by Venus (trine to Uranus, quincunx to Jupiter). The Jupiter-Uranus square encourages expansive visionary schemes that may be brilliant but are often unsound. The Venus aspect is responsible for the poetic quality with which Schneider's system, unlike most of its kind, is imbued. A nearly exact conjunction of Mars with the Dragon's Head (north node of the moon) lends tremendous energy to the central task of his life, aptly pictured in the Sabian Symbol for their common degree (the 12th of Libra): "Miners are emerging from a deep well into the sunlight" (Rudhyar's reading). Schneider digs deep indeed: his mine is the primordial condition of the cosmos, from which he brings forth into the reddening light of dawn the unforgettable image of man uttering the praise song that is at the same time his own self-sacrifice.

It would be impertinent to comment on the life and horoscope of Rudolf Haase, who is still at the peak of his career. But his biography alone is sufficient to illustrate the remarkable ways of providence, which supports the work of all speculative musicians. The prisoners in his POW camp, where, as he says, a high level of intellectual interest prevailed, organized a large-scale exhibition with the motto "Man and Knowledge." Of the 50 displays, one was dedicated entirely to Harmonics, the ancient discipline revived by Hans Kayser (1891–1964), and Haase decided then and there to devote himself to this subject as soon as his academic course was completed. After graduation from the University of Cologne in 1951 he duly entered correspondence with Hans Kayser in Switzerland, who sent him all his books to study, welcomed him as a frequent visitor, and eventually appointed him his biographer. But Haase stayed in Cologne just long enough to meet the other great man of speculative music, Marius Schneider, who in 1952 gave his first seminar on Comparative Musicology there—a seminar which Haase in turn was able to enrich with his own knowledge of Harmonics. In 1963 he was finally able to bring together his two mentors at a congress on symbolism organized by Julius Schwabe in Basel. I do not believe that our three authors were ever in the same room, but I like to think of them that summer in Hans Erhard Lauer's hometown, perhaps standing together innocently at some street corner.

In the remainder of this introduction I will map out some of their intellectual common ground. Speculative music, like any science, makes the same revelations to anyone who works in it sincerely, irrespective of his other persuasions. But whereas the consensus in a haptic science such as biology or chemistry is a superficial one, leaving its deeper assumptions untouched, in speculative music, as in any esoteric study, the case is reversed. All biologists agree as to the observed behavior of organic substances: but the ways in which they define Life, the subject of their science, will vary according to their philosophical or religious convictions. In our science, on the other hand, surface opinions and practices may differ as widely as Western music does from Chinese, yet the principles behind all of them are identical. Consequently one cannot take up this study unless one is ready to assent to these principles, for just the same reason as a materialist or positivist can practice chemistry, but not alchemy.

The first postulate of speculative music immediately sifts the believers from the profane. It is that *sound* (or tone, or music) *is ontologically prior to material existence.* One way of giving assent to this is through recognizing that underlying the apparent solidity of matter there is nothing but a network of vibrations, which may be allegorized—as no doubt they have been since time immemorial—as "sound," the name given to vibrations in the human audible frequency range. However, according to this view none but sound vibrations are actually perceived as sound. Speculative music often goes further and asserts that the whole cosmos is audible in its superior modes of existence, just as heaven and its inhabitants are visible to certain mystics, even when there are no light vibrations striking the eye. The principle is easily grasped by considering the existence of a world of sights and sounds, devoid of a material substratum, that everyone knows in his dreams.

This priority of the sounding cosmos over the visible or material one may be due to the fact that this was its first form of existence, or it may have less to do with precedence in time than with an ever-present hierarchical superiority. Marius Schneider and Hans Erhard Lauer have similar ways of putting it. "The world first created," writes Schneider, "is a pure sound world" (p. 40). He explains that it may contain sounds *as of* rushing water, animal cries, etc., but that these are not the sounds *of* those things, since things do not yet exist. Concrete objects are secondary creations, not causes but consequences of their sounds (p. 59). Any other conception we may form of the primordial world is merely our own

visualization of its pure sound events (p. 60). Hans Erhard
Lauer has precisely the same idea of the tone world as an independent world owing nothing to matter, though he views
it from the opposite side, saying that the natural sounds of
water, wind, animals, etc., are "only a closer or more distant
echo of this tone world" (p. 172).

Schneider does not hesitate to trace the hierarchy of being
still further back, or upward. "In the beginning there was
nothing but an absolute stillness"—by which I understand
him to mean both the state of God before creation, and
its eternal unmanifested self-containment irrespective of
whether there is a cosmos or not. In this silence, says
Schneider, "the first thoughts, inaudible rhythms, arose.
Such rhythms were the model for the coming concrete creation . . . Then the first act took place; and this act was the
utterance of the thought in the form of rhythmical sound . . .
Rhythm is the creator and upholder of the world" (p. 58).
These stages of creation correspond to the successive
"worlds" of every emanational doctrine. We can compare
Schneider's sequence of events to the Plotinian hypostases:

The One	Absolute stillness
Being	"The first thoughts, inaudible rhythms"
Intellect	Rhythm as "creator and upholder of the world"
Soul, Nature	Praise Song, sacrifice
Body	Concrete existence

or to the Four Worlds of the Hebrew Kabbalah:

	En Soph The Unlimited	Silence
1	Azilut World of Emanation	Inaudible rhythms
2	Beriah World of Creation	Rhythmical sound or cry
3	Yezirah World of Formation	Praise Song, sacrifice
4	Asiyyah World of Action	Concrete existence

The Lambdoma diagram, which will be explained by Rudolf Haase (p. 23), represents this ultimate silence, the God
beyond creation, by the symbol o/o which lies outside the
field of manifested tone numbers. As Haase points out, the
lines that join identical tone numbers all meet at this o/o
point.

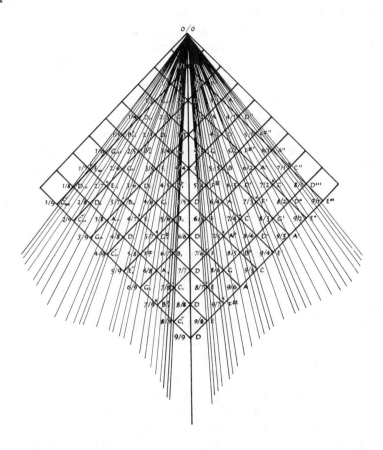

The above version of the Lambdoma (based on one in Hans
Kayser's *Orphikon*, p. 43) is drawn so as to emphasize the
equal tone lines, although to avoid graphic confusion they
are not all prolonged to their source at o/o. The Lambdoma
as filled out here with its tones and numbers is the fruit of a
highly intellectual development, whether ancient Greek (as
von Thimus and Kayser believed) or modern German (as

others claim, attributing it to von Thimus' fertile imagination). Yet Haase's conviction that it is a natural formative law does receive confirmation from the most disparate sources. For example, one could not ask for a better illustration of the picturesque myth recounted by Schneider from the Dogon tribe of West Africa, concerning the genie who creates the world at the dawn of each day (p. 63). Here in the equal tone lines are the threads that grow in a bunch from his throat, and are parted by his teeth at the level of creation, 1/1. With his forked tongue he weaves the diagonal overtone and undertone lines that connect the tone numbers in multifarious ways. For harmonic thought this is no coincidence, but rather evidence that both Lambdoma and African myth depict an actual "norm": an archetypal idea beheld by the authors of both and then elaborated in ways appropriate to each one's culture. Schneider himself says (pp. 43, 59) that the earliest prehistoric symbols — the curves, spirals, etc., of the most ancient art — are attempts to render for the eye those primordial energies that have their being in sound alone.

Schneider's dawn weaver is described as an "ambassador from the creator of the world" (p. 71), a phrase readily associated with Haase's extended comparison of the Lambdoma's symbolism with the attributes of the "King of the World" (i.e., the Demiurge) and his ambassadors (p. 97). Haase's discussion of some ideas of René Guénon and of Antoine Fabre d'Olivet opens a door to connections that deserve to be more fully explored. In his more metaphysical works, especially *The Symbolism of the Cross*, Guénon expounded a geometrical symbolism that corresponds in many ways to Hans Kayser's use of the Lambdoma table. The figure of the cross, of course, underlies the whole Lambdoma as the principle of intersecting tone lines: wherever two lines meet, a tone is born. The fundamental meaning of this figure for Guénon is also the intersection of two principles, a vertical ray with a horizontal plane, that brings a being into existence. But this is only the beginning of a comparison that could well lead to a book on "*Geometrical* Keys to the Interpretation of Reality": for it goes without saying that any of the subjects of the classical and medieval Quadrivium (Arithmetic, Geometry, Music, Astronomy) can be taken as the basis for a complete system of cosmological and metaphysical explanation. The work of Guénon, and more recently that of Keith Critchlow (*The Soul as Sphere and Androgyne*) and Robert Lawlor (*Sacred Geometry*) is a modern re-creation of speculative geometry comparable to the present revival of speculative music.

In the case of Fabre d'Olivet, Haase reminds us of this important member of the chain of Pythagorean philosophers, active in the early years of the nineteenth century (at the very time that Thomas Taylor was introducing Pythagoras, Plato, and their successors to English readers). Fabre d'Olivet shares with harmonicists and anthroposophists alike the view that music played a vital role in the earlier history of man—and not merely in his cultural history, but as a subject inseparable from his worldview and even his politics. "Music," he writes at the beginning of *La musique expliquée . . .* , "envisaged in its speculative part, is, as the ancients defined it, the knowledge of the order of all things, the science of the harmonic relationships of the universe; it rests on immutable principles which nothing can assail."*

The weaving of the creator God or gods is also their song: what Steiner calls "the gods' cosmic music of jubilation, as the expression of their joy at the creation of the world" (p. 178). But he adds that it is also their lament over the possibility of mankind's fall. For as soon as manifestation takes place, duality is born. In the Lambdoma it begins with the innocent twinlike closeness of the first two harmonics 1/2 and 2/1, sounding harmonious octaves above and below the originating 1/1 note. But the lines thus generated will spread indefinitely to become the opposites of good and evil between which the whole world conflict is played out. The Pythagoreans are reported variously as having attributed evil to the number 2 and to ∞: it comes to the same thing, for both

* For more on Guénon and Fabre d'Olivet in relation to music, see my *Harmonies of Heaven and Earth* and my English translation of Fabre d'Olivet's *Music Explained as Science and Art* (Inner Traditions, 1987, 1988).

both are in a sense "opposites" to the initial 1/1. The whole Lambdoma is constructed from the opposition of two series of tone numbers (the overtones and undertones), and it can be used to illustrate more than one theory of the nature of evil. Rudolf Haase has a very interesting passage on the subject (p. 103f.) in which he uses it to demonstrate that good and evil, while complementaries, are not equals.

  The primordial world of Schneider (and the reader should note that this plethora of "primordials" is only an English approximation to the German philosopher's favorite prefix, Ur-) is of the essence of time. "The primordial world knows no space at all, but exists strictly in time; hence such expressions as the cavity, egg, or head at the beginning of all things should not be considered as concrete objects, but as figurative expressions for wholly abstract functions" (p. 40). While Schneider moves easily among abstractions, Hans Erhard Lauer treats the same stages of metaphysical descent as definite periods of cosmic or human history. His information comes from Rudolf Steiner's clairvoyant reading of the cosmic memory or Akashic Chronicle, one of the pillars of anthroposophical teaching. Lauer also describes primordial man before speech even existed as singing a "wordless primordial song" (p. 177), but it is as a member of the Lemurian Root Race, the first of humanity to incarnate in quasi-physical bodies during the period called by geologists the Tertiary Era. Now to sing is to surrender one's breath, that is, one's life. Schneider makes us well aware that the law of all incarnate life is self-sacrifice, performed willingly or unwillingly in that one either accepts "singing death" as the companion of life, or else has to be dragged to it ignobly protesting (p. 66f.). And though Lauer does not have cause to mention it here, Rudolf Steiner also taught that death began for mankind only in the Lemurian Period.

  Many esoteric doctrines teach that ever since the time of his incarnation, man has progressively lost his original, spiritual perception. Schneider says that this has worked to divorce both music and language from the natural harmonies and rhythms (p. 66) which, we will recall, were and remain the primordial condition of all things. One result of this obscuration is the invention of conceptual thought and logical language; another, the acquisition of the hard physical skeleton (p. 69). Anthroposophists agree in regarding the human bone structure as quite a late development. (This explains why there are no human remains to be found in the Tertiary fossil beds.) And the dawning of a clear but deceptive day which Schneider so beautifully describes is exactly parallel to Steiner's more literal account of how the mists that shrouded the earth in the Lemurian Period gradually cleared during the succeeding Atlantean Period, enabling Paleolithic man to see the stars—whose gods he had formerly known so much more intimately through supersensible perception.

Distrust or rejection of daylight is a favorite theme of German Romanticism that runs from Novalis' *Hymn to the Night*, through the nocturnal second act of Wagner's *Tristan und Isolde*, to its more sinister appearances in the mythology of national socialism. For it is easy to take a wrong turn and to mistake the chthonic darkness of pure matter, greedy for annihilation, for that other one, the thrice-unknown darkness of Orphic theology, from whose point of view there never was or is anything to annihilate. Thus the Nazi ideologue Alfred Rosenberg could believe himself a disciple of the medieval mystical theologian Meister Eckhart, the greatest German exponent of the *via negativa*.

The Lambdoma makes the difference between these two darknesses quite clear. The one which is dark through excess of light is o/o. For most individuals, represented by the different tone numbers or "values of being," this is reached only by way of the spiritual sun which is $1/1$, and its avatars $2/2$, $3/3$, etc. The chthonic darkness, on the other hand, lies at the very extreme of manifestation: it is the limit represented by numbers of the form ∞/n or n/∞. As René Guénon explains it in *The Reign of Quantity*, this is the extreme of pure quantity totally devoid of quality: of matter totally devoid of spirit. It can have no real existence, but it seems to draw all things either to total solidification (∞/n, the infinite lump of matter) or to total dissolution (n/∞, infinite fragmentation).

Schneider's vision of cosmic and human descent, reached through his meditations on the Vedas, so much resembles Lauer's, reached through the clairvoyant perceptions of Rudolf Steiner (if not also through his own), that one suspects some central core of truth underlying both. This would be on the level of metahistory or "hierohistory," the term coined by Henry Corbin for the sacred history that bears the same relationship to historical events as does cosmic to practical music.

All our authors agree that even in historical times man has suffered further separation from the spiritual and alienation from the cosmic order of which, in all but his highest self, he is a member. Even Rudolf Haase, though not inclined to Theosophy or Anthroposophy, shares this attitude, expressed through the Hindu doctrine of the four Yugas or world ages: the first a legendary Golden Age, the last (our own), an Age of Iron (p. 105). Catastrophes mark the downward path of man in all traditional cosmogonies, such as the volcanic fires that destroyed Lemuria and the flood that ended the Atlantean Period, according to the Akashic Chronicle. But the Catholic Schneider blames them all on the "refusal to sacrifice" (SS, 17) by gods and men, whereas for the Anthroposophist they are seen rather as ending inevitable periods in man's evolutionary progress.

Here we must touch on a fundamental difference between Schneider and the Harmonicists on the one hand, and Lauer and the Anthroposophists on the other. Schneider's philosophical range is metaphysical in the strictest sense, whereas all of Lauer's realities are actualized (even if their actuality is that of the astral plane). Nor does Lauer conceive of humanity as existing outside temporal evolution. Hence his idea of the goal of man is quite different from Schneider's negative way. Lauer speaks of the necessity to bring to birth the "I" (pp. 158, 163) and to take the step from ordinary consciousness on the soul level to a higher consciousness whose vehicle is the spirit, man's innermost nature (p. 172). For him this is the task of Western civilization, and it could not have been achieved ever before. Therefore he says that the "general return toward the spirituality of the ancient Orient . . . in answer to the need to escape the materialism and egotism of Western civilization . . . cannot truly further evolution because [it denies or abandons] what made that evolution effective: the unfolding human *I* (individuality). Rather than extinguishing it, it would be better to develop it further, to enable it to conquer its entanglement with subjectivity and to find in itself again the spiritual world from which it once emerged" (p. 216). For Schneider, on the other hand, the whole spirit world, even though filled with the rhythms of creation, is already a deception, a *Maya*, "because for ancient Indian philosophy *the ultimate truth is not sound, but silent nothingness and the complete absence of concepts and form*" ((p. 42; my italics). And later, "The praise song is the highest conceivable form of sacrifice, because the sound sacrifice means, beyond any material sacrifice, the offering of the Word. The only higher level is the triumph over death by entrance into the *nothingness that protects one from all rebirth* . . ." (p. 50; my italics). Employing the symbolic language of Harmonics, we can say that Lauer is not concerned with o/o; whereas for the primordial tradition this ultimate reality both of the cosmos and of the human being is attainable by individual men or women at no matter what stage of collective evolution (or devolution): indeed, this potential is what defines humanity. As Schneider says, echoing the teachings of Hinduism, Buddhism, and the Orphics, such attainment liberates a person from the necessity for further rebirth.

But from the musical pont of view o/o is silence, hence beyond consideration, whereas music is the reminder of man's place as he is repeatedly incarnated in the cosmic community. As Schneider says, referring in harmonic terms to the level 1/1 regarded as the higher self of man: "this inner center of man is a cosmic center, not an individual, personal one. Achieving this center presupposes depersonalization, and nothing stands more in the way of the realization of this *conditio sine qua non* than the individualism through which the European mystic of romantic stamp turns away so consciously from the community" (p. 51); I should add that he also includes modern orientalizing mystics in this censure, and that he is not speaking in a narrow social sense but in that of the "so-called world and life community ... founded on the assumption that acoustic rhythm is the primordial ground and meeting point for all beings" (p. 81). It is precisely rhythm, says Schneider, that links the microcosm to the macrocosm (p. 57); "singing and hearing represent the most refined forms of higher cognition" (p. 56). For Haase the discipline of Harmonics reveals nature's norms, structures, forms, and goals (p. 92), i.e., it puts us in touch with the unfallen condition of things as they were designed by an intelligence we may call God (p. 93). The natural sciences that attempt to understand this design through quantitative methods will never come as near the truth as Harmonics, which deals not merely with quantities (numbers) but also with qualities (tones), moreover linking the two domains inseparably through the tone numbers of the Lambdoma. Lauer refers to a cognate idea in mentioning the possibility of a "qualitative mathematics" (p. 170), which George Adams and other anthroposophists were to follow in their development of projective geometry, and which is another facet of the modern revival of the Quadrivium alluded to above.

Music is the archetype of the cosmic order, and as such "the most genuine expression of a world restored" (p. 67), but this holds good only "so long as it has not fallen victim to a chaotic way of thinking" (p. 58). In Schneider's Basel address he mentions the "subhuman forms that [man] has assumed that have descended into the grotesque" (p. 36). Lauer is more explicit: "the characteristic healing power of music has been increasingly crippled in recent times" (p. 166), so that many have "lost the desire even to listen to music owing to the sheer strident noise of the era of extreme materialism (p. 219). And Haase speaks of the "catastrophic narrowing of our field of vision" (p. 91) by philosophic positivism and materialism. He points out that as soon as man ceased to trust the intuitive knowledge that formerly enabled him to create in accord with the harmonic nature of things, the traditional foundations of music were replaced with "increasingly new-fangled, clever, intellectual schemes, causally rather than teleologically generated. No wonder that music then became incomprehensible to an increasing degree" (p. 123). So what is the solution to our predicament at the end of the twentieth century?

Haase finds one answer in the revaluation of Johannes Kepler: an empirical scientist of the highest stature who was nevertheless free from the false worldview that seemed by the end of his century (the seventeenth) to be the unavoidable concomitant of scientific progress. Kepler's contributions to physical science were in fact only secondary effects of his primary concern with cosmic harmony (p. 119): a scale of values which perfectly reflects the ontological primacy of tone over matter, even of music over mathematics (p. 124). All our authors share this scale of values, Haase making bold to say that "not only is Kepler's harmonic world image correct in every respect, but also . . . further pursuit and elaboration of his methods and perspectives permit a truly all-encompassing worldview to emerge" (p. 126). Haase has taken on the courageous role of a preacher to unconverted, presenting to his academic colleagues irresistible evidence for regarding the cosmos as primarily a harmony. Unfortunately, "scientific" evidence carries little weight when to accept it also implies the acceptance of an "all-encompassing worldview" which has such deep metaphysical and ethical consequences. Such evidence is mainly going to confirm the expectations of those who have already accomplished this change in themselves. In this respect Haase's arguments rather resemble the proofs of God of scholastic philosophy — to which in fact he contributes another one (p. 93) — which surely never changed anyone's life. Kepler's own conversion came through his early vision of the harmonious relationships between the spheres, long before he achieved empirical proof of them. It seems that Haase, too, underwent an initiatory experience in his youth (taking place, appropriately enough, in Egypt, where Pythagoras before him had journeyed in search of a more ancient wisdom than his native land could provide), long before establishing the new science of "research in harmonic principles".

Schneider and Lauer make no such claims to be scientific in the technical sense of the word. Schneider is a highly regarded scholar, of course, but one who has succeeded, with almost incredible sleight of hand, in presenting a spiritual worldview under the guise of the scholarly discipline of ethnomusicology. His message in these essays is that the dimension of the sacred, so notably absent from our present world, is attainable especially through the experience of tone, its first creation: thus he asks us above all to listen. Lauer differs from the others in already addressing a group with very particular convictions—the Anthroposophists. His musical writings, impressive as they are, retire into the background when seen in perspective against his work as a whole, in which the major themes of anthroposophic Christianity and the evolution of thinking are paramount. Nevertheless, I feel it is important to make them available to a wider audience because anthroposophic attitudes toward music—as to education, agriculture, politics, and much else—are of great value even to those who do not embrace those larger dogmata. Eventually every universal system has to be weighed against other universal systems, and this collection gives, in its limited way, just such an opportunity.

As concerns the present state of music, the hope of the Harmonicist must be for a new recognition of the cosmic laws. Hans Kayser himself was active as a composer throughout his life, though his works, which certainly applied harmonic principles, are as yet unpublished. The only well-known composer who was at all influenced by him was Paul Hindemith, whose opera about Kepler, *The Harmony of the World*, and whose system of relative consonance and dissonance based on the harmonic series already betray leanings in this direction. Yet although he corresponded briefly with Kayser (see R. Haase, *Paul Hindemiths Harmonikale Quellen*), his interest in Harmonics was practical rather than speculative. He was intrigued, for example, by whether two themes could be linked by harmonic methods. In fact, when the two men met they talked mainly about their model railroads, and Hindemith eventually alienated Kayser by never publicly mentioning him, at a time when a word from a famous composer would have been a real encouragement to the obscure theorist.

What Harmonics does offer to a modern composer is a firm reason, beyond the vicissitudes of fashion, for holding fast to tonality and to the hierarchy of consonance. It explains *why* atonal and serial compositions are so unattractive to most musical people: it is because they are based on artificial principles, divorced from the harmonic laws of creation, with which the human soul can have nothing in common. More positively, in accepting the inaudible undertone series as complementary to the audible overtone one, Harmonics suggests new possibilities for tonal structure and contrast that might replace the old dialogue between tonic and dominant which sustained Western music for three hundred years but is now thoroughly exhausted. Moreover, it gives every encouragement to experiments that go beyond the tyranny of equal temperament, for the harmonic series itself has no two intervals alike. Hans Erhard Lauer touches on this in his acceptance of the unequal but harmonically derived modes proposed by Kathleen Schlesinger in her book *The Greek Aulos*. Though her theory is generally discredited as history, the subtleties of these modes and their intervals remain as a harmonically valid and unexplored resource, and one which, almost impossible to realize on existing instruments, would particularly lend itself to generation by computer. Composition according to the principles of Harmonics, in short, would neither compel one to sound like another second-rate Hindemith, nor restrict one to the incestuous play of the "twelve notes related only to one another," nor force one into the harmonic blandness of current postmodernism.

Hans Erhard Lauer anticipates some of these possibilities with his sympathy for the microtonal explorations of the Czech composer Alois Hába (whom he knew in Prague). This, together with his openmindedness toward the serialists Hauer, Schoenberg, and Webern, is the consequence of the evolutionary scheme, first outlined by Rudolf Steiner in 1923, that Lauer makes the backbone of his long essay. According to this, the human race has lived musically in the experience of intervals that have decreased progressively from ones larger than the octave in the Lemurian Period to the tones, semitones, and even microtones of today. The end point of this progression, says Steiner, will be a new experience of the unison. Therefore music which exploits the sound of the smallest intervals could be regarded as furthering this goal, though Lauer's sympathy for the atonal school is unusual among Anthroposophists.

I do not know what credence to give to this theory of interval experiences. Historically it is true that the feeling for what interval constitutes a consonance (i.e., a satisfactory point of musical repose) has moved from the octave, fifth, and fourth (the only "perfect" consonances of Greek and medieval theory), through the thirds and sixths in the common practice period (1600–1900), to the whole tone (e.g., in Debussy), and finally to the semitone, major seventh, and tritone. But acceptance of the latter intervals as "consonances" inevitably marks the dissolution of the whole harmonic hierarchy as the human ear perceives it (see pp. 39, 40), which is certainly not Lauer's desire any more than it is the Harmonicists'. The French writer Albert Roustit, in his book on musical prophecy, sees this exhaustion of the interval series as a clear indication that the end of our world is at hand. In fact this dissolution did occur (in the freely atonal works of Schoenberg) only a few years before the political rule of the proletariat was first established by the Russian Revolution of 1917, similarly dissolving the entire social hierarchy—which was to be replaced in the 1920s, at the same time as Schoenberg was inventing the twelve-tone system, with the purely manmade system of "communist" bureaucracy. Those who believe that life imitates art will find this a satisfying parallel; the principle is inherent in Steiner's and Lauer's analysis of human evolution *through* (i.e., to a large extent by means of) interval experience. But the explanation probably lies in some sinister event in the "hierohistorical" dimension—a veritable War in Heaven—which our century has seen reflected in every field of activity.

The deeper currents of history are also the subject of Lauer's essay on "Mozart and Beethoven," which is included here to show how one who thinks in cosmic terms—that is, in terms which refer to more than earthly realities—approaches practical music and its creators. Speculative music alone is not enough for Lauer: I doubt that it is enough for anyone today. The Platonic Ideas with which it deals have to be incarnated in the *musica instrumentalis* which the theorists of antiquity could afford to despise, but which, as he says (p. 166), is the very lifeblood of a civilization in thrall to materialistic thinking. Lauer suggests that when, as in the eighteenth and nineteenth centuries, divine revelation no longer took place via the channels of traditional religion, the task of bringing the heavenly down to earth fell to composers. By this means, the great number of sensitive and intelligent people who could no longer recognize the sacred behind the trappings of exoteric Christianity were still enabled to know an immaterial realm, and to encounter there certain archetypal figures and truths of the cosmos.

Yet why, against the background of those cosmic laws, need music itself ever have descended to that "Prometheanism" which Lauer so penetratingly shows as the archetype behind Beethoven's life and work? Why set itself such problems that it needs a Fifth Symphony to work them out, or that find their resolution in the Bacchic craziness of the classical finale (be it that of *The Magic Flute* or of the Ninth Symphony), instead of in the peace that surpasses understanding?

Such heretical questions are bound to arise when one reads Schneider, who has evidently passed through the experience of Western classical music to quite another conclusion. In his article "On Gregorian Chant and the Human Voice" he calls the religious music of the eighteenth and nineteenth centuries "a splendid but entangled path full of obstacles born out of egocentricity, which is the source of its most inspired melodic lines. One needs only to cast a glance at the triumphal way of the liturgical [i.e., plainchant] *Te Deum* and the magnificent but tormented shortcut of the Latin version of Handel's *Dettingen Te Deum* to see the difference" (pp. 10 f.). And one wonders about Schneider's attitude to the piano, which he studied seriously for years, when he writes of the "insolent lie" (p. 77) of playing without respect for the "singing dead" whose bodies have provided one's instrument. Surely the mechanistic piano and its virtuoso repertory are the antithesis of the sacral and sacrificial approach to music which he admires in primitive cultures. Yet "through music making one sets out on the path that leads to participation . . . at the river of cosmic rhythm. And even if one does not reach the ultimate goal, i.e., the completely empty form, by this kind of musical meditation, not the completely empty form, one nevertheless senses through the sound the nature of this ideal, most subtle and fluid filling of the empty rhythmic form by sound" (p. 75). These empty forms, as he has made clear, are nothing less than the gods themselves. And although in our time, long after the dawn of creation, music has become a conscious, manmade art, "the material that it uses remains the sound that reaches deep into our dark subconscious" (p. 84).

I imagine that Schneider might have found some common ground with the American composer, astrologer, and speculative musician Dane Rudhyar, who describes his musical ideal in *The Magic of Tone and the Art of Music* in such terms as "holistic resonance" and "pleromas of sound," and characterizes each culture cycle as having its characteristic tone that both molds and constricts its psychic space. (Perhaps Lauer's interval experiences have to do with these same tones.) But from the point of view that Schneider represents, the development of Western man since the Renaissance has simply "distract[ed] him from his metaphysical mission, reducing him to terrestrial positivism and an erroneous over-evaluation of his personal capacities" ("On Gregorian Chant," p. 10). It might better not have happened at all: liberation was already within man's reach. And whatever *Maya* is woven in earthly time, the spheres sing on undisturbed in their region of perpetual certitude.

Although complete in itself, this book is part of a larger movement that seeks to deepen and broaden the current understanding of what music is, and what it can be. Several books in English have appeared recently with the same intention, such as Dane Rudhyar's *The Magic of Tone and the Art of Music* (Boulder, Colo., and London, Shambhala, 1982), and David Tame's *The Secret Power of Music* (Wellingborough, England, Turnstone Press, 1984). More particularly, this collection of essays should be grouped with the English translations of Hans Kayser's *Akróasis: the Theory of World Harmonics* (Boston, Plowshare Press, 1970), Peter Michael Hamel's *Through Music to the Self* (Tisbury, England, Compton Press, 1978), and Rudolf Steiner's *The Inner Nature of Music and the Experience of Tone* (Spring Valley, N.Y., Anthroposophic Press, 1983) in giving access to a lively world of ideas current today in German-speaking countries but almost totally unknown to our musicologists and philosophers. This collection also forms part of my own threefold effort in this direction, with its companions *Music, Mysticism and Magic: a Sourcebook* (London and Boston, Routledge and Kegan Paul, 1986) and *Harmonies of Heaven and Earth* (London, Thames and Hudson; Rochester, Vt., Inner Traditions, 1987).

I am very grateful to Frau Marta Lauer, to Frau Birgit Schneider, and to Professor Rudolf Haase for permission to publish these essays, and to Christopher Bamford, President of the Lindisfarne Press, for his vision and support.

JOSCELYN GODWIN

Works cited in the Introduction

Critchlow, Keith, *The Soul as Sphere and Androgyne*, Ipswich, Golgonooza Press, 1980.

Fabre d'Olivet, Antoine, *La Musique expliquée comme science et comme art*, Paris, Pinasseau, 1928.

Guénon, René, *The Reign of Quantity and the Signs of the Times*, trans. Lord Northbourne, London, Luzac, 1953.

——, *The Symbolism of the Cross*, trans. Angus Macnab, London, Luzac, 1958.

Haase, Rudolf, ed., *Paul Hindemiths Harmonikale Quellen—Sein Briefwechsel mit Hans Kayser*, Vienna, Lafite, 1973.

Kayser, Hans, *Akróasis: The Theory of World Harmonics*, trans. Robert Lilienfeld, Boston, Plowshare Press, 1970.

——, *Orphikon: Eine harmonikale Symbolik*, ed. Julius Schwabe, Basel, Schwabe, 1973.

Lawlor, Robert, *Sacred Geometry, Philosophy and Practice*, London, Thames and Hudson, 1982.

Roustit, Albert, *La Prophétie Musicale dans l'histoire de l'humanité*, Paris, Horvath, 1970.

Rudhyar, Dane, *The Astrology of Personality*, Wassenaar, Servire, 1963.

——, *The Magic of Tone and the Art of Music*, Boulder, Colo., and London, Shambhala, 1982.

Schlesinger, Kathleen, *The Greek Aulos*, London, Methuen, 1939.

Schneider, Marius, *El Origen musical de los animales simbolos en la mitologia y la escultura antiguas*, Barcelona, Instituto Español de Musicologia, 1946.

——, "On Gregorian Chant and the Human Voice," in *World Music*, vol. 24, no. 3 (1982), pp. 3–21.

Steiner, Rudolf, *The Inner Nature of Music and the Experience of Tone*, ed. Alice Wulsin, trans. Maria St. Goar, Spring Valley, N.Y., Anthroposophic Press, 1983.

——, *Cosmic Memory: Prehistory of Earth and Man*, trans. K. E. Zimmer, Englewood, N.Y., Rudolf Steiner Publs., 1959.

MARIUS
SCHNEIDER

MARIUS SCHNEIDER was born July 1, 1903 in Hagenau, Germany (now Haguenau, France), the child of Alphons Schneider, an hotelier, and Josephine Schneider, née Geiger. From 1919–24 he attended the Conservatory of Strasbourg and passed his examination in piano. From 1924–27 he was at the University of Paris, concurrently studying piano with both Philippe and Alfred Cortot. From 1927–30 he attended the University of Berlin, graduating as a Doctor of Philosophy in 1930 with a dissertation on "*Ars nova* of the Fourteenth century in France and Italy." From 1930–39 he was assistant to Erich van Hornbostel at the Phonogrammarchiv of the Museum of Ethnology in Berlin, and from 1933 he was head of its archive, making transcriptions of over 1000 phonograph records which remain unpublished. During this period he also studied piano with A. Liebermann, musicology in London and Oxford, and native music in Africa. In 1934 his *Habilitationsschrift* for the University of Berlin was denied because his thesis on the history of Gregorian chant was unacceptable to the Nazi authorities. It was published (*Geschichte der Mehrstimmigkeit*, 2 vols., Berlin, 1934–35), however, and accepted by the University of Cologne in 1955.

From 1940–43 he was recruited by the German Foreign Office and the D.K.W. (Supreme Command of Armed Forces) for radio broadcasts and POW work in North Africa. In 1943, thanks to the influence of Higinio Anglés, he was invited by the Spanish government to establish an institute for musical folklore. In 1944 he founded, and headed until 1951, the Ethnology Department of the Instituto Español de Musicología, Barcelona, working concurrently as Professor of Musicology at the University of Barcelona (1947) and with UNESCO (1948). In 1951 he returned to the Federal Republic of Germany. In 1955 he married Birgit Siller and joined the music faculty of the University of Cologne, also heading the department of musical ethnology at the Musicological Institute there as

Professor from 1966 until his retirement in 1968.

Marius Schneider wrote five books and over a hundred articles. For his bibliography, see Robert Günther's article on him in *The New Grove's Dictionary of Music and Musicians*, supplemented by Günther's "Special Bibliography: Marius Schneider," in *Ethnomusicology*, vol. 13 (1969), pp. 518–26. At his death in 1982 he left a great deal of material on the cosmogony which had occupied him for forty years, and it is hoped that this will be published in due course under the direction of Birgit Schneider. [Sources: *MGG*; *New Grove*; Birgit Schneider.]

"The Nature of the Praise Song" was first published as *Die Natur des Lobgesangs*, no. 2 of *Basilienses de Musica Orations* (Basel, Bärenreiter, 1964). "Acoustic Symbolism in Foreign Cultures" was first published as *Klangsymbolik in Fremden Kulturen*, no. 11 of *Beiträge zur harmonikalen Grundlagenforschung*, edited with an introduction by Rudolf Haase (here omitted) and published by the Hans-Kayser-Institut für harmonikale Grundlagenforschung of the Vienna Hochschule für Musik und darstellende Kunst (Vienna, Verlag Elisabeth Lafite, 1979). A version of this work was given in the form of three talks on Austrian radio in August 1973.

The Nature of the
Praise Song

SURELY one of the greatest errors commited by nine-teenth-century religious historians and their successors was the attempt to explain the origin of religious feeling as lying primarily in the human fear of natural forces and to consider supplication, consequently, as the actual core of the relationship between gods and man. Theologians have always disputed this on the basis of their tradition, and the thorough researches of nontheologians have at least shown that such a view reduces the multifaceted and subtle phenomenon of the religious to an expression so coarse that its true content can no longer be adequately evaluated. It is like explaining the phenomenon of the love a woman feels for a man, that is so closely related to the religious, as a mere feeling of defenselessness in life's struggles. In both cases the situation is too complex to be resolved by means of simple utilitarian thought.

Fearful pleading certainly plays an important role in the realm of religion. If fear of life were the true basis of religious feeling, however, our century surely would be the most pious of all time. Fear characterizes both love and man's reverence for God only insofar as in the depths of this phenomenon what one loves is also feared. It is obvious that this irrational fact, independent of the antinomy of feelings, remained beyond the reach of the basically suspicious "rational experts" (as Alfons Rosenberg called them) of the past century. Yet what primarily binds love and religion together so intimately is in their common assumption: the ability to trust.

Three great currents of religous feeling seem to flow from this trust on which all man's dignity is based: the first, to a certain extent feminine, grows from a need for protection; the second, masculine, manifests itself in praise and reward; and the third, common to both, in thanksgiving. All three aspects naturally exist in each person, although one may prevail over the other. Religiosity and love are so closely linked that grieving for love and religious mourning as protection for the souls of the dead have always been mainly the duty of women, whereas the song of praise — whether of the lover or of God — has been principally assumed by men. Without confusing the terms, therefore, we can speak of the act of love within religion, and of the religious character of love. The actual connecting element, that is, the *religio*, is gratitude. Naturally this is only true on condition that, despite the spirit of our time, we emphasize the dignity to which man is born, rather than those subhuman forms he has assumed that have descended into the grotesque.

The facts show that praise and glorification, the specific act of love in religion, are at least as important and emphasized as supplication. Of course the vast hymn literature could be perceived as ultimately designed by poets for the deliberate flattery of the gods. One might ask, though, whether this facile assumption does not contain a serious error in logic. In any event, such an assessment of the praise-giver necessitates pointing out another, somewhat embarrassing dimension, arising from the relationship between the researcher himself and his object. As a rule, omniscience and the ability to see all are ascribed to the highest God, or the most important of gods. The deception of God by hypocrisy, therefore, is practically impossible, and by its very nature irreligious. One cannot deny that such purely self-serving attempts are still being made. However, well-documented discoveries of attempted deception do not constitute a specific character trait of religious feeling, but an overt error which transgresses the highest principle: God's omniscience. Of course, documents are vital for research, but they can only serve as evidence if they are evaluated with the correct assumptions.

As far as the emphasis on goals is concerned, in all religions, at all times (and the same applies to researchers) there have been those who are inspired by a utilitarian idea, and others who are spontaneously enthusiastic about a higher meaning of life. Here objective research fails, simply because of its own uncontrolled human assumptions. Yet the worldwide notion of sacrifice proves how intrinsic spontaneous giving and praise is to the nature of things. Acknowledging that the ability to sacrifice forms man's greatest power is often easier for those living in more primitive circumstances than for modern urban dwellers. But this in no way alters the fact that the start of every true advance must be accompanied by a readiness for sacrifice and involvement. In addition, one must also have the capability fully and willingly to acknowledge something greater than oneself. Naturally, both irreligious primitive man as well as the modern researcher can also consider the sacrifice as a kind of bribery of God, but this overlooks the fact that the sacrifice is not merely a material offering but is primarily a spiritual and vocal process. As we shall see, it is ultimately a sound sacrifice, a song by which man surrenders his word, which is his innermost substance.

In order to understand this better, we must realize that song, according to the ancient concept, did not accompany the sacrifice but in fact formed the core of the sacrificial process. The *Shatapatha Brâhmana* and *Taittirîya Brâhmana* say explicitly that the powerful Asuras (the fallen gods) lost their war against the much weaker gods of light only "because they sacrificed in their own mouths."[1] The Asuras knew the mechanism of the sound sacrifice just as well as the gods. Their fall was brought about by the fact that "they did not sing the holy formulae in truth, but with pride."[2]

In the total religious phenomenon, three spiritual attitudes are always interlinked: first, that of the person who is innately prepared to admire and revere the greater; second, that of a being who is thankful from his innermost nature; and third, that of the eternal beggar. None of these three attitudes is especially primitive or culturally advanced: they exist everywhere and at all times. Irreligiosity, however, is not the product of a higher spiritual evolution but of a disposition that can also be found at all times. Yet one cannot deny that in some religions fear manifests itself so blatantly that the irreligious researcher sees nothing more than this facade. Within these walls, though, praise is still valued as the true power, indeed, as the actual sacrificial power, because it is the most productive. In the Vedic tradition, it is no accident that praise stands at the head of the creation myths.

In the *Brihadâranyaka Upanishad* we read the following account: "At the beginning there was nothing here, for this world was shrouded in death and hunger, for death is hunger. He then created the *Manas* (will for existence), for he desired to be a (physical) self. He was transformed while singing praises; because he sang praises, water appeared, for he spoke: 'Because I sang praises (*ark*), I became joyful (*ka*).' This is the essence of light (*arka*), for the light is water. What had been the cream in the water was curdled. Thus the earth arose. He thereby grew tired. Because he grew tired, he grew hot, because his strength and his juice became fire."[3]

Before analyzing this account in detail, we should remember that what resounds at the beginning of all things is a praise song. This song represents the first sacrifice. The *Rigveda* says: "First the gods created the song, then *Agni*, then the dispenser of sacrifice."[4] In the *Shatapatha Brâhmana* it says: "Whatever the gods do, they do by song. The song is the sacrifice."[5] All things are summoned by this praise song and encouraged to come joyfully into being. The Sanskrit word for singing praise, *ark*, signifies in the Vedic vocabulary the equivalent of "to achieve, swell, or let something grow through song."[6]

One can see that the whole creation begins to a certain extent on an almost purely psychological plane. The praise song, that inner preparedness to acknowledge and stimulate things by praise, is the power from which everything later arises: joy, water, earth, and fire. Sound is the basic matter of the primordial world. Praise is the dynamics of this sound.

To understand correctly the position of the praise song as a primordial phenomenon and later as a ritual event, we must occupy ourselves a little more closely with the nature of the process of creation.

If the beginning of all things is not directly portrayed as the product of a sound (*Nada* or the syllable *AUMm*), then the discussion generally centers on an egg, cave, or Brahma's head, in other words, a primordial resonating body from which the first sonorous energy springs. The true creative force, however, is always *vâc*, *vox* in Latin: the voice. But though *vâc* is the actual creator of all things, she does not represent the absolute "Good" and the "True," but something neutral that must first be given a specific direction by *manas*. Thus the voice alone is sometimes compared to a lightheaded woman, but one who is nevertheless indispensable, because without her no creative rhythm can be made to sound.

The resonating body (cavern, egg, or mouth) from which *vâc* flows forth is the archetype of the three central life organs that still formed a single indivisible entity in the primordial era. It is the shared point of departure of the mouth, the heart, and the womb. In this empty resonating cavity, which can significantly enough also be replaced by the image of hunger or a yawning mouth, the vacuum also operates as an attractive and productive eruptive force. The first act of creation to issue from this hungry cavity is the voice, which creates all things in their primal form as pure acoustic rhythms, or, as the literature generally says, as meters or names. Obviously these names have nothing in common with those designations that various languages give to objects. The first names are the rhythms that constitute the essence of created things. They form the primordial substance of every object, and thus also form the core of its being when in the course of creation the objects have become concretized or even silent.

The primordial world knows no space at all, but exists

strictly in time; hence such expressions as the cavity, egg, or head at the beginning of things should not be considered as concrete objects, but as figurative expressions for wholly abstract functions. The world first created is a pure sound world. The *Atharvaveda* expressly states that *kâla*, time, is the primordial form of creation. By her magic incantation she has created all that is and that is to come.[7] If the primordial sound is the "word" or the praise song of the creator, then the individual rhythms of time arising from that word are the word or the primordial acoustic matter of every created object.

With regard to a person in the concrete sense, however, this word not only reveals itself in the fact that he speaks and that his body is molded according to the model of his primordial acoustic rhythm. It also manifests itself in each of his productions. Thus, for example, a basket that he has woven is his word, just as much as a promise he has given. The actual core of the creative individual and his power to create is still the primordial acoustic matter whose power of praise brings things into existence. This word can even reach far beyond his physical boundaries, inasmuch as it can be heard and then transmitted by other people, even if it has already become faint. Since the influence of the word is not tied to the immediate personal surroundings of the speaker, he lives on acoustically even after his death, and remains responsible for his word.

If we analyze more closely the concept of the word that makes everything arise, we see that it actually expresses the continuity of life. One repeatedly encounters the idea that the word is sacrificed, the word is time. Man is born only to sacrifice and be sacrificed, for according to the laws of nature, every day he must surrender a part of his allotted lifespan and life force. Yet this word can be "true" or "untrue" depending on how willingly or unwillingly the natural sacrifice of breath is carried out. The sound sacrifice is only true, that is, real, when it is recognized and assented to as a life value, a gesture analogous to that of creation, and consequently is offered as a praise song. It is untrue insofar as it is carried out unwillingly and on a purely material level, i.e., merely in the way dictated by physical nature. Sacrifice is the crimson thread that runs through the whole of human life. If this sacrifice is a sound sacrifice, a praise song, then man taps into the primordial acoustic energy of creation, which in the final analysis is the holy syllable *AUMm* that "fastens" everything together: the past, the present, and the future. This is of great significance, insofar as all that is present actually issues from the sum total of the past. The way in which man carries out his life sacrifice, that is, his word, constitutes the holistic rhythm of his existence. For what he is today, he can thank his yesterdays.

Only the gods of the acoustic primordial world have been granted the power to maintain the original sonorous laudatory nature of the word free from any confusion or restriction brought about by material corporeality. The true gods are pure songs of praise. The *Aitareya Brâhmana* states that all their limbs are meters;[8] in the *Shatapatha Brâhmana* it says: "All that the Gods do, they do through song."[9] The praise song is the body of the invisible and the primordial matter of all that has come into being.

Only on the basis of this meaning of sound can one understand the high estimation in which ancient Indian philosophy held all sound relationships, particularly where mystical languages were concerned. For example, if the word *Brâhman* (the complete power of formulation) is associated with *bhrat* (to be strong), on the basis of the sound *bra*, even though they have nothing etymologically (in our sense) in common with one another,[10] it is because a particular power has been ascribed to this sound itself.

Just as the creation partially converts its original, purely acoustical existence to a concrete, physical one, parts of the primordial acoustic substance of the world have become deeply concealed. Thereupon begins the second epoch of creation. Whereas the gods remain as pure sound beings in the dark primordial night of creation, the other creatures enter the second period that lasts from the gray dawn to the red dawn, and is marked by the sudden appearance of light. The third period is the brightly lit world in which things that had previously only been visible in blurred, semimaterial or foglike form finally take on clear and concrete shape.

In the course of this evolution, then, the once purely acoustical rhythms become visible. As the pure proportions of time take on visible and palpable proportions with the irruption of light, space develops, and with it come the delineations of figures, individuation, and finally solid, conceptual thought. What was impalpable and inconceivable in the primordial night becomes palpable and conceivable. Nevertheless, the primordial acoustic matter lives on, audibly or inaudibly, as a metaphysical core in everything that has been created, even if it has become deeply concealed in this process, especially in the case of mute objects. This does not prevent the net of *Maya*, that is, the confusion of our senses, from continually becoming denser, because the growing light and increasing corporeality gradually cloak the acoustic background so heavily that man can easily mistake the appearance of corporeality for the truth. This *Maya* does not even begin *de facto* with the advent of light. It already starts with the primordial sound, because for ancient Indian philosophy the ultimate truth is not sound, but silent nothingness and the complete absence of concepts and form. Thus the ultimate truth is already limited by issuing as sound from the vacuum of the resonance body. However, the rhythms of creation arise precisely from this limitation, as the illusions brought about by the praise song of death hungering for life. Dualism begins with death, this hungering for life. The ultimate truth is the overcoming of this hunger. This truth is by its very nature formless; and because it lacks form and rhythm, it cannot be manifest. If every manifestation implicitly means a limitation, then the only possible way of at least hinting at the truth of nothingness is by a purely acoustic, musical formulation of the truth, because it sounds without concepts and without being confined by material, concrete symbols. The purely acoustic formulation comes closest to formless truth. Of all existing modes of expression, music is the most ephemeral and dissoluble. Its medium, vibrating air, may be considered the finest of all fabrics. In addition, nowhere is the evolution and crystallization of clear concepts more strongly suppressed than in music. As the creator of the primordial rhythms and forms of the world, music surpasses all cosmic energies, because its rhythmic possibilities are greater and more multifaceted than those of any other energy bound to concrete matter.

Music is the multivalent, fertile primordial growth of creation. It knows as yet no space, and lives only in time, as if in the primordial world. Devoid of conceptuality, unbound to any stable form, it can continuously change, reverse, or shatter its form in order to reassemble later at will, like the primordial world-dragon—its primal symbol—that ceaselessly transforms itself. To a great extent, it can even draw absolute silence (rests) into its realm of influence. And yet the actual onset of *Maya* already lies in this acoustical entanglement, not only because music provides truth with a shape, albeit a fleeting one, but because even its very silence is charged with tension, while by seemingly high and low, "thin" and "thick" tones it can evoke the first illusion of space.

To visualize the imprinting of the invisible acoustic rhythms that occurs in the dawn grayness of creation is not easy, especially since it is not a case of a simple transposition of temporal relationships to spatial ones. The pitch, color, and intensity of the sound must also have played a part in the process. One thing is certain: the linear and visible figures resulting from the primordial rhythms (by the transposition of the heard into the seen) are primarily totally abstract diagrams constituting a fixed canon in the spatial composition of cultic images. Let us take for example the form Y, the symbol of the sacrificial post. Whether this shape appears in the form of a larynx, a tree, a person with raised arms, two snakes with tails intertwined and their heads far apart from each other, or any other fabulous animal, is irrelevant to its primordial meaning. What is crucial is the reduction of all appearances to the same linear rhythm whose origin is purely acoustical. This is demonstrated by a closer comparison of the spatial compositions of ancient cultic images.[11] Yet as long as we possess no documents of history or experimental psychology that would permit us to decipher the nature of these relationships, their acoustical interpretation remains a problem that can scarcely be solved. The case here is quite different from the one treated in *Singende Steine*[12] (*"Singing Stones"*). In the Romanesque cloisters we were dealing with simple, documented evidence of transposition from animal representations into individual tones, whereas here we are dealing with an optical impression of whole rhythmic forms.

Nevertheless, there is no doubt that music is the primordial language of all the most ancient, visible symbolic forms. The fact that this transition from the acoustic to the optical in values has to do with quite a specific world, difficult to grasp intellectually, is principally due to the cosmic moment at which this metamorphosis of things takes place. The entire process occurs in the intermediate world, i.e., the moment between the gray and the red of dawn. This world that stands between the purely acoustic primordial time of creation (night) and the concrete present (the day- or light-time) is the light-tone world of dream. Since in the analogical system of this cosmogony the primordial time also corresponds to heaven and the present to earth, the light-tone world, in which the transition from quasi-immaterial tone to concrete matter takes place, represents the light-dark cultic space of the universe. It is the atmosphere.

On the basis of the same analogical system these three worlds have also become identified with the states of deep sleep, dreaming, and waking, or with the subconscious, the semiconscious, and the conscious. We thus arrive at the following formula in which the spatial and the temporal continuously overlap.

I	II	III
Primal Time	Intermediate Time	Present
Acoustic world	Light-tone-world	Concrete world
Night	Dawn grey/Dawn red	Bright day
Deep Sleep	Dream state	Waking state
Heaven	Intermediate Realism (Sacred space/ Atmosphere)	Earth
Subconscious	Half-consciousness	Consciousness

Perhaps at this point we should mention an important point upon which so many works on the ancient cosmogonies have foundered. Since the world expands from a midpoint in concentric circles, one must imagine the three realms accordingly. The acoustic primordial time always lies in the center, remaining in the creation even in its present completed form. The other realms congregate around this center so that the world egg (the primordial mouth or the holy of holies) always stays in the middle of the cultic space. Things are never perceived as lying behind or beside one another, even if they follow each other historically, but always

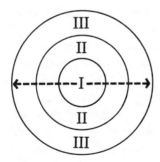

as lying within one another. Thus they are in a constant state of mutual interchange.

To a certain extent, then, the primordial time stands at the heart of the cultic space in the intermediate world. It represents the subconscious within the semiconscious light-tone realm of the cult. Nothing is yet visible in it; it is the dark, self-contained cavity in the penumbra of the sacred space. In it the yet unformed being rustles slowly to life, because it is the locus of the so-called primordial waters of creation, from whose rhythm all things have arisen.

What then are these primordial waters? Nothing other than the rhythms of flowing time. The primordial world is spaceless, that is, it exists only in the time dimension. The sound that exists audibly or inaudibly in the substance of every created object is the only form of existence of this object in the primordial time. These primordial waters, therefore, so often called the proto-element of creation, could never have actually been water, but only the sound thereof. The so-called primordial waters are only the acoustic expression of flowing time, which is the true nature of the primordial world. The *Shatapatha Brâhmana*, for example, says that Prajâpati the creator god made the waters out of his voice.[13] According to *Tandjamâya Brâhmana*, he makes his voice resound so that it develops like a drop of water.[14] According to *Shatapatha Brâhmana*, the water was at first liquid and sounding, and because it flowed eight times it was the *Gâyatrî*, an octosyllabic meter that later became the foundation of the world.[15]

This concept, like many others particularly in European usage, survived right into the music theory of our Middle Ages: for example, in the explanation of music as an "aquatic science" in the *Compendium de Discantu Mensurabili* of Petrus Frater.[16] Simon Tunstede similarly states that music is a "scientia juxta aquam inventa,"[17] a "science invented near the waters." Most authors attempted to explain music's aquatic character from the analogous sound of *musica* and *moys-ica*:[18] a confusion exactly similar to one of the ancient Indian "etymology." Then in *Summa Musicae* the first rational attempt was made to explain the connection between music and water by the sound made by rain falling on roofs and stones.[19] The author, Pseudo-Johannes de Muris, was evidently the first of the rationalistic experts, thanks to whom these conceptions, rooted in the deepest layers of the human psyche, could at a later date simply be rejected as foolishness. In fact, the entire concept of the primordial world is nothing other than the depiction of purely acoustic or light-tone events in the semiconsciousness of dreaming man.

If the primordial world represents the subconscious human psyche, then the light-tone world of the cultic space corresponds to a semiconscious dream state that constitutes the transition from the purely acoustic, only psychically experiential primordial time, to the physically bound, concrete present.

This light-tone world of the ritual that mediates between heaven and earth is just as difficult to comprehend as the bridge linking the purely spiritual functions of the human brain with the physiological organism. It can neither be weighed nor measured. It is a nature *sui generis* resulting from the confluence of two utterly different structures, mechanisms, or realities, to which neither the earthly nor the heavenly can lay sole claim within the context of the cult. For this situation, Vedic literature employs the term *satyam*. *Satyam* designates a truth "that conceals in itself the mortal as well as the immortal,"[20] or, similarly, "is both true and false, but the false dominates."[21] It is fundamental to the cult in the intermediate world to seek to unite heaven and earth, which if they stood apart unmediated could never be joined. This explains the very specific nature of ritual: from the false it makes truth, and from the true, falsity. It confers spirituality upon the purely material by imbuing it with form and content. Ritual recalls the primordial world not only by means of the voice but also by extolling it in song or speech with the concrete or mute means and actions of the present time. This permits the ritual to suffuse the earthly with the divine, the purely physiological with acoustic spirituality, and transforms the untrue into that musical truth that is closest to the primordial act of creation.

The duty of the light-tone world is to let the rhythm of primordial time resound as far as the frontiers of visibility and to reawaken in earth's material objects the awareness of their acoustic primordial substance. It is obvious, therefore, that only praise song can assume the essence of this responsibility, for this song is *rita*, that is, the unspoken truth, the nature of the primordial world that made everything come to be in its purest and truest form.

Such a song not only bestows a common basis on heaven and earth, but also even brings about purification and rebirth, because in the cult the praise song is indeed a process analogous to the act of creation. Through it, *Maya* is reduced to a minimum. The blatant contradiction vanishes when the concept of space is suppressed. In the world of sound, dualism becomes amalgamated resonance, and in rhythm it becomes flowing time.

Where is the organ allowing man to experience this very specific nature of the cult simultaneously as a spiritual and a physical reality? We can produce no ancient Indian literary evidence of its location, only practical experiences and statements by Indian authorities. Through bone resonance, the singer experiences the reality of pure sound and its intimate link with the physical world, that is, the concrete reality of the spiritual. The spiritual then becomes physically perceptible and the physical is experienced spiritually. The bodily locations of the different sounds vary from school to school, but ritual singing always strives to arouse the sounds of the primordial world. Hence the technique of interspersing within a poem certain sounds, called "strewing a sacred *Brâhman*," which logically and linguistically speaking appear to have no relationship to the text (unless at important places in the text certain often-repeated vowels are chosen for the purpose of being a sort of leading vowel). The *Nrisinhapûrvatâpanîya Upanishad* says explicitly: "If now and then in the midst of song one murmurs the *Brâhman* in the form of the sound *AUMm*, one will become a member of the song 'Prajâpati,' that is, a Creator oneself."[22]

What happened in a purely acoustical way in the primordial world, the light-tone world of the cult, also expands tangibly in space. The sacred *Shruti* that is heard becomes visible through ritual action (in particular through the use of sacred numerical proportions) in that the acoustic primordial event is used as a model for concrete forms and acts. But in order to let these concepts, things, and acts become effective, i.e., true, the priest must enunciate every one of his actions while he does it. He must sing or speak, for the heart of ritual lies not in concrete acts but in singing and speaking. Nevertheless, the ritual would be incomplete if there were only singing and no action, for concrete celebration amidst song is the way matter is made sacred by the word, the "false is overcome by truth,"[23] and man is also led from the false to the true. The praise song stimulates this exaltation, because it is the best conceivable formulation of the truth.

Praise singing does not only mean the act of lavishing praise or bestowing power and magnificence on another being, but bringing one's own innermost nature into harmony with the word of creation from which all creatures have sprung. In the religions of the Brahmans, both of these duties of the praise song were one and the same because Atman, the highest God, resides in the innermost part of every person, and his redemptive power and truth must be revealed through song alone. Thus from the praise song, singing death became joy, i.e., a complete being, and every being who has found his true center and hence his perfection sings in the same way. The *Shatapatha Brâhmana* says: "When the Earth was created and felt itself perfect, it then sang the Gâyatrî verses . . . and ever since, every being who feels perfect begins to sing, or to rejoice in song."[24] When the *Rigveda* states that the rivers sing their own praise song (*Alalâ*),[25] it elucidates above all their power of purification. Music and water are the primordial elements of purification. The same *Alalâ* also cleanses Indra of the secret shame that overshadowed his birth.[26]

The praise song is genesis, purification, perfection, and affirmation of all that is created. This helps explain the following tale taken from Greek antiquity. When Zeus created the world he summoned the gods to show them his work. The gods came and admired the creation in silence. Since none of them said anything about this work, Zeus asked whether anything was still missing. Then the gods answered: "Your work is great and glorious, but the voice that would praise the great work is missing." Thereupon Zeus created the Muse, for the existence of things is not complete as long as there is no voice to express it.

Disregarding the identity of God and creature, this idea of perfection through song cannot have been far from the hymns of Judaism and the Christian Church, for their poets never tire of involving all creatures in the continuous praising of the Lord and his creation. But those lengthy lists — "Praise the Lord, you works, you Angels, Sun and Moon, rain and dew . . ."[27] — are probably to be understood mainly as joyful and affirming proclamations of the orderly existence of all created things. For the Indian, ritual praise singing is as important as living in the right state of being. The praise song is the highest conceivable form of sacrifice because the sound sacrifice means, beyond any material sacrifice, the offering of the Word. The only higher level is the triumph over death by entrance into the nothingness that protects one from all rebirth, for all singing, no matter how primordial its nature, implies affirmation and hunger for life. Singing death, therefore, can also be briefly described as hunger. Those gods who require praise songs for themselves are hungry, i.e., seized by the first *Maya*, because — since they are of pure sound — songs are their only food.

It is no literary frivolity in the *Rigveda* when the terms food and hymn are used practically as synonyms. "May my hymn and prayer be food for the unequaled master (Indra)."[28] "Although Indra is fully grown, may his body grow even more when celebrated with songs and words of praise."[29] "A song of praise like sweetmeats shall be offered to Indra."[30] But the God Indra also feeds himself by song: "As a means to grow I recited a *Bráhman* for myself."[31] With this we come to our last point: self-praise. Self-praise is a very widespread trait among the gods, because it is the way they maintain their sound bodies. That person who also rediscovers his divine acoustic primordial substance in his innermost center and strengthens it by praise songs is singing self-praise. And this is the same stumbling block upon which both non-Christian European mysticism and the mysticism recently adopted from the Orient easily come to grief. They forget that this inner center of man is a cosmic center, not an individual, personal one. Achieving this center presupposes depersonalization, and nothing stands more in the way of the realization of this *conditio sine qua non* than the individualism that makes the European mystic of romantic stamp turn away so consciously from the community.

Notes

1. *Shatapatha Bráhmana* V, I, I, 1–2.
2. *Taittiríya Bráhmana* VI, 3, 4, 8.
3. *Brihadáranyaka Upanishad* I, 2, 1–2.
4. *Rigveda* X, 88, 8.
5. *Shatapatha Bráhmana* VIII, 4, 3, 2.
6. A. Bergaigne, "Etudes sur le lexique du Rig-Veda," in *Journal asiatique*, vol. 8, no. 4 (1884), p. 198.
7. *Atharvaveda* IX, 53, 5–6; 54, I.
8. *Aitareya Bráhmana* VII, 8, 2.
9. *Shatapatha Bráhmana* VIII, 4, 3, 2.
10. P. Thieme, "Bráman," in *Zeitschrift der Deutschen Morgenländischen Gesellschaft*, vol. 102 (1952), pp. 91–129.
11. The author will treat this question thoroughly in his *Altindische Kosmogonie*. [Unpublished—ed.]
12. M. Schneider, *Singende Steine* (Kassel, Bärenreiter, 1955).
13. *Shatapatha Bráhmana* VI, I, I, 9–10.
14. *Tandjamáya Bráhmana* XX, 14, 2.
15. *Shatapatha Bráhmana* VI, I, 3, 6–7.

16. "Et dicitur musica a moys, quod est aqua, et ycos scientia, quasi scientia aquatica." Petrus Frater, *Compendium de discantu mensurabili*, 1336, ed. J. Wolf, "Ein Beitrag zur Diskantlehre des 14. Jahrhunderts," in *Sammelbände der Internationalen Musikgesellschaft*, vol. 15 (1913/14), p. 507.

17. "Musica enim dicitur . . . a Moys graece, quod est aqua latine, quasi scientia juxta aquam inventa." Simon Tunstede, *Quatuor principalia musicae*, Principale I, cap. 7, ed. H.E. de Coussemaker, *Scriptores de musica* IV (Paris, 1876), p. 203.

18. M. Schneider, "Die historischen Grundlagen der musikalischen Symbolik," in *Musikforschung*, vol. 4 (1951), p. 125.

19. "Quidam dicunt, quod musica dicitur quasi moysica a *moys*, quod est *aqua*, eo quod aqua pluvialis, vel quaecumque alia, dum cadit super diversam materiam, nunc super tecta, nunc super lapides, nunc super terram, nunc super aquam, nunc super vasa vacua, nunc super arborum folia, sonos diversos reddere videatur, a quibus ad invicem comparatis antiqui dicuntur musicam invenisse." Johannes de Muris, *Tractatus de musica* (*Summa musicae*), cap. I, ed. M. Gerbert, *Scriptores ecclesiastici de musica sacra* III (St. Blasien, 1784), p. 193.

20. *Chândogya Upanishad* VIII, 3, 5.

21. *Brihadâranyaka Upanishad* V, 5, 1.

22. *Nrisinhapûrvatâpanîya Upanishad* I, 17.

23. *Brihadâranyaka Upanishad* V, 5, 1.

24. *Shatapatha Brâhmana* VI, 1, 1, 15.

25. *Rigveda*, X, 95, 7.

26. *Ibid.*, IV, 18, 5–7.

27. Medieval antiphon to the *Gratiarum actio post missam*. Poem after the Song of the Three Holy Children (Daniel 3, 17) and Psalm 150.

28. *Rigveda* I, 61, 1.

29. *Ibid.* VI, 24, 7.

30. *Atharvaveda* XX, 35, 1.

31. *Rigveda* X, 49, 1.

Acoustic Symbolism in Foreign Cultures

The Rites of Creation

The symbol is the attempt to render transparent an underlying reality not perceptible by pure thought through another reality. Thus the symbol is not the reality of what is symbolized. It allows us to recognize the mode of operation of the symbolized by way of another medium, consisting of the symbol. This implies that the symbolized is present to us not in its being and essence but only in its radiance.

An electric lamp is not electricity itself, but it symbolizes the power of electricity in that it radiates light. But electricity can also be manifested as warmth and motion. The lamp, consequently, is only a partial symbol. If the symbol were to bring all these different manifestations of electricity under a common denominator, it would have to consist of a formula tracing all these different modes of operation back to their elemental essence. According to ancient cosmological doctrine, this common elemental denominator is the flash of lightning.

You might ask why one does not simply use the word "electricity" as a general denominator. We must answer by saying that the word "electricity" is not a symbol but only a concept, not a radiation of electricity. The crucial element of the symbol lies in the fact that it is not a designation, but that it can be an experience of the symbolized. The symbol is not an intellectual bearer of meaning that can be expressed via any conventional sign, because it seeks primarily to provide a psychological, soul access to the object. A symbol first becomes a symbol when it becomes an internal experience, i.e., where internal participation in the mode of operation of the symbolized takes place: for example, when one takes fright at lightning, or plainly and simply electrocutes oneself. The ultimate common denominator of all the different manifestations is described graphically as "empty form." The essence of a latent creative primordial force, a rhythmically flowing fundamental energy that one can never imagine in sufficiently abstract terms, can be symbolized by just such an empty shell. Although one can recognize its mode of operation, its inner essence cannot be described in words. The only possibility of bringing to life the dynamic, flowing play of pure form within ourselves is offered by music, which is likewise a meaningful but verbally inexpressible play of empty forms. In the course of creation this original void becomes concrete, realizing its potentiality without shedding its pre-existent emptiness. Seen anthropocosmically, it fulfills its emptiness as one would a desire.

The primordial energy is a force of desire generating both fullness and the first rhythmic movement on the basis of its emptiness. By this movement it manifests all the phenomena of nature. It begins with the element of air and the sounds that hover there and extends to the coarsest material formation.

Examples of such rhythmic fundamental energies are the latent forces of expansion, contraction, circulation, evolving, building vortices and concave spaces, etc. These empty forms precede the things in which they come to expression. They are the latent energies of all things, imparting to them their origin, specific existence, and form. They are the primordial principles within which the patterns, the prototypes, and, ultimately, individuals come into being. Thus, for example, the pattern "man" arises from the empty form in which particular types evolve and from which individuals emerge as innumerable variants. Thus the ultimate fulfillment of the empty form's desire is individuation.

Nevertheless, every type is simultaneously permeated with numerous different energies. Within an apple tree, for example, a variety of patterns interact: germinating, expansion, curling, circulation, formation, etc. If just one of these energy patterns is also present in another object, then the tree is related to that object in this particular aspect, even though it is vastly different from it in its other properties.

In each case the symbolic relationship depends on the model according to which an object is being considered and known. There are a host of symbolic relationships based on the principle of breathing and circulation, for example, although the manner (the individuation) of circulation can be very different from one object to the next. In regard to the common empty primordial form of circulation, however, there remains that primordial relationship upon which rests the mystical "universal consciousness," which knows man and the whole of nature finally as a unity.

Symbolic relationship makes more of an impression by an accumulation of common rhythms, especially when observing external shape and the form of movement. The contours of a pear or an apple, echoed in the crowns of their respective trees, are then registered as shapes analogous to the head or to the female breast. The relationship is even closer when two figures stand in "rebus" relationship and complement one another like the casting and the mold. It is so in the case of the water snake or the jellyfish, for example, who fit the mobile shapes of their bodies to the water in order to be carried along by its flowing form.

Another kinship is produced from number: triangle; funnel; maelstroms; candlelight; future, present, and past; heaven, intermediate world, and earth; or a song with three strophes. These can be grouped together without regard to the differences of their categories on the basis of their threefold rhythm, if they are reduced to their empty, dimensionless formative force.

But the most powerful kinship lies in tone. The tone of voice is inherited. It is transmitted from father to son. But when a human being can imitate perfectly the call or the

rhythmic movement of a particular animal, a primordial kinship is disclosed even there—it is known as totemism. The
relationship between speaking and listening is still more intense, for what the listener receives is what the speaker gives.
This means, ultimately, that the attentive listener becomes
what the speaker is. In all ancient cosmologies, air or periodic
breath counts as the first and subtlest content of the empty
form. It is air that makes the word of creation audible, and
thereby leads to the first individuation of the empty form. In
contrast to this flowing and sounding individuation, all other
material and static individuations possess only a relatively
low degree of reality and truth, because the full truth, the "immutable and immortal," can come to pure expression only in
the primordial principles. In an individuality, perfect truth is
materially as unattainable as the geometric point. The only
possibility of approximately reaching the empty form in the
individuation is through sounding rhythm. This is why singing and hearing represent the most refined forms of higher
cognition and are the basis of a ritual that organizes its songs
according to meter, that is to say, after numbers or sounding
patterns.

If the depiction of external events in ancient tales often appears so improbable and inconsequential, we now know that
they are only the fluctuating individuations of higher patterns. The external events are the individuation. The real
meaning of the story is the pattern on which the many wise
and universally valid observations of life are formulated. For
example, when the youngest of three brothers is always the
lazy, weak, and stupid one who prefers to lie behind the stove
and sleep, and then unexpectedly becomes such a strong, intelligent, and enlightened hero that he completely overshad-
ows his two elder brothers, what is implied is the superior
power or talent whose development requires a longer period
of maturation than ordinary intelligence.

But why is it always demanded of this third brother—who
perhaps must free an enchanted princess from a spell, fetch
from a dark forest the water of life for his old and ailing father,

or conquer some giant—that he complete three difficult, normally quite impossible tasks in order to achieve his goal? Why is the nature of this hero's deed so different in every fairy tale? Answer: because the number 3 is the symbolic number of the highest power (namely 3 as a unity), and it does not matter in the least where, what, and how something occurs, but only whereby it occurs. It need only be pointed out that the unusual and indomitable power and courage symbolized by the number 3 appear everywhere in some form, as much in man as in nature.

The number 3 is the entirely neutral expression, or as it were the code, of an extraordinary function. In such tales, therefore, the most varied conceptual planes can be blended with one another. For example, Venus is sometimes considered either the son or daughter of the sun and moon; sometimes the three heavenly bodies are considered three brothers who are supposed to bring daylight, but only the third, the youngest, i.e., the sun finally succeeds in this task.

This mixing of man and nature, two such different concepts, not only indicates a nature-bound quality in man, but even more a *spiritual bond of Nature with Man.*

The doctrine of the anthropocosm is based upon this interrelation. The world is a large universe, man a small but analogous one enclosed in the larger.

What constitutes then the connecting link between the large and small worlds? The connecting link is the periodic rhythm to which all thinking, living, growing, and dying in the world is subject. Rhythm is the actual basis of an organizing set of laws, the power of flowing time that shapes things, regulates their course, and lets them disintegrate again.

The founders of the ancient cosmologies, who from the Neolithic Age onward meditated a great deal on the origin and meaning of music, recognized in this rhythm the creator of the world expressing himself, at first inaudibly and then audibly. "Silent and still was the creator! An iceberg! Dumb as a stone!" Thus says the Mexican mythology. Yet one day he cast the mountain away from himself (that is, he broke his silence), because he could no longer resist his deepest desire to create the world and men. Then he sang: "This world shall be!"—and the world arose.

This is the mythological setting for the following cosmological reflections. In the beginning there was nothing but an absolute stillness (symbolized by the iceberg) in which the first thoughts, inaudible rhythms, arose. Such rhythms were the model for the coming concrete creation, similar to the way in which every newly created concrete work first exists only in the mind of its maker. Then the first act took place; and this act was the utterance of the thought in the form of rhythmical sound. Naturally this first formulation of the thought of creation was not a definite sentence in the linguistic sense, but the spontaneous expression of a will to existence, sometimes described as a cry. Mythology also depicts this voice as a kind of primordial drum, even, at times, as the heart of the creator. Such primordial drums are never an attribute of the creator, but rather represent the creator himself. His voice does not speak of anything; it is simply the manifestation of his existence. It is the empty form whose individuation is confined to a minimum of form, namely, to a form of pure sound.

This voice is often called the "son" of the speaker. Yet this too suggests that this son is none other than the speaker himself, or the spoken that proceeds from the father. This son or sound can to a certain extent distance itself from its creator, but it cannot leave him entirely, else it would fall silent.

The rhythm is the creator and upholder of the world. It is the law of periodically flowing order. It is the archetype of circulation that permits no congestions, coagulations, or obstinate resistance.

Nowhere is this more clearly expressed than in music, whose so-called strong and weak beats are not irreconcilable opposites but form an unbroken stream. Music, therefore, so long as it has not fallen victim to a chaotic way of thinking, has always been regarded as the archetype of the cosmic order.

This first segment of the history of creation is considered

the winter or deep sleep of the world. It is dark and cold, and there is nothing save the sonorous rhythms that make up the beginnings of movement in the subconscious of the anthropocosm. These prototypes of all things in the unconscious primordial world are invisible voices that according to ancient Indian tradition speak at first only "incomprehensible things." "Incomprehensible," however, does not mean "nonsensical," for what are resounding here are the sounds of nature.

It is like the blowing of the wind, the murmur of a spring, or the rushing of a mountain stream: a sound that has no *meaning* that can be reproduced in words, but one that truly has a *sense* that addresses us if we are collected in the depth of our consciousness. Indeed, ancient symbolism has always linked wind and water closely with sound.

Just as rhythm in sound was always regarded as the acoustic archetype of fire in water, so too the ritual song borne on the breath was considered as that moist breath or warmth whose power allows everything to grow and flourish.

The Indian Brahmanas, such as the *Rigveda*, state explicitly that the resounding primordial rhythms were joined in one roaring praise song, and thereby became the water that encouraged creation to grow and flourish.

One can see how nature is treated exactly like a human being whom one stimulates to action by praise.

The singing of the wind that blows in the breath of the unconscious primordial world is likewise the cradle of music as well as water.

That the roaring arises before the water is a most surprising reversal of the actual physical event to our way of thinking. But we are dealing here with a creation *ex nihilo*, from the void, and the standpoint of the ancient cosmogonies is that during the birth and early formation of things, it is the thought, invention, and expression, i.e., the sounding of the idea, that must precede the concrete existence of the object in question. In other words, in the acoustic primordial world, what is now the effect preceded the cause, and consequently the first roaring must have preceded the water.

In the Brahmin mythology this primordial music is depicted as the threefold intelligence of a personified creator, who at the beginning of his work is characterized as a head, and occasionally even as an embryo. With his tongue and his spittle he creates a resonant chamber in the hollow of his mouth in which the so-called primordial ocean is situated. This roaring resonance chamber in the head of the creator conceals the archetype of the creative power, namely the voice, that will be amplified in the course of later development by androgyny. The feminine element thereby becomes the water, and the male part the fiery tongue that conjures or enhances the waters, in order to transform them into the so-called fiery speech or into the fertile waters.

This analogy between head and sexual organ can be explained by the anatomy of the anthropocosm, in that the head of the creator is located in the middle of the world, and accordingly assumes the same position in man, the microcosm, as the embryo in the womb. This shared place, depicted as the "navel of the world,"—where the original act of creation is repeated at every birth—corresponds to the so-called solar plexus where the singer begins his note, and from which the sound of creation also proceeds in the anthropocosm.

It is obvious that such visual concepts as the head or womb in this purely acoustic primordial world are only mythological visual aids for the prefigured rhythms that comprise the acoustic archetypes of the functions that will later become concrete.

The world as it exists in human thought only partially represents reality, since we all too often conceive of objects only in their static condition. In truth, however, the fixed form is no more real than that of a towering wave, for all forms—regardless of how solid they may appear—are results of an impulse toward movement, i.e., of a rhythm whose field of action and qualifier is time. But in no kind of rhythm is the essence of its own nature so open to man and so readily assimilated by his soul as in that of music. The perception of its temporal movement is easily identifiable as a clearly grasped and audibly completed chain in which past, present, future (or expectation) must continuously flow into one another for the hearer. The value of each single tone can only be heard from its position within the whole.

The more immutable and rigid a figure appears to be, the more it conceals from our eyes the flowing reality of things. Religious and musical philosophy denies this illusion by ascribing a far higher truth content to all that flows than to solid, palpable, and measurable shape. If, according to ancient Indian teachings, resounding rhythm is the best conceivable formulation of truth and reality, then it attributes a similar power to water too, although the latter element does not represent formlessness quite as well as sound, insofar as it tends naturally toward meandering and spherical forms.

Despite this, water dispenses easily with its own outer boundaries. It adapts itself continuously to the form of its present environment, and, by its roaring, leads the person capable of hearing back to the primordial sound of the world. Nor does it know any rivalry. Two water currents in the Gulf Stream, for example, can come into contact or intersect with one another like two contrapuntal melodies without being separated by a dividing wall. According to Lao-Tse, water is the symbol of the soul's peace. Like sound it contains all the requirements for undisturbed higher cognition.

"The best of Man is like water;
Water helps all things,
And strives with none of them.
It tarries in low places
That the whole world disdains,
And therein it stands close to the origin of things."
(TAO-TE-KING, CHAPTER 8)

With this meaning of water, it is not surprising that the ancient Chinese drew the tonal center of their harmonic system from the sound of their sacred Yellow River and valued dripping water as a source of musical inspiration.

The intake of breath for the vocal reproduction of this water music should always proceed from the navel, because the navel is "the most highly honored center" in which man's rootedness in and attachment to the cosmos are particularly strongly felt.

Indeed, this feeling of the middle can only be maintained by deep breathing; when breathing is superficial man remains incomplete. The whole of man first arises when breath extends to the stomach.

In contrast to later Far Eastern musical aesthetics, the ritual practice states: "He who tries to speak deep and true things using only the chest or larynx voice or just the top of the head, cannot be believed." This categorical assertion is corroborated by the manner in which Brahmin, Buddhist, or Islamic worshippers intersperse their ritual songs with mystical syllables such as HUM, HIN, HA, etc.

The yogi uses them during spiritual contemplation in order to establish contact with the acoustic primordial world. In other rites, the sounds of nature are imitated in order to allow the primordial music of the world to resound in one's own body and to be able to experience it vibrantly.

Besides water, one other linking of the fluid with the sonorous rhythms of creation should be mentioned. We spoke earlier of a primordial ocean whose waters resounded in the oral cavity of the creator. Mythology adds that these waters, as they left the mouth of the creator in four streams, called into life a second ocean. This second ocean was the so-called Sea of Milk, the acoustic archetype of the Milky Way that is churned by the gods with a whisk.

With these mythological assertions one arrives at the first solidification of the liquid, the appearance of crystals from the water, and the formation of the first food, whose power is due to the rumbling motion of a whirlpool.

Musical Instruments as Expressions of the Animate and Inanimate World

In the ancient cosmogonies, rhythm is prized as the basis of the whole universe. Its origin lies in the primordial breath that sacrifices itself as it utters the word of creation in the blowing of the wind. This word, depicted as an empty form, is an impersonal, latent energy whose significance or power cannot be described in words. But nothing in the range of our experience stands as close to this energy of the empty form of rhythm as music, a play of pure form. The latent primordial energy fills out sonorous patterns whose rhythms prefigure all things to come. This conceptless movement occurs in the primordial time of the night of creation and remains invisibly present to this day, especially in the life of the subconscious. Now the acoustic patterns of creation gradually evolve concrete individuations. Thus, for example, the dual basis of rhythm, that is, its flowing to and fro and its alternating link with sound, becomes fire and water. Rhythm becomes fire, sound becomes water, and both together generate moist warmth.

After the conditions for growth had arisen, parts of the more or less fluid matter must have changed into soft, pliable tissues or into crystals. The rhythms that previously emerged as sounds from the mouth of the creator are now depicted as threads, especially as gossamer. These threads that progressively impart a concrete shape to the creative rhythms also symbolize man's link with the sound of his creation. A Californian Shaman relates his dream experience: "When I saw the creator, he sang a song, which I must always sing now. Something like a thread went from his mouth to my head."

This nightly singing and spinning that also occurs in the dream consciousness of man falls silent at the first light of day. But before the flowing rhythms finally take on a concrete and fixed shape, all the sonorous threads are once more gathered into a multicolored web. This web is the first reddening of dawn.* In the tradition of the West African Dogon, this new world is woven by a semidivine genie. They say that from his throat grew threads. Some passed between the teeth of his upper jaw, others between those of his lower jaw, and the upper jaw thus served as a weaver's reed. When this ancestor of humanity sang, he moved his jaws and thus set the weft in motion, the jewelry of his lower lip serving him as a shuttle. With this shuttle the ancestor, thanks to his extremely agile and forked snake tongue, pulled the weft laterally through the warp threads.

If the first word of creation flowed forth in the waters in the obscurity of primordial time, then the second word, by way of the rhythmically woven band, reached the light of the outer world on the breath of the weaver. This second world was the red morning sky.*

According to the *Atharvaveda*, the upper jaw was the sky and the lower jaw the earth. "This sacrifice," it states verbatim, "that with its threads fans out in all directions, is woven by the primordial fathers. They sit at the stretched thread and turn the melodies into shuttles."

There is much evidence suggesting that this singing loom of the dawn was represented in the ritual by a harp, and the snake's tongue that led the shuttle by the playing hand rapidly weaving the melody of the dawn from string to string.

Thus in a world becoming lighter and more concrete, the creative work of the singing tongue is replaced visibly by playing hands. We are also told what was being sung there: the verse *Gâyatrî*, which lets the concrete earth arise and become bright; and also *Trishtubn*, whose meter attracts the god Indra, so that he may draw the sun across the horizon with his seven horses. This number 7 is nothing more than a joining of the forces 3 and 4 of the primordial world, the 3 which we previously recognized as the number of the fiery water song, and 4 as the lowing of the cow. During the outbreak of light, this number 7 is a last backward glance at the dark sounds of the unconscious primordial world that fades into the background during the day, but still remains the moving force of cosmic life. The dark, creative voice of the primordial night time becomes light, or, as they used to say, instead of the black cow there came the red cow — the red of dawn.

The *Rigveda* says: "Invoking the dawn, the fathers drove out the red cows that were penned up in the rock of night. As the herds were freed, they sang the song of triumph. They found

---

* "reddening dawn," "red morning sky," "the red of dawn," and "red rosy dawn," are all attempts to capture the rich content of the single German word *Morgenrot*. (Ed.)

the light for which they had longed in their thoughts, for they once again remembered the first name of the cow. As this herd recognized their names, they answered with a loud lowing. Through the singing of the gloroius name of the cow, the rosy dawn appeared."

In the *Atharvaveda* it is said that this famous name was only rediscovered after lengthy meditation. This leads one to suspect that something catastrophic must have taken place, causing this holy song to slip into oblivion. Indeed, there is no cosmogony that does not mention a petrification of the world: a deluge, a global fire, or some other catastrophe brought about by the wickedness of one or several generations of men.

The root of this sin is often given too. With the approach of light, men believed that they knew more, and even that they *were* more than they had been previously. The zealots of progress of that time refused to submit themselves individually to the inescapable law of a creation that can only survive from generation to generation on the basis of an individual readiness for self-sacrifice.

Yet one must understand this notion of sacrifice correctly. Modern man would like to substitute the concept of social service for the idea of individual sacrifice in order to preserve the ego. But at the same time, the deeper background becomes only more obscure, then as now, because of the usual vagueness of the concept or the limitations of perspective. The ancient notion of sacrifice is obtained from the nature of song: for what blooms more readily and fades faster than tone?

The ancient notion of sacrifice proceeds from the idea that considering life's evanescent nature each breath is already a personal sacrifice to time that nobody can avoid. What is decisive, though, is whether one consents to this sacrifice or whether one makes it reluctantly; for both the temporary and the ultimate value of the sacrifice, its relative and its ultimate absolute value, depend on one's inner attitude. He who lets his breath, hence his life force, flow consentingly as a willing sound sacrifice from the depths of his body, sings his life; for singing means to affirm life, to free oneself, and thereby to bring happiness and prosperity to oneself, and consequently to one's fellow men. On the other hand, he who grimly and stingily holds back his breath, or with nasal, strident, or sluggish voice endures the sacrifice as an unavoidable ill, croaks out his life. He denies his manhood, his *conditio humana*, to his own disadvantage in particular but also to the horror and detriment of his environment.

According to mythology, this generation, petrified in sterile egotism, refused to "*sing* the sacrifice," that is, to commit a *personal* sacrifice, preferring instead to burn fruits on altars or to immolate animals and slaves. In order to acquire more light or, as they thought, more freedom, they pushed the resounding primordial sky, at that time very close to earth, far up and away from themselves. Since they placed greater confidence in the eye than the ear, they destroyed the sacrificial post, the spinal column of the universe or the world axis, whose symbol is the hollow tree which, singing and listening, connects heaven and earth, or higher with lower consciousness. The fall of the sacrificial post means nothing less than the careless and fateful division of consciousness and subconsciousness. Thereby men lost their nature-given center, for the original locus of man's power was neither in the head nor in the sexual organs, but in the navel. Sin came not from the flesh but from the spirit that threatened to destroy the very basis of life.

At the same time, naturally, music and language also moved further away from natural sounds. As this primordial language was gradually suppressed, a new, distinct but truly unnatural rhythm and vocabulary also arose that no longer reflected the rhythm of things and consisted only of conventional terms. Because people immediately began fighting about these terms, that is, about these names that had not sprung from the truth, there arose confusion, a multiplicity of languages, misunderstandings, and finally strife and enmity. Instead of balanced dualism, irreconcilable contradictions appeared. In the place of musical ambiguity, or pure meaning, came concept-bound, alternative, and logical thinking and speaking.

And woe to the poet who still dared to think and to speak musically!

In this situation the mythical ancestors are said to have sought an escape: by correct song they strove after the power to recover the true center. Finally they were also granted a ritual of redemption. This ritual, designated as the "new *rita*," was a way in which one more or less acknowledged the newly acquired clarity of light and the unequivocal meaning of terms, but restricted the onesideness and inadequacy of logical language by singing the texts to pre-existing melodies. The song was intended to complete what language lacked, for true knowledge cannot emerge from abstract formulation, but must be uttered in a true-to-life, holistic form, if it is not to become a caricature.

The ancient Indian term *"rita"* means "order, law," in particular the truth of this order as it resounds in pure, wordless rhythm. But the truth of this order resides in the fact that it is not a rigid order but a constantly flowing rhythm that periodically tightens and releases, and never surrenders to congestion, abrupt contrasts, or edges that could lead to states of chaos. Rhythm is the energy potential of the true center in which the opposites are neutralized, and for us humans the subtlest manifestation of this rhythm is still to be sought and even experienced in music. Music is, therefore, the most genuine expression of a world restored.

With the intention of restoring this true rhythm of the *rita* to men, the gods of the primordial world are supposed to have built a place of worship whose seat is located in the red of dawn, between the dark and the light world. Here music was primarily put to the service of restoration, and it served this regulating and pedagogical duty for many centuries. When government and society fell into disarray in ancient China, the first concern was to reform the degenerate music. Only through hearing could people once again come to realize their true position in the cosmos and the meaning of the flowing order within their deepest unconscious.

Usually this duty is taken over by so-called saviors or cultural heroes who are also depicted as twins, since they live between the light and dark or the conscious and subconscious worlds. They are twins because to an extent they represent two equal aspects of the same being. Because they stand on the border between the dark, invisible realm of music and the concrete, visible world, mythology says that their songs are their *hands*, that they shoot with musical bows, eat from drums, and drink from cymbals. Their true being and their true nourishment is sound or the "word," but their external appearance is concrete. Now and then they are even described as self-sounding, walking musical instruments. In other words, they are concrete figures who act musically. After the sounding of the dawn, this mythological condition of dream consciousness turns to the bright consciousness of day. From now on, musical bows are no longer transformed into shooting bows, but the latter have become the archetype for the former. Drums are no longer the archetype of pots, but are now made from pots, grain holders, and mortars.

The mythical khuei, player on a lithophone (stone instrument), belongs to the ranks of the legendary people who carried out this reform. In order to understand the meaning of his playing on the stones, one must first realize the symbolic value of stone. In the acoustic primordial world, stone, rock, or iceberg do not correspond to any material reality. They are only visual aids that refer to the concentrated silence that precedes the sounding of the word of creation. But in the concrete world, stone refers to the heavy, hard, and dumb matter that arose in the course of creation. This heavy stone or rock is the symbol of guilt, generally unconscious, but nevertheless weighing heavily on man and nature: guilt for having neglected the flowing rhythm of the cosmic order by a lack of readiness to vibrate and listen. The spiritual attitude that is closed to the flowing order of the world (a condition that serves also as the root of stubbornness, stupidity, and dullness) wants all motion to solidify into a fixed form. In fairy tales this petrification is often traced to the deed of an evil sorcerer, in whose castle the prisoner awaits the liberating hero.

Yet under the circumstances, one must admit that a similar guilt is planned in the course of every creation. That is why man and nature *must* become sinful when the seductive light comes over them.

And yet man, whose mortality and rigid skeleton were caused by this petrification and numbness, can nevertheless release himself from this attachment to the aging cosmos. This is the duty of sacred games and ritual song, which can make man's soul and even his skeleton vibrate once again. Basically the hardening is inescapable, but to a certain extent it can be delayed and overcome psychologically, and especially musically.

Rapid movements, easy for youth, are hard for the aged. A rapid musical tempo is as easily grasped by the young as by the old. But whereas the comprehension of children enters kinetically into every detail, the older person grasps the rapid tempo by his superior overview, which keeps his musical participation young. By this maintenance of youth through music, the numbness, petrification, and blockage that are associated with maturity, melancholy, or indeed with death itself, can be overcome.

From this body of thought the meaning of playing on stones and later on gongs is revealed. Striking them makes the mute stone or metal ring out. Striking humans or animals is one of the most widespread forms of fertility magic. The last vestiges of that custom can still be seen in the customs of our carnival. But stones, too, made to sound by striking, are supposed to attract and release fertility, make the cripple once again feel the will to live, and move hardened hearts to tears. Even the dead, who lie there stiffly and whose souls have gone into the stone, are supposed to be transported into the "house of songs," i.e., to eternity, through the freedom of sound. If the dumb stone is the symbol of numbness, then the sounding stone is the symbol of the power to overcome.

The task of the saviors who introduced such redeeming musical instruments to the ritual was, of course, not limited to music alone. They also taught man the arts of chronology and medicine. But here too, just as with their concern to eliminate every sort of hindrance, from channeling marshes to allowing passage for the winds, they always work to restore life's free flow by setting the frozen rhythms in motion again. Furthermore, nothing appears to be more important than the percussion instruments, especially the drum whose membrane is made of the skin of a *sacrificed living being*. No hide can resonate if it is not dead and stretched taut and if it is not dry as the skin of an ascetic. The power of the drum's sound resides in the sacrificial power of self-abnegation. Siberian traditions say that the sound that becomes audible through the skin of the instrument is the voice of the being that was sacrificed to make the drum. The same applies to stringed instruments, whose sounding material must be made from gut, and even more so for the flutes made from human or animal bones. Such instruments are always viewed as the dead or as magic tools, sacrificial wagons, or as speaking and oracular riding animals, who first lend humans, heroes, and gods the power to act through sacrifice and singing. The sun itself subsists by this primordial power. Ancient Indian mythology states that the sun's chariot has an axle that consists entirely of praise songs. The horses must be harnessed by the rhythms that set the sun in motion.

This power of sound is none other than *rita*, the truth that unfurls its power when it is piously uttered, and better yet, piously sung. Axle and horses symbolize the clearly oriented direction of the striving for truth.

Thus one repeatedly encounters a spiritualization of nature, which on the basis of sound forms an entity with man, thereby becoming a hearing and responding being.

Naturally this connection of harmony with concrete representations has nothing to do with tone painting. It does not transfer something primarily visible to an acoustic plane, but rather returns the visible, as something secondary, to its originally musical rhythms.

Musical instruments are the tools of a half-dreaming, half-waking middle world. They are concrete, visible appliances that allow invisible energies to arise, thereby serving as mediators between the dark and the light world. In them the transition from sonorous symbol to concrete symbol is complete.

If one looks at the world from the standpoint of the beginning and unfolding of the process of creation, then it is sound that produces matter. Seen from *our* vantage point (that is, looking back on history), it is matter that is the cause of harmony. On the two sides of the dawn, things behave in exactly contrary ways. The sonorous rhythm that prefigured the functions of things to come during the acoustic primordial night is the invisible symbol of tangible matter. In contrast, in the concrete, light world that determines our usual thinking, visible writing and material instruments become the symbol of sound.

The play of colors of the dawn, whose forms (as in a polyphony of visible sounds) constantly permeate and color each other without clashing, also belongs to this median world of transition. It is no accident that until the high Middle Ages the dawn was described as a singing light, and that Vedic literature speaks of a light-colored or seven-colored song that raises the gods of day up to the horizon. Ancient ritual placed marriage in this period of dream consciousness as a human act analogous to the marriage between heaven and earth, primordial and present era, dark and light, sound and material, and also between truth and falsehood, until the short lifespan of the dawn is overpowered by the hard clarity of daylight.

In India and West Africa, as we have already heard, this dawn is *woven* by an ambassador from the creator of the world. This envoy lets the thread slide between the teeth of his upper and lower jaws, and while he sings, opening and shutting his mouth, his tongue pulls the shuttle sideways through the threads. In the musical ritual of waking consciousness, this loom of the dawn becomes a harp. The threads become strings. The tongue that shuttles the weft now corresponds to the hand that executes the woven pattern in numerous melodies. As is said in the *Atharvaveda*, one has "turned the melody into a shuttle."

This is the way in which cosmological ritual symbolized the twilight of dawn: a situation in which sonorous and dream images crossed with images from daylight consciousness. The custom of hailing the dawn by ritual string playing is very widespread. In Psalm 57.9 it even says: "Awake, psalteries and harps! I will awaken the dawn!"

Inherent to the mediating role of the dawn—like the evening—is the link to a number of fables that relate to the redemption of a cosmic guilt by the *rita*.

At nightfall a melancholy girl arrives at a lake. Close to shore she notices a harp lying on a rock. She reaches for the instrument and suddenly sinks into the water. The harp is the hook used by the water sprites to drag the body of the girl to the depths, while the soul, robbed of its body, finds refuge in the stone. After a while the corpse floats to the surface of the water. It clings fast to the shore of the lake and becomes a tree. One morning, shortly before sunrise, the inconsolable bridegroom of the girl arrives at the shore. He sees the young tree, fells it, and carves a harp from it. Thereupon the quiet plaintive voice of the girl is heard as if from afar, and the young man is taken with such despair that he shatters the harp on the very stone that sheltered the soul of the girl. But hardly has this happened than the girl, released from the spell of the stone, stands alive once again before her bridegroom.

This highly symbolic tale is a typical instance of spiritual renewal or so-called second birth by the power of *rita*. The girl, rendered numb by sadness, is plunged at evening into the waters of the primordial world. After the symbolic death and rebirth in the shape of a tree, she returns to the world. The tree, carved into a harp, strikes the stone, which by resonating frees the soul at dawn.

The harp also very often appears as a ship that plunges at evening into the resounding primordial night world, and at dawn reappears on the surface of the water. It is the ship that carries the sun at night through the underworld. This underworld, which corresponds to our deep subconscious, is frequently symbolized in ancient mythology as an undefined melancholy, a subliminal grief, or even the realm of the dead, or at least as a disposition toward death. In the *Kalevala*, the famous Finnish epic poem, it says: "Only of tears was the harp, only of sorrow was it built. Hard days gave it its arch and sounding board. Only grief stretches its strings, another sadness makes its pegs."

Aside from the fact that every instrument serves as a vehicle of sacrifice, the harp, depending on its position, is viewed as the baited hook of the water sprites, but also as a swan with arched neck.

An Irish tale tells of a harp player's son named Ongus, who once had an ominous dream. In this dream he saw a most beautiful woman who accompanied her singing on the harp so wonderfully that he become sick with yearning for her. He left his parents' house in order to look for her, and after wandering around for a whole year, he finally found her in the castle of her father, the king. But the king could not grant him his daughter, because he had no power over her. The young woman, Caer, had two forms: sometimes she was a person, sometimes a swan maiden. So Ongus wandered to the Swan Lake. There he waited a long time in vain. Finally, on All Saints' Day, he saw her swimming in the lake with fifteen other swans. Hopelessly she looked at him. But in desperation he plunged into the lake, dived three times under the water, and was also turned into a swan. Both then sang the most beautiful songs, the swan song of the harp, the song of longing for death, and the whole of Ireland sank into a deep sleep for three days and three nights.

In all tales, the harp always stands on the borderline between life and death. Sometimes it leads to death, sometimes back to life again. It is not only a coffin, a tree of death, but a tree of life, even a "tree of joy." This term "tree of joy," also known in Ireland, remains to be analyzed.

Among all sonorous symbols, the tree is the most important because it is the ancestor of all cultic musical instruments. Whenever it is given a more precise description in the literature, it is portrayed as a hollow, singing tree that grows up out of a pond or a spring. Its three roots, which reach to the waters of the land of the dead, end at a stone that blocks the entrance to a funnel-shaped cavern.

The translation of this symbol reads: the water is the sound of the unconscious. The spring and the hollow tree are the resonant cavities of the body, the stone is the dead heart, and the funnel is the larynx from which the all-enlivening word of creation comes forth. But this voice, which ancient Indian tradition calls the "inaudible tone," remains silent as long as the heart blocks its passage. Only when the roots of the tree of sacrifice succeed in crushing this stone can the voice rise up through the tree, and the tree of death can become the tree of life or of joy.

Ritual Music as a Penetration into the Subconscious Life

In the previous section we saw that rhythmic sound and water in the old cosmogonies form the basis for the periodic movement of the universe, and that the origin of life is explained by the moist warmth of the silent and periodically passing breath of creation. Since man and cosmos originally form a self-enclosed unity, this primordial world represents the subconscious. The first rhythms, regarded as the prefiguration of the functions and forms of all things to come, are the so-called empty but dynamic forms that only achieve substantiality in the course of creation, and can then individuate into a particular form. As empty but dynamically flowing abstract formative forces, these rhythms are the quintessence of truth, that is, the *perfect* reality. In contrast, their many concrete and static manifestations contain only a limited degree of truth, because they are only inconstant and imperfect disguises of the primordial forces.

If symbolism assigns the ideal principles of the formative force to the so-called primordial night, or primordial time, then the substantiation of the empty formative force is transferred to the dawn. The first fulfilling of the empty form is accomplished by abstract sound, which, as long as it sounds in the primordial night, does not manifest itself in language, words, or concepts, but in nature sounds and in the spontaneous utterances of human feeling, usually in specific syllables which certainly have a sense, but no semantic content. If these syllables are consciously embedded in the dynamic flow of the empty form during the ritual, the *sound sacrifice* arises. A sound sacrifice is accomplished by a singer who surrenders his breath and individuality in order to bring expression to an impersonal empty form and pushes his own personality into the background in order to make himself the sounding board of a higher principle. Of course this possibility dwindles in proportion to his adaptability to the flowing nature of rhythm, that is, when the nature-given abilities of intellect, of the heart, or of the life instinct become rigid, or as they used to say, "turn to stone."

Of all the means for identifying oneself with the flowing cosmic rhythms, ancient ritual recommends music making as the best and most suited to man. Musical rhythm is unencumbered by any intellectual activity; it reaches down into our deepest unconscious because in its empty form it constitutes the basis of that existence. It is the reality always operating in man, yet remaining inexpressible. Through music making one sets out on the path that leads to participation (or as they say, "drinking") at the river of cosmic rhythm. And even if one does not reach the ultimate goal, i.e., the completely empty form, by this kind of musical meditation, one nevertheless senses the nature of this ideal, most subtle and fluid filling of the empty rhythmic form by sound. There is in fact no kind of form filling of a material or static kind that can match for truthfulness the acoustic individuation of the empty rhythmic form. The flowing primordial energy can never become as transparent in solid form as it does in the fluid, or in particular the acoustic form.

Not only does music making reveal the first and most palpable filling of the empty form, it also provides direct experiences of the contact between matter and spiritually significant sound, because this sound also sets the body of the singer in perceptible vibration.

In wordless song, and in playing musical instruments, primal energies become transparent through matter in the purest conceivable form. Music making is a borderline occurrence between the tangible and the intangible, whereby the intangible is actually produced out of the tangible. If one considers that the ancient cosmologies had the intangible and invisible precede the material and tangible, then one begins to understand the pre-eminent significance of music in cultic activity. Whereas the sonorous word of creation gradually becomes enshrouded by the mute matter it is producing, the ritual strives toward making mute matter resonant. Music making is a borderline occurrence between intangible sound and tangible matter. Its cosmological position in the reddening dawn between light and darkness springs from this borderline nature.

The dawn, then, is the rightful place of musical instruments, since its light also suggests the *expansion* of the world, just as music also suggests certain spatial representations that even become palpable in concrete instrumental playing. The *Brihadâranyaka Upanishad* states that sound as ultimate reality would certainly be intangible, but with this reality, it says, "it is as if a drum is being struck. One cannot grasp the sounds that spring from it. But if one has the hand drum or the drumstick in one's hand, then one has also grasped the tone."

This also implies, however, that a new means has been placed at man's disposal with which he can offer a sound sacrifice — the selfless realization of an empty rhythmic form — without having to surrender his own life's breath by singing. Naturally he still uses rhythmic energy, even if he does not sing, but this energy no longer flows from the narrow zone of contact between breath and body, but only by the secondary way of muscular activity. With this we touch on a sore point of the ritual, one that is of decisive significance for the nature and history of instrumental music. As we have already said, a substantial part of every cultic instrument should be made from the material of a sacrificial being. Strings should not be made of steel, but of gut. Drumheads should be made of hide and flutes of bone.

Whenever a musician makes these instruments sound with total devotion, or even brings them into sounding by singing with them, he obviously takes part in the sound sacrifice. However, if he performs for his own sake or only for virtuosity, without becoming aware of the sacral nature of the instrument and without identifying with the nature of these "singing dead," he is abusing the sound sacrifice, and with it the singing dead. In such a case he is playing untruthfully and loses his credibility. Furthermore he is even summoning the noisy demons or those who seem to speak the truth, who know the power of the sound sacrifice but being incapable of truly consummating it themselves are eager to fake it. Instrumental playing thereby becomes an insolent lie, indeed an effrontery whose noise grows in proportion to its untruthfulness. It is no accident that the inanimate musical instrument should lend itself particularly well to the portrayal of the demonic. A typical example is offered by Tibetan rites that use this kind of music to lay bare the unreality or nonbeing of those bloated figures of terror.

Not surprisingly, our medieval music theory, crossed by many ancient lines of thought, differentiated between *musica mundana, musica humana*, and *musica instrumentalis*. The first was cosmic music, in particular the harmony of the spheres. The second was song. The third category corresponded to instrumental music, which was wisely distinguished from the specifically human.

The following tale from the Sudan tells how an instrument is empowered to let truth ring out only by the player's readiness for sacrifice. A musician goes to a smith to have a lute built for himself. (In this culture smiths have the priestly function that permits them to build musical instruments.) After the instrument has been completed, the musician attempts to play it and declares that the lute has a bad sound. The smith answers: "This is a wooden thing. As long as it has no heart and experience, it cannot sing. It is you who must give it a heart and experience. The wood must go into battle on your back. The wood must echo with the sword blow. The wood must soak up the dripping blood: blood of your blood, breath of your breath. Its pain must become your pain and its fame your fame."

One more problem must be resolved at this sacrificial place in the rosy dawn, before the bright day puts man in danger of letting the invisible flowing rhythms of the dark-rooted life force wilt. After the sense of sight gradually replaced the sense of hearing as a means of thinking and perception, people began to understand things much more easily by means of a language based on the visual rather than by means of pure sound. But while they gained these new possibilities for cognition, they also lost the greater part of their earlier power of empathy. They no longer sought to come closer to the traits of nature that lie dormant in the subconscious, but limited their exploration to the realm bounded by their own linguistic logic.

With that, the search for the essence was steered in a formal direction. Under these circumstances, ritual seeks an opportunity to link music and language together again. Whereas the ancient cultic music consisted essentially of imitations of natural sound—spontaneous, psychologically motivated cries or sacred syllables with significance but no semantic meaning—there now appear grammatically and logically connected words whose pictorialism forces the nature of the empty form far into the background. After the universal meaning or pure sense quality of sound came the constricting meaning of syntactical words. Thus arose the "truth" offered by the words in cultic song that can naturally never be the complete truth, because the primordial rhythms of the sound and its natural noises do not mix well at all with conventional word and phrase rhythms. If one considers simple conscious breathing to be an important form of religious practice, one can easily gauge how profound the rupture is that takes place in symbolism after the irruption of daylight. The best expedient was made possible by the composition of praise songs, which were already prized in the ancient Indian

Genesis as the primordial rhythm by which the creator called
all things to life and stimulated them to grow and flourish.
What interests us from the standpoint of rhythm is the fact
that the texts of such praise songs always reiterate the same
thought in numerous variations, like a litany, and furthermore are conceived on the musical principle of repetition.

By setting texts to originally pure sounds, the ritual was
made more accessible, but there is no doubt that this took
place at the expense of profundity. It is a kind of adaptation to
the world we also experience in our own day that is really a
disquieting denial and refusal of the truth existing in the subconscious. In the long run it will not endure repression without harm to mankind. In any event, the gap widens with each
concession to superficial consciousness: a gap that the man
who is visually and intellectually one-sided (and not musical)
can hardly ever cross, much less close. During the ritual, it
goes without saying, logical thinking is overtaken by the musical dynamic nature.

What appears as matter in our waking consciousness on
this side of the dawn is sound on the other side of this turning
point in our dream consciousness. The concrete symbol so familiar to us and the pictorial word of prosaic language itself
become, with respect to night and ritual consciousness, a
purely sonorous experience that is ultimately released in the
empty forms of mediation. This is why the ritual permits the
solidified forms or images of the concrete world to exist fully
but only as transitional phenomena, in order to return them
to their original and mysteriously moving fluid and empty
rhythms.

The Indian soma sacrifice offers a classic example of the return of the external phenomenon to its sonorous essence in
the ritual. Soma is a plant and thus a concrete object. It is pul-
verized between two stones in order to obtain the ritual soma
juice. As soon as the hard stem is crushed and turned into liquid, it becomes a ritual drink, personified as the god Soma. It
is said that the sacrificial stone press crushes the squeaking
soma stem in a drumlike rhythm, so that the yellow juice
flows *murmuring* into the sacrificial vessel. This murmuring

tone generated by the liquefication of the hard plant was gathered with great reverence by the Vedic priests by placing resonators before the sacrificial vessel. Once again we encounter the sound-water relationship to which the ritual attempts to return all solid forms. "Many meditators"—thus says the *Rigveda*—"must join in the song. They will thereby move the king of the waters with their mouths."

This Soma also acts as a "word maker." Indeed, since he is simultaneously god of thunder and of water, he does not use his strength to place the word of formal speech in the foreground, but rather to subdue it. Although texts were in fact appended to the *Sâman* song and sung during the soma sacrifice, they were only of secondary importance. For one thing, their words were only set to pre-existing melodies; for another, the texts were often distorted to the point of incomprehensibility. Without regard for grammar or logic, individual vowels were expanded or totally foreign syllables interspersed in order to provide greater freedom for the diffusion of the primordial power of sound. Furthermore, each rhythm had a specific property. There were rhythms for causing expansion or contraction, others for fire and water, still others for animals and plants. We know nothing more precise about these rhythms, unfortunately, but the given number of syllables can hardly coincide with the actual number. The vital power lay rather in the delivery, as we can observe today in primitive hunting people, for example, who are able to paralyze animals by certain sounds without killing them.

Brahmanic philosophy views the ritual song as the focal point of all sacrificial forces. Whenever man sings the *Sâman* correctly, the so-called world and life community will fall to his share on the basis of the acoustic substructure of the world. This community is founded on the assumption that acoustic rhythm is the primordial ground and meeting point for all beings. Moreover, the *Brâhmanas* say: "The *Sâman* song is the air of life and bestows immortality. It is the truth." Here these observations are given their most concise form. The nature and power of sonorous rhythm are the truth, and truth is immortal.

From this universal life community, man develops through sound such an equal relationship to the gods that earthly musicians' praise songs are considered "a true meal and help" for the gods who are always thirsting after music. Nevertheless it must be noted that this parity rests only on a reciprocal relationship. The gods are the same creative empty forms from which the meals proceed in the form of concrete individuations of rhythmic energies; and those very meals which men offer to the gods can be seen as the return of these concrete individuations to their empty forms. In the *Shatapatha Brâhmana* it says: "When the gods have exhausted the power of their meters, the earthly singers must intercede for them, so that the power of the sacrificial meal may rise up to them through song." Often too the rhythms are portrayed as the dairy animals that nourish the gods. A singer of the *Rigveda* says: "May my song from which oil trickles and that is filled with sweetness be a fine tasting meal for Indra."

It is also characteristic that the rite that persistently strives to link the relative truth of outward appearance with the whole truth of the empty form is actually surprisingly pictorial in its technical language. Clearly, the purpose of this pictoriality is to carry the image (as an adequate expression of the truth) to absurdity, or to substitute for one expression another that springs from the same empty form. Thus, for example, the verb "to milk" is applied to numerous acts by which a valuable item is acquired. The expression of milking is often used especially for ritual speaking or singing that one milks from oneself. Musical instruments too are milked like a cow, not only because this animal is the source of all nourishment, but because its voice is supposed to be similar to the sound of the word of creation from which all things came forth.

According to the *Yoga Upanishad*, each of the ten steps of meditation is supported by a particular tone color. The first two are made up of human voices. The third step is marked by the sound of a bell that turns the spirit away from the external world. The fourth tone, produced by a conch shell, makes the meditator doubt the reality of the phenomenal world. The string playing of the fifth step inflames the desire for higher knowledge. On the next two, the clapping of hands becomes a divine drink, and the sound of the flute reveals sacred knowledge. The eighth and ninth steps inspire with a drum a final discourse followed by deepest meditation. Finally the yogi reaches the highest state of universal consciousness at the clap of thunder.

This pictoriality is also found when rhythm is mentioned. Very often meters are depicted as birds. In the *Aitareya Upanishad* it states: "Just as one travels in stages on earth, each time harnessing horses or oxen that are a little less tired, so one comes to the heavens in stages, each time using new meters that are not tired." Just how highly the significance of rhythm was esteemed is manifest in many lapidary sentences. "Meters are the limbs of Prajâpati," i.e., the god of creation. In himself "Prajâpati" unites all holy formulae. The first sacrificial offerings and the first gods were meters, and the seven ancestors of mankind were rhythms. The further one moves from the apparent imagery in order to come closer to the empty forms of the original rhythms, the more the image becomes replaced by sound.

We saw earlier that the combination of invisible sound and visible matter is situated in the twilight of the mediating dawn. From the perspective of this unique, dual connection between seeing and hearing in the dream consciousness, what is fluid and formless in the deep sleep of the unconscious represents the revealer of truth. What is concrete and formed, indeed the very language of waking consciousness as determined by imagery, notions, and logic, reproduces the untrue or only relatively true. This is why the task of *rita* in the waking world is "to conquer the false by the true," that is, to deepen the image by sound. Although the visibility of an act in our concrete world is both normal and hence necessary in ritual, it only becomes effective and comprehensible by the simultaneous uttering of this event. The *Shatapatha Brâhmana* states categorically: "When the priest takes hold of the sacrificial goblet, he is the exalted singer who is introducing power by song."

To do this, one needs the so-called "right voice." The right voice is man's most precious possession. The struggle that the gods and demons waged with one another during the dawn is one of the most amusing tales of Indian mythology. After the voice had been recognized as the creator's indispensable aid, the gods of the dawn tried every way to acquire her for themselves. But Vâc—the name of the personified voice—behaved hesitatingly at first. Perhaps other admirers would present themselves! Vâc is a fickle, unpredictable woman. When summoned for the first time, she nodded her head, and nobody quite knew what that signified. Yet one day she did decide to go over to the gods and remained because she found a pleasant home there. Nevertheless she did vanish now and then in order to play around on earth in the rustling of trees, squeaking of cart wheels, or in musical instruments. One day she even visited the demons, and another time the heavenly musicians who like to have women about them. This filled the gods with the greatest fears, however, for they knew that they could be done far worse harm by the heavenly musicians who continuously dealt with magical formulae than by the demons. In desperation they took up the vina and sang for bodily powers, so as to be able to offer Vâc an unparalleled spectacle. And thus they acquired Vâc for themselves, who is neither good nor bad, only without judgment. Her power lies in the fact that during the performance of the ritual she cannot be dispensed with, because the voice is the carrier of the holy formulae. Yet the success of the sound sacrifice does not depend only on the voice, for this is understood by the demons just as well as by the gods. If the gods, although they were weaker, defeated the demons who had fallen from the truth, it was because the demons sang the holy formulae with the voice of pride, and "sacrificed in their own mouths," instead of offering them in truth and with the whole breath of life. Hence the demons were left with only the hollow barbaric language of pride after the gods had defeated them with truth.

The truthfulness of a formulation can be recognized in the tone that produces it. To strike the correct tone was the constant concern of the Brahman, who led an ascetic life and whose song was considered a "sieve" that tested and purified all that was spoken. This correct tone cannot be learned. It is the pious tone that finds itself when it springs from the truth when all pride is absent, and the being addressed is acknowledged with spiritual greatness, by which we mean reverence. Where this is not the case, there can be no acknowledgement, but only a devastating lack of contact that strikes the irreverent one with the blindness of his own pride. The home of the tone lies in the unconscious.

With this we reach our conclusion. Let us briefly summarize the essentials. The role of music in our concrete world is that of a *mediator*. It is no longer a primordial sound, nor a natural one, because since the dawn of creation it has become a conscious, manmade art. But the material that it uses remains the sound that reaches deep into our dark subconscious. According to the sayings of ancient cosmologies, music's place of origin lies in the breath, in the soughing of the wind and the roaring of the water. The home of music is the reddening dawn. There it has its castle with that high tower which, as it says in the fairy tale, sometimes even reaches beyond the borders of dawn into the bright daylight. As a purely sonorous phenomenon, music is the archetype of movement insofar as rhythmic sound forms the basic structure of the world. Since man is also rooted in this early cosmos, he preserves this substructure in his subconscious, where the archaic and the truthful are ever present. The rhythmic substructure is the anthropocosmic primordial memory. As an *art*, music—particularly in its connection with language—is a mixture of truth and falsity, and if the falsity of daylight is not overcome, music will become a bearer of illusion.

In order not to forget the true nature of sounds, it has been customary over the centuries to greet the rising sun with instrumental music and thankful feelings. Hence, for example, the following words: "The morning song of seven verses has set the sun in motion and has raised it up high with powerful songs. He who glows there should be revered as a burning song. Let us praise this sun, because it sings all the wonders that it has heard during the night."

Such morning rites have remained with us for a long time in Europe, too: in the playing of the alphorn, in waking songs, and later in tower music. This early morning music making incarnates music's own hour that gradually leads us out of dream into the waking day.

It is a frequently recurring mythologem that important messages or gifts are brought to people at the early morning hour. At a similar hour—according to one widespread legend—the promise of immortality was once upon a time supposed to have been made to mankind. But when this message was announced, people were asleep. And only because they failed at this decisive hour—not listening, perhaps, simply out of laziness—they succumbed to the power of death.

The call that the dawn directs toward *us* is a different one. It announces that by music we can maintain the health of our unconscious life, if we really want to, in the midst of a world obsessed by the compulsion to analyze and dissect. For to make music means to be wide awake, without driving out the creative power of the dark unconscious. Therefore when the sun lets its first light ring out like a quiet trumpet call, the eye should calmly dream on. But the ear should be more awake than ever, so that this time at least, the hour of music will not be slept through!

RUDOLF
HAASE

RUDOLF HAASE was born February 19, 1920 in Halle/Saale, to a civil service family. He studied technology and natural sciences from 1942–43 at the Technische Hochschule in Berlin and then was drafted. From 1945–48 he was a POW in a British camp in Egypt, where he continued his education, discovering Hans Kayser's revived science of Harmonics. From 1948–51 he studied musicology and philosophy at the universities of Münster, Bonn, and Cologne, graduating in 1951 with a doctoral dissertation on Brahms' piano music. He studied privately with Hans Kayser in Bern until he embarked on independent harmonic research in the late 1950s. In 1955 he was Dozent and became Geschäftsfuhrender Direktor at the Conservatory of Wuppertal, in 1957. He was appointed Gastdozent at the Institute for Applied Psychology in Zürich in 1962, a position he held for three years. From 1965 to the present, Haase has held a newly founded professorial chair at the Vienna Hochschule für Musik und darstellende Kunst. Since 1967 he has directed the Hochschule's Hans Kayser-Institut für harmonikale Grundlagenforschung.

Haase has published ten books, some of which are collections of his articles. His institute, which houses the Hans Kayser papers, also issues a regular bibliography of writings on Harmonics. [Sources and Bibliography: Rudolf Haase, article in *MGG* Supplement; his biography of Kayser: *Hans Kayser, ein Leben für die Harmonik der Welt* (Basel, Schwabe, 1968).]

The following three articles are collected in Haase's *Aufsätze zur harmonikalen Naturphilosophie* (Graz, Akademische Druck-und Verlangsanstalt, 1974). They first appeared as follows: "Harmonics and Sacred Tradition" as "Harmonik und heile Überlieferung," in *Antaios*, vol. 12, no. 3 (Stuttgart, 1970), pp. 253–73; "Sequel to the Keplerian World-Harmonics" as "Fortsetzungen der Keplerschen Weltharmonik," in Catalogue of the Kepler Exhibition in Linz, 1971:

Johannes Kepler, Werk und Leistung (Linz, 1971); "Kepler's World Harmonics and Its Significance for Today" as "Keplers Weltharmonik und ihre Bedeutung für die Gegenwart," a lecture given November 8, 1971 at the Hochschule für Musik und darstellende Kunst in Graz, and November 19, 1971 at the Österreichische Gesellschaft für Musik in Vienna.

Harmonics and
Sacred Tradition

THIS essay treats metaphysical problems, attempting to link together a variety of ancient traditions on the hypothesis that if these traditions are equally true and significant, some connection must exist between them. At our focal point is the harmonic Pythagoreanism which, though its transmission had been only fragmentary,[1] Albert von Thimus[2] and Hans Kayser[3] were able to reconstruct during the past hundred years—Johannes Kepler's grand harmonic synthesis[4] having remained a phenomenon limited to its own time. This tradition, pursued today as research into harmonic principles[5] and therefore as a science, contains in addition an important metaphysical element: indeed, in antiquity it may well have been of metaphysical significance alone, as Thimus and Kayser lead us to believe.

In modern times, of course, skepticism toward metaphysical problems has become the rule. Since Kant, it has seemed preferable to entrust oneself to positivism and materialism, though thankfully this catastrophic narrowing of our field of vision is not the last word in wisdom. In this respect, Kayser has already developed a harmonic metaphysics which offers some magnificent ideas, though, like Plato before him, he taught it largely deductively,[6] since for him as an adherent of mysticism this mode of reflection was entirely self-evident: hence, a mystical postulate is also a notable feature of this "Kayserian Harmonics." At this point, however, this harmonics becomes dependent on religious presuppositions, and since, besides, it shows strong ties with German idealism, it is difficult for many people to accept it as a whole. We have therefore undertaken to reconstruct the study of harmonics through inductive and empirical methods, putting it on a scientifically secure basis. This provides an epistemological road toward a harmonic metaphysics that can be pursued logically and consciously excludes any speculation.[7] Since this epistemological foundation will be assumed in what follows, we must first sketch its most important lines of thought.

Harmonic cognition begins with the discovery of harmonic analogies in the most varied areas, compiled (often in ignorance of this meaning) by the individual sciences. These ubiquitous harmonic laws are not simply interval ratios but far more comprehensive, interrelated figures, such as the major triad, the overtone row, or the Lambdoma. (The relevant examples can be consulted elsewhere.[7] Harmonic laws thus allow for interconnections between different areas, which since they often prove significant, cannot be dismissed as accidental or side effects. It is far more a matter of norms, structures, and forms occurring at the endpoints of evolutions: therefore in nature we must designate them as goals or aims. This important fact necessarily gives harmonic research a teleological perspective. Kepler was already applying it logically.) Consequently its methodology is characterized by finalistic thinking, as opposed to the causal thinking of the natural scientists.

These epistemological foundations of Harmonics allow some most important inferences. If identical structures have appeared in fields otherwise unrelated to one another (we are thinking above all of the Lambdoma, discussed below), some common plan must obviously have existed; for the complexity of these norms excludes chance. The inevitable recognition of this plan necessitates acceptance of an author for it, hence a higher spiritual being. Moreover, the acknowledgement of goals and aims in nature (for this is how harmonic norms appear) brings one to conclude, analogously, that these goals and aims reveal a will that has established them.

It already manifests in the microstructures of the cell's nucleus recently discovered by natural science as the "programs" for those goals and aims. Only in this area we are not accustomed to speak in terms of a programmer, but rather for millenia have called this power "God"! In other words, with the help of consistent and firmly based analogical and teleological thinking, harmonics is in a position to produce a morphological proof of God. At this level, of course, one can say no more about God; it must remain open whether God is a person or a principle, whether he is to be considered transcendent or immanent to our world, whether or not the architect of the plan and its executor are one and the same, and other questions. We have not yet reached the end of harmonic metaphysics, however, and a whole series of metaphysical assertions could still be formulated which, at least in part, contain a high degree of cogency, and whose identity with ancient ideas Hans Kayser has already shown with many examples.[8] We cannot present all the conclusions here, but their inductive origins can be studied fully elsewhere.[9]

For present purposes it is enough to highlight some metaphysical principles that we wish to bring into contact with other traditions. We refer especially to René Guénon's writings on the "King of the World,"[10] and to Fabre d'Olivet's penetrating commentary on the so-called "Golden Verses of Pythagoras":[11] two works that, surprisingly enough, have been overlooked until now from the perspective of harmonics. The connection involves the Lambdoma, already mentioned, which we must now examine a little more closely.

This diagram, named after its resemblance to the Greek letter Lambda, was rediscovered by Albert von Thimus,[12] who found it drawn as follows in neo-Pythagorean sources:

$$
\begin{array}{c}
1/1 \\
2/1 \quad 1/2 \\
3/1 \qquad 1/3 \\
4/1 \qquad\quad 1/4 \\
5/1 \qquad\qquad 1/5 \\
\text{etc.}
\end{array}
$$

He followed logically the indications for filling out the diagram, and also, on practical grounds, turned the whole figure 45° so as to produce the following scheme:

1/1	1/2	1/3	1/4	1/5	etc.
2/1	2/2	2/3	2/4	2/5	
3/1	3/2	3/3	3/4	3/5	
4/1	4/2	4/3	4/4	4/5	
5/1	5/2	5/3	5/4	5/5	
etc.					

Kayser adopted this format and used it as a basis for his many-layered interpretations. In the process he discovered that this numerical table possesses an astonishing number of different applications; thus he was able to corroborate the old traditions which spoke of the universal validity of a legendary "Pythagorean Table." In fact the Lambdoma in its complete form can be detected in arithmetic, geometry, acoustics, crystallography, and cybernetics, and allows many philosophical and theological interpretations as well. The amazing wealth of its functions naturally cannot be demonstrated here, but has been elsewhere.[13] We can only observe that this diagram, whose regular construction of rational fractions is easily grasped, is first and foremost a table of tones or intervals, strictly organized according to what today are called the "overtone series" and "undertone series."

We begin our actual theme with an illustration[14] of the Lambdoma which already contains something of the consequences proceeding from the basic form:

Note first those tones that all relate to the common generating note 1/1c as fractions or multiples of its frequency. (The diagram is only developed here as far as the seventh index; theoretically it could be continued to ∞.) All rows of tones connected by solid lines slanting down to the left are overtone rows; those slanting down to the right are undertone rows. Thus every tone is at the intersection of an overtone and an undertone row. Next one can see that in the vertical line forming the axis of symmetry the tones are all identical with the generating note, just as the fractions have identical values: 1/1, 2/2, 3/3, etc. That is why this is called the generating-tone line. The most remarkable feature of the figure as drawn here is the straight dotted lines that come together at the point o/o above the Lambdoma. These lines are not part of the fundamental structure, but only arise subsequently by virtue of inherent laws. For if one examines the tones more closely, it appears that several are repeated: the c′ in the left

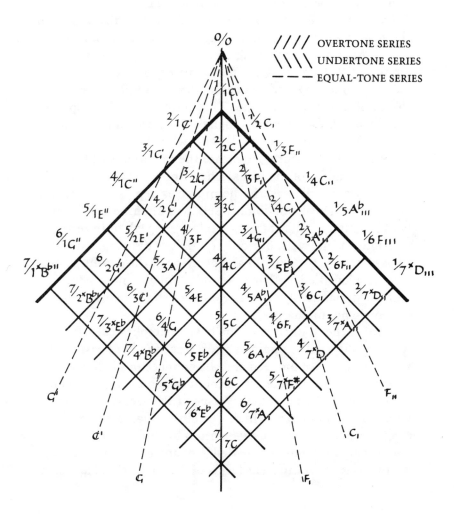

half, for example, which is an octave above the fundamental, recurs at the fractions 2/1, 4/2, 6/3. If we connect these identical values we will find that they fall on straight lines which we call "equal-tone lines," and that the equal-tone lines, when extended, all meet at a point *outside* the Lambdoma. The Lambdoma thus has an inherent structure that points beyond the diagram: something certainly not noticeable at first sight, and anything but obvious. No wonder, then, that Kayser proceeded at this point with metaphysical reflections, leading to some remarkable findings that agree with many mythological and philosophical traditions.

Above all, these discoveries associate this diagram with the dual concept of God, as taught in many different traditions. Without mentioning here the illustrations and examples that form a significant portion of Kayser's work[15] (and which justify our procedure), let us simply refer to Plato's notion of the demiurge. This is the idea, developed in the *Timaeus*, that there is a highest divinity who created the ideas (the plan of the world), and who then instructed an undergod, the demiurge, to create the material world according to the model of the ideas. The symbol for the highest divinity is o/o, whereas the demiurge is represented by the symbol 1/1. The Lambdoma itself will then be the created world, which at this stage we no longer speak of in terms of fractions or intervals, but only of "values of being." (We note in passing that the symbol and position of the demiurge may also be identified with the founders of religions—Buddha, Christ, Mohammed, etc.—as well as with the many so-called "saviors" and "mediators.")

In this general outline of the basic metaphysical situation we have purposely remained brief, since further possibilities will emerge as we proceed and the connections become even clearer. Now let us take a statement by Fabre d'Olivet, whose annotations to the "Golden Verses of Pythagoras" go far beyond the actual text (which certainly originates from Pythagoreanism if not actually written by Pythagoras himself), and reveal outstanding knowledge of ancient writings. Fabre d'Olivet says that different levels of divinity exist. He distinguished[16] the divinity as observed by the intellect, and describes it as being under the sign of the number three. Observation derived from reason, on the other hand, leads, "like nature," only to the number two. Finally, the instinct observes a multiplicity of properties and attributes "like matter." Although these ideas do not cover the entire layout of our harmonic scheme, they fit some aspects of it all the more closely.

As Kayser has pointed out, the connection of the number three with the notion of God, plainly seen in many ancient trinities, appears harmonically at the apex of the Lambdoma where the three tones $1/1c$, $2/1c'$, and $1/2c_1$, simultaneously provide the key, as it were, to the diagram's further development. The twofold idea of God in correspondence with nature—one thinks primarily of Zoroaster—is paralleled in the reciprocity of the two number and tone series that stem from $1/1$ and determine as coordinates the order of values of being on the Lambdoma. (Hence Kayser speaks of "partial-tone coordinates.") They may be equated with the principles of creation or with similarly functioning intelligences. Once again, the multiple attributes of the divine lead us to a mystical notion of God: to the inherence of the divine in all that is created, symbolized in the Lambdoma by the equal-tone lines by which every value of being (if the diagram is infinitely extended) is directly connected to the symbol o/o. These remarks by Fabre d'Olivet are identical to the assertions of Kayser, and serve principally to familiarize us with the Lambdoma and its metaphysical analogies.

For the moment, however, we will focus on the symbol $1/1$, namely on the notion of the demiurge or mediator, which we will attempt to correlate with the idea of the "King of the World" as found in René Guénon's work. Guénon is the founder of the doctrine of "integral" or "restored tradition," imparted to him in secret Oriental orders (he converted to Islam and was a member of a Sufi order) on the basis of ancient wisdom, and which he was entitled to expound.

The King of the World, about whom Ferdinand Ossendowski also made interesting remarks,[17] is in the strictest sense a designation for the universal lawgiver Manu,[18] whose name is found in various ancient traditions, for example as the Greek Minos. Of course, this name does not conceal a historic or legendary personality, but rather a principle, a "cosmic intelligence that mirrors the pure spiritual light and grants the law that underlies the conditions of our world and the cycle of our existence." At the same time this principle is the archetype of man, especially in his thinking aspect. It can also manifest on earth in a spiritual center, an organization whose leader has the duty to confer the primordial wisdom on those able to receive it, and who himself bears all the titles and attributes of Manu. This leader will also identify with Manu on the basis of the knowledge that is a prerequisite of this office.

There exists, then, a science of primordial wisdom consisting of specific principles functioning as laws for our world; and there is a mediator who is identical with these principles. This aspect corresponds exactly to the position of the symbol 1/1 on our Lambdoma figure, and it is very interesting to compare it with the characteristics of the King of the World mentioned by Guénon.

According to Guénon, the King of the World wields a twofold power, both sacerdotal and royal. The Lambdoma is similarly dualistic: it is constructed from the two principles (coordinates) 1/1, 1/2, 1/3, 1/4, etc., and 1/1, 2/1, 3/1, 4/1, etc., whose intersection with the central vertical line occurs at the value 1/1. (Multiplication of the same values is always equal to 1, a mathematical operation perfectly reflected in tone.) The 1/1 principle, permeating the whole "world of values of being" like an artery, proves to be a synthesis of two polarities. But the function of the king of the world is also a dual one, namely to care for justice and peace; and the outcome should then be equilibrium or harmony. The construction of the Lambdoma is indeed harmonic, in the perfect correspondence of all values to the left and right of the fundamental line, and in the foundation of its laws on the intersection of two principles. All values are found here in a state of equilibrium. Behind this apparent balance and symmetry, however, lies the fact that the two halves of the Lambdoma are structured in exact inversions like mirror images, or more precisely as reciprocals of one another.

Kayser has shown convincingly that the mirror-image imbalance of apparent symmetry corresponds exactly to the difference between right and left,[19] and he cites sources[20] suggesting that the preference for the right, which is in no way innate, goes back to archaic religious ideas. The dichotomy of right and left has a cosmic basis in the orbit of the sun, and still manifests in language today, for example in the association of the right hand with right as opposed to wrong, righteousness, etc. This situation allows the dichotomy of values to be transferred to the Lambdoma, giving the key to further metaphysical interpretation. On the basis of these reflections of Kayser's, we can now include the attributes of the King of the World in our discussion.

To describe justice and peace as attributes of the King of the World fits perfectly with what we have outlined. Peace, of course, is the positive ("right") condition, whereas justice, i.e., the execution of a judicial function, assumes at the very least the occurrence of offence and punishment, and hence the existence of the negative. This is even more explicit in the Hebrew notion of *Shekinah* that denotes the "King of the World" and actually means "true presence of the divinity."[21] This designation also embraces the two aspects of justice and mercy, leading (with a certain shift of perspective) toward the idea of the chosen and the damned at the Last Judgment. Incidentally, the same properties, with their aspects of grace and righteousness and the duties of high priest and high ruler, are also ascribed to another Hebrew appellation, *Metatron.*[22]

These qualities apply above all to Melchisedek, in whose encounter with Abraham (Genesis 14. 18 ff.) Guénon sees the act of linkage of the Hebraic with the great Primordial Tradition.[23] Melchisedek is also both king and priest; his name signifies "king of justice" and he is described as the king of Salem, translated as "peace," which is not at all the name of a city, but rather a symbol of the "seat of the King of the

World." Furthermore it is said of Melchisedek that the "Almighty," *Elion* (whose symbol in the Lambdoma is o/o), is set over him,[24] and that he is "without father, without mother, without gender . . ." (Hebrews 7. 1–3). This introduces a new concordance with the Lambdoma. We have already mentioned that every value of being in it is situated at the intersection of an overtone and an undertone row; in other words, it is "generated" as a result of these two principles. Curiously enough, in older music theory major and minor were spoken of as two "tonal sexes" (*Tongeschlechtem*). Since their fundamental triads are identical with tones 1–5 of the overtone and undertone rows, one can actually say that every tone of the Lambdoma is generated from these two tonal sexes, which is why it is such a fundamental diagram, even for modern music theory. Regardless of the level at which generation is being spoken of, one thing is certain: there is only one value on the Lambdoma whose generation is not "sexual," and that is 1/1. It alone stands at no point of intersection; thus the reference to Melchisedek in the Epistle to the Hebrews agrees quite literally with the configuration of the Lambdoma.

A further attribute of the King of the World is that of the "unmoved mover," as it is generally known in the metaphysics of Aristotle. This concept may be interpreted thus: that the ruler of the universe, implying the royal aspect,[25] is simultaneously the pole of all things, which causes all movements without itself participating in them. This principle is more closely defined by an attribute of Metatron, namely that he is connected with the earthly pole on the world axis. A glance at the Lambdoma makes it clear that this axis is symbolized by the generating-tone line at whose uppermost point is the pole 1/1. This amplifies Julius Schwabe's statement that in symbolism, the generating-tone line is identifiable with the world axis.[26]

Now we must address one of the chief problems of this train of thought, also connected with an important aspect of the Lambdoma. According to Guénon, the king of the world also possesses three principles or functions, designated[27] as *Brahatma*, the supreme being ("support of souls in the spirit of God"), *Mahatma* ("representative of the world soul"), and *Mahanga* ("symbol of the whole material organization of the cosmos"). We will just add here that the mention of the world soul immediately recalls Plato's description of this world soul as a Dorian scale, given in the form of an esoteric harmonic text[28]—one of the oldest and most important examples of harmonic symbolism. Similar formulations are found in Ossendowski: Brahatma can speak to God face to face, Mahatma knows the future events, and Mahanga controls the causes of those events. One infers from the latter that together with these "intrapersonal" aspects of the King of the World, a causal principle (the control of the causes of events) as well as a final one (future events) are also represented. What scientific methodology promotes today as the so-called laws of nature corresponds to the causal principle, while the final principle must be classified as astrological and harmonic knowledge, since, as already stated, it deals with norms, structures, and forms, i.e., with goals and aims in nature. Guénon also distinguishes three functions in the figure of Melchisedek:[29] *Adoni-Tsedeg* ("Lord of Justice"), *Kohen-Tsedeg* ("Priest of Justice"), and *Melki-Tsedeg* ("King of Justice").

Here, then, we have a situation corresponding closely to the Christian dogma of the trinity, insofar as it portrays a trinity within a unity; for obviously, despite their different names, we are not dealing with three Melchisedeks but with a single one. This is precisely what is found in a prominent section of the Lambdoma, already mentioned in passing: the three numbers at the apex, $2/1c'$, $1/1c$, and $1/2c_1$. The two flanking numbers are important as the means for the construction of the Lambdoma, namely the principles of multiplication ($2/1$, $3/1$, $4/1$, etc.) and division ($1/2$, $1/3$, $1/4$, etc.). But most importantly, these three numbers refer to a single tone: the fundamental and its upper and lower octaves (c' and c_1); for in music theory the octaves of a tone are viewed as its recurrences or identities on another level. Consequently this pole or point of the Lambdoma symbolizes nothing less than the mystery of the Trinity,[30] and corresponds exactly in form to the intrapersonal principles of the King of the World.

Having discovered a whole series of remarkable parallels between the Lambdoma and the characteristics of the king of the world, we will now briefly expand on them. Among other things, Guénon also knew of the existence of secondary centers of the primordial tradition, different from the main center that nevertheless legitimizes them. For example, Moses was endowed with lawmaking power by Manu;[31] while the highest trinity of Lamaism (Dalai Lama, Tashi Lama, Bodo-Khan)[31A] presents an image of the trinitarian nature of the King of the World. In this context it is interesting to see how Guénon relates Christianity to the King of the World. In the three Magi, or Kings, of the Gospel he sees representatives of the Primordial Tradition, emissaries of the King of the World, so to speak. They possess both royal and sacerdotal authority, and their number incorporates the three aforementioned principles. Hence Guénon considers them as "a support for the complete legitimacy of Christianity from the viewpoint of this tradition." He also sees a further manifestation of this in the twelve disciples of Jesus, but we will treat that issue separately. We have already mentioned that the dogma of the Trinity is reflected in the primordial tradition, although it should be added that it is not of biblical origin but must stem from another tradition, entirely possible in the early Christian era (Synesius, for example, to whom Fabre d'Olivet often refers, was simultaneously a Neoplatonist and a Christian bishop).

We will now leave Guénon in order to draw some conclusions. In the foreground stands the dual conception of God, which takes on undeniable importance from the data concerning the king of the world. According to this ancient tradition, a superior divinity (o/o), not further defined in this context, ordered our world initially on clearly established principles embodied by an intermediary, the King of the World, who was also charged with supervising them. One of the most significant aspects to emerge is an implicit dualism symbolized by the concepts of peace and justice. We have just stated that these words conceal polarized values, one positive and the other negative. It is well known that the construction of the world on the basis of two antithetical principles is an age-old concept: it is best known as the yang and yin of Chinese tradition, but also forms an important element of Pythagorean philosophy, which is why Kayser revived this dualism in referring to the similarly dual structure of the Lambdoma, regarding it as the foundation of the latter.[32]

It must be emphasized that this dualism does not issue from the highest divinity (0/0) but only from the demiurgic one (1/1); in other words, that this dualism is by no means all-encompassing, but merely proper to "our" world. This involves a fundamental problem shared by all religions and philosophies and considered insoluble until now: the question of an explanation for the evil in the world. Fabre d'Olivet discusses it extensively in connection with Pythagorean ideas,[33] though admittedly he is also unable to solve it, and refers only to ancient esotericism. We believe, however, that we are justified in treating this question too, in the light of the Lambdoma, since, as we have shown, the Lambdoma appears to be in very close agreement with the features of the King of the World, and hence with our world's own principles.

Since in ancient traditions this cosmic dualism is mentioned in paired terms such as day and night, light and dark, etc., we can immediately assign everything negative, or evil, to one side of the Lambdoma (the "left," as it were). If we look more closely, however, at the acoustic series, a new fact reveals itself: the overtone and undertone rows that give the diagram its apparent external symmetry are not equal principles in nature. As a natural law, only the overtones exist: it has never yet been possible to demonstrate undertones. Therefore the so-called undertone rows of the Lambdoma are merely reflections, introduced subsequently as it were: inversions of the mathematical law of the overtone row. They can be re-created not only in numbers, but also in the individual tones easily produced on a monochord. Unlike the overtone row that automatically appears at every generation of sound, however, the undertone row does not exist as a holistic natural phenomenon.

Consequently the second, "negative" principle of the Lambdoma is only a derived one, extracted from the positive law by way of inversion (reciprocity) and thus artificial. We could almost apply the same words metaphysically (and the justification for that we have already provided above). Accordingly, the evil in the world does not proceed from the highest divinity (o/o), nor is it an equal partner in a strict dualism, but it derives secondarily from a superior good by way of inversion. In other words, the evil in the world is in no way a property to be derived directly from God, but is only something "ordained": intended, as it were, for our world, and having a very specific function.

It is important to note now that those equal-tone lines to which we have alluded several times, and which indicate a direct link between each value of being and the highest divinity in the mystical sense, are present not only in the "positive" sector of the Lambdoma, but also in the other one. Seen this way, the antimony of good and evil clearly does not exist for the divinity, which is consistent with the Christian notion of God's mercy. Significantly, Fabre d'Olivet transmits the teaching of Synesius that "the soul of man draws its origin from two sources: a light one that flows down from the heavens, and a dark one that springs from the depths of the earth."[34] The point of view is reversed, yet the Lambdoma convinces us of the remarkable concordance, if the values of being are taken as individual souls. Our notion of evil as a purposeful arrangement also agrees, in one respect, with the writings of Julius Evola. In discussing the validity of moral codes for initiates,[35] he states that they serve a useful purpose for the initiation process, but for the initiate, i.e., for one who has risen above ordinary human existence, they are not necessary. This "instrumental conception of moral codes" that forms a pendant to our discussion of the preordination of evil (of which here the actively wicked is considered a subsection), Evola finally explains through the

Buddhist allegory of the raft: "Sila, the essence of moral codes, is comparable to a raft, built and used to cross a river. When the raft has served its purpose, however, it makes no sense to keep dragging it along." Our interpretation of the Lambdoma has therefore brought us by another way into agreement with the primordial tradition, reconfirming our view of its symbolic power.

Initiation apart, the evil in the world appears for normal mankind as a necessity not only in the causal sense, because it is given as a firm and inextricable part of our world's plan, but also in the final sense, namely as a motive force that facilitates the further evolution of the individual as well as of mankind. This evolution would have been impossible in an exclusively positive world without knowledge of evil; such was perhaps that paradisal state of the legendary Golden Age. We find ourselves, however, in the Iron Age, the last and lowest of the four Yugas, and evil, as a means to an end and a motive force, is part of its destiny. Since in this darkest of all ages the veil of Maya is becoming increasingly opaque, and thus the recognition of the good ever less self-evident, religious founders were needed, all of whom appeared just at the onset of the Iron Age, whose moral codes lead us on a path through the valley of darkness. They are, in part, leaders of those secondary centers already mentioned, and their indication of the good along with the contrasting evil constitutes the motive force for further evolution as a dialectic principle.

It is essential for man's fulfillment that he freely choose the upward path; that is why he has free will. As Fabre d'Olivet puts it clearly in his discussion of evil,[36] it is man's state of tension between destiny and will that exactly defines him. Of course destiny is not the same as evil—we define that only as one possible destiny—but the sum of all conditions to which we are bound in our existence. Examples are the inheritance of certain dispositions (we will recall that the Mendelian laws of heredity are harmonically structured),[37] the nationality, language, and religion into which one is born, and one's social environment. To these

destined factors of our being must be added numerous conditions of character and fate, as scientific astrology can show.
And this thought brings us back to a connection with the
primordial tradition and with harmonics.

At this point we must mention the King of the World
again, and say that to his mysterious center belongs an "inner circle" of twelve members,[38] who represent among other
things the twelve signs of the zodiac, as reported by Guénon.
This shows clearly that the zodiac also belongs to the order
of this world, which is hence subject to astrological laws. It
follows that the world governed by this King cannot be our
earth alone, but comprises at least the entire solar system,
and furthermore that the astrological connections put into
dynamic effect that which already exists statistically in harmonic laws and schemata, in particular the Lambdoma. The
various creative principles are combined according to their
effect over a given time. "Astrology, seen in purely formal
terms, is one of the most impressive attempts at a system-
atic and constructive worldview ever attempted by the human spirit,"[39] said Ernst Cassirer from a neutral standpoint.
According to the findings of scientific astrologers, and because it clearly belongs to the primordial tradition, hence to
the principles governed by the King of the World, astrology
might be considered as much more, but this topic should be
treated by experts. Let us just say that astrological laws are
also partly of a harmonic nature, namely in the theory of aspects that Johannes Kepler treated harmonically.[40]

Incidentally, the number twelve is also to be found in the
secondary centers, for example in the "Round Council" of
the Dalai Lama that consists of twelve great Namshans; the
twelve Knights of King Arthur's legendary Round Table;[41] the
twelve tribes of Israel issued from the twelve sons of Jacob,[42]
and the twelve Adepts of the Rose Cross.[43] As already mentioned, Guénon regarded the twelve apostles of Jesus as an
essential sign of the harmony between Christianity and the
Primordial Tradition.[44] In this context, let us add that the eu-
charistic offering is part of this tradition, inasmuch as it
stems from the "Order of Melchisedek;"[45] for at his appear-

ance he brought forth "bread and wine" (Genesis 14. 18). It is no coincidence that this Order of Melchisedek is constantly mentioned in connection with Christ, most obviously in the Epistle to the Hebrews with the words: ". . . Jesus, made a high priest in eternity, according to the order of Melchisedek" (Hebrews 6. 20).

The twelvefold order that reveals itself in the zodiac and is the guiding principle of astrological laws also shows a harmonic basis, if we divide the octave into twelve so-called semitones, following an ancient tradition that prevailed not only among the Greeks but also in ancient Chinese music theory. The allusion to ancient tradition is important because that is what we are speaking of here, but in fact I could also demonstrate that this twelvefoldness is precisely prescribed by the anatomical structure of the ear, and is therefore a law of nature.[46] This basis of our music is no accident, then, just as the use of intervals of simple mathematical ratios, the differentiation between consonance and dissonance, and the construction of major and minor modes are not accidental. All these musical laws may be derived exactly and scientifically from the disposition of our sense of hearing. In fact, our music has unconsciously evolved in a teleological manner, governed by man and his specific way of hearing. This point is significant, since during our investigation we have often drawn our attention to the importance of the teleological, finalistic point of view.

The scientifically verifiable existence of twelve tones in analogy with the twelve signs of the zodiac recalls the ancient connection of the signs of the zodiac with the twelve tones in the most varied symbolic traditions. With the link between planets and tones, this is part of the doctrine of the harmony of the spheres, which can certainly be traced to Pythagoreanism, though such concepts were common knowledge in ancient cultures. Unfortunately we cannot offer a complete taxonomy here, since the various sources contain thoroughly different systems and a comprehensive explanation would be long and extremely difficult. We will only mention the research of Marius Schneider, who has treated the theme primarily in relation to one of the most famous documents concerning the harmony of the spheres, Plato's *Republic*.[47,48] He concludes, most interestingly, that for the ancients the association of planets to tones could have led to the fact that every scale had, so to speak, its own horoscope, and thus its own individual characteristics. This suggestion is significant because in Greek antiquity individual modes were in fact ascribed different influences (also reported, significantly enough, in the legends of Pythagoras). This so-called doctrine of ethos was so self-evident that Plato, in the *Republic*, in regard to the republic's legislation, seriously considered banning the "harmful" modes.[49] The psychological influence of music is a reality today, when (as in antiquity) music is being used scientifically as a psychological treatment. At present these things can only be considered theoretically, but as conjectures that lead back to very ancient traditions.

We have come to the end of our study, naturally without treating these problems exhaustively, but proving the existence of a far-reaching agreement between ancient traditions. In particular we have shown the justification for including harmonic research in this context, not only in the form of so-called harmonic symbolism, notably the Lambdoma, but also in recent scientific findings, which we can use for the constant expansion of our thinking. Most important is the realization that the events of our world are governed by a plan, and that this plan is recognizable even when the events appear to us as incomprehensible and harmful. Hence our life is woven into a manifold connection of goals and aims, over which the King of the World watches. This makes it clear that the proper way of thinking for our world is a finalistic one directed toward goals and aims, whereas natural scientific thinking, necessarily causally oriented, can only conceive of the world in a partial manner. It is, therefore, highly significant that awareness of the limits of scientific methodology is widespread among leading scientists today, and that the teleological outlook is being promoted as an urgently needed complement. Walter Heitler,[50] one of those who has undertaken this, has referred specifically to Kepler and Pythagoras, thereby recognizing from a purely methodological standpoint (for at the time he did not know of harmonics), the importance of a way of thinking that has led us here to such consequential results.

Notes

1. R. Haase, *Geschichte des harmonikalen Pythagoreismus*, Vienna, 1969.
2. A. v. Thimus, *Die harmonikale Symbolik des Alterthums*, 2 vols., Cologne, 1868, 1876, reprinted Hildesheim and New York, G. Olms, 1972.
3. H. Kayser, *Lehrbuch der Harmonik*, Zürich, Schwabe, 1950.
4. J. Kepler, *Harmonices mundi libri V*, Linz, 1619; ed. Max Caspar in *Gesammelte Werke*, vol. VI, Munich, Beck, 1940.
5. R. Haase, "Harmonikale Grundlagenforschung-eine neue Wisssenschaft," in *Musikerziehung*, Jg. 22, no. 3 (Vienna, 1969), pp. 120–23, no. 4, pp. 164–67.
6. H. Kayser, *Orphikon*, Basel, Schwabe, 1971.
7. R. Haase, *Leitfaden einer harmonikalen Erkenntnislehre*, Icking bei München, ORA, 1970.
8. Kayser, *op. cit.*
9. Haase, *op. cit.*
10. R. Guénon, *Le Roi du monde*, Paris, 1927. [Translated by A. Cheke as *The Lord of the World*, Ellingstring, Coombe Springs Press, 1983. Citations are from this edition. Ed.]
11. A. Fabre d'Olivet, *Les Vers dorés de Pythagore*, Paris, 1813. [Translated by N. L. Redfield as *The Golden Verses of Pythagoras*, New York, Putnam, 1917, reprinted N.Y., Weiser, 1975. Citations are from this edition. Ed.]
12. Von Thimus, *op. cit.*, vol. I, pp. 129 ff.
13. Kayser, *Lehrbuch*, pp. 56 ff.
14. J. Schwabe, *Archetyp und Tierkreis*, Basel, Schwabe, 1951, p. xxxix.
15. Kayser, *Lehrbuch*, pp. 87 ff.
16. Fabre d'Olivet, *op. cit.*, p. 133.
17. F. Ossendowski, *Beasts, Men and Gods*, New York, Dutton, 1922. [See also the important article by Marco Pallis, "Ossendowski's Sources," in *Studies in Comparative Religion*, vol. 15, no. 1/2 (1983), pp. 30–41, and J. Godwin, "Saint-Yves d'Alveydre and the Agarthian Connection," in *Hermetic Journal*, no. 32 (1986), pp. 24–34, and no. 33, pp. 31–38. Ed.]
18. Guénon, *op. cit.*, pp. 5 ff.
19. Kayser, *Lehrbuch*, p. 76.
20. H. v. Meyer, "Über den Ursprung von Rechts und Links," in *Zeitschrift für Ethnologie*, vol. 5 (1873).
21. Guénon, *op. cit.*, p. 11.

22. *Ibid.*, p. 16.
23. *Ibid.*, p. 33.
24. *Loc. cit.*
25. *Ibid.*, p. 9.
26. Schwabe, *op. cit.*, pp. 294 ff.
27. Guénon, *op. cit.*, pp. 18 f.
28. Plato, *Timaeus* 35 A. f.
29. Guénon, *op. cit.*, p. 34.
30. Kayser, *Lehrbuch*, p. 120.
31. Guénon, *op. cit.*, p. 19.
31A. Without invalidating Haase's thesis, it is only correct to note here Marco Pallis' statement that there is no question of a third associate to the Dalai and Tashi Lamas ("Ossendowski's Sources," p. 35). Ed.
32. H. Kayser, "Pythagoras," in *Abhandlungen zur Ektypik harmonikaler Wertformen*, Zürich, 1946, pp. 75 ff.
33. Fabre d'Olivet, *ed. cit.*, pp. 41
34. *Ibid.*, p. 115.
35. J. Evola, "Über das Initiatische," in *Antaios*, vol. 6, (Stuttgart, 1965), pp. 184 ff.
36. Fabre d'Olivet, *ed. cit.*, pp. 41 f.
37. R. Haase, "Die harmonikale Struktur der Mendelschen Gesetze," in *Zeitschrift für Ganzheitforschung*, Jg. 9, no. 4 (Vienna, 1965). [Also in his *Aufsätze zur harmonikale Naturphilosophie*, Graz, Akad. Druck- und Verlagsanstalt, 1974, pp. 28–35. Ed.]
38. Guénon, *op. cit.*, p. 23.
39. E. Cassirer, *Begriffsformen des mythischen Denkens*, 1922, cited in W. E. Peuckert, *Astrologie*, Stuttgart, 1960, p. 7.
40. W. Koch, *Aspektlehre nach Johannes Kepler*, Hamburg, 1952; R. Haase, "Musik und Astrologie," in *Musica*, Jg. 5, no. 12 (Kassel, 1951). [See the first extract in our Appendix. Ed.]
41. Guénon, *op. cit.*, p. 23.
42. *Ibid.*, p. 63, n. 18.
43. *Ibid.*, pp. 47 f.
44. *Ibid.*, p. 23, n. 13.
45. *Ibid.*, p. 33.
46. R. Haase, *Die harmonikalen Wurzeln der Musik*, Vienna, 1969, pp. 56 ff.
47. Plato, *Republic* 616 B ff.
48. M. Schneider, "Die musikalischen Grundlagen der Sphärenharmonie," in *Acta musicologica*, vol. 32 (Basel, 1960), pp. 136–151.
49. Plato, *Republic* 398 D ff.
50. W. Heitler, *Der Mensch und die naturwissenschaftliche Erkenntnis*, Braunschweig, 1966.

Kepler's World Harmony
and its Significance for Today

JOHANNES KEPLER, whose 400th birthday was celebrated throughout the world on December 27, 1971, is well known to us as a great scientist and mathematician of the past. Since our schooldays we have all known the three laws of planetary motion named after him. Yet this picture of Kepler, apparently so self-evident, is in need of some correction; for our idea of a scientist who came into the world, so to speak, in order to discover these planetary laws and much else of significance for the scientific worldview is very one-sided, if not entirely false. This was absolutely not the case with Kepler: in fact, most of his deservedly famous discoveries, which we certainly do not wish to demean, were made, as it were, in passing, while pursuing a different goal entirely—a goal that he also ultimately achieved. To put it quite plainly, Kepler was possessed all his life by an idea that dominated his whole work and that he never lost sight of: he was seeking evidence for a harmony of the world such as was handed down as a legend from antiquity. He was unshakably convinced of its truth and was finally able to demonstrate its existence in the form of musical laws. This proof is contained in his *Harmonices Mundi Libri V* (completed in Linz in 1619), or "Five Books on World Harmony," as Max Caspar appropriately translated the Latin title.[1]

Kepler's self-imposed life's work was not so outlandish for his own time. On the contrary, Kepler is by no means the only thinker of the Baroque era to have concerned himself with the idea of world harmony. The concept also emerges, indeed even forms a central premise, with Paracelsus, Athanasius Kircher, Robert Fludd, Marin Mersenne—to name but a few of the most important universal savants of the time—and they, too, were thoroughly familiar with the musical disposition of harmonic laws. All of them, including Kepler, began from traditions that originated in antiquity and had been revived by the humanists. This idea of world harmony with musical laws goes back to the Pythagoreans, who hardly left any written documents behind because they observed strict secrecy in the manner of the ancient mystery religions. The idea then surfaced in Plato and Aristotle, albeit still in the form of barely comprehensible cryptograms. It was transmitted through the centuries as a legend, and during the Renaissance it was reborn.

We cannot go into this historical transference in detail here, but we can say that this doctrine of a musical world harmony was practically common knowledge among humanist scholars, and that many were convinced of its truth. Certainly evidence was lacking, and besides, these ideas were usually linked with magical, cabalistic, Rosicrucian, and other speculative and enigmatic doctrines, which have made this "Pansophia" (a word of Paracelsus) less attractive to subsequent schools of scientific thought. This may be correct, but as one moves further from that era, one discovers a profound error. When Pansophia was thrown away, so was the premise of Johannes Kepler. Thus it was totally overlooked that his contribution to this topic differed radically from that of the others. Despite their common roots in the Pythagorean tradition, it was Kepler alone who approached his self-imposed questions with critical understanding and set himself to the task with scientific precision and responsibility.

Kepler's world harmony, in contrast to his contemporaries', is not a dogmatic belief in legend: rather he proceeds heuristically,[2] checking his research with unremitting self-discipline. In a letter to Fabricius dated July 4, 1603,[3] he said, to that effect: "You believe that I first think up some pleasing hypothesis and amuse myself embellishing it, and only then submit it to the test of observation. You are quite wrong. The truth is that when a hypothesis has been built up and buttressed through observations, I then feel a wonderful longing to discover whether I can reveal in it some natural and satisfying relationship. But never do I first propose a judgment." This, then, is the decisive difference from Kepler's contemporaries, who blindly bowed to tradition.

Kepler has been identified, quite unjustly, with the followers of Pansophia, and his image has thereby been distorted. Later it was thought necessary to excuse him for what had been imputed to him, and finally these components of his work were entirely suppressed, one person copying from another for two centuries. What remained was Kepler the scientist, discoverer of the famous planetary laws and other notable things, while his true premises remained virtually unknown until well into our century. Now we must briefly sketch Kepler in his true colors, at the same time providing evidence for what has already been said; and this we will do as far as possible in Kepler's own words.

Kepler was, of course, already famous in his own lifetime, though it is less generally known that he first aroused interest by a work devoted to the idea of world harmony: the *Mysterium Cosmographicum*,[4] written in Graz and published when he was twenty-three. This publication, the first of his great scientific works, immediately brought him to the attention of those in his field, including Tycho Brahe. The book contains a geometric construction of world harmony in which Kepler, not yet having discovered the elliptical form of the planetary orbits, observed that the five Platonic solids (cube, tetrahedron, octahedron, dodecahedron, and icosahedron) could be imagined as fitting between the spheres of the planets. It was a work in tune with its time: a revised edition was called for twenty-five years later, although Kepler in the meantime had discovered that the planetary orbits are elliptical, so that much of its content was actually superseded.

Kepler wrote a preface for this second edition in which we find these astonishing words on the first edition: "Almost all the books on astronomy that I have published since then can be related to one or another of the chapters of this little work, as representing either its extension or its completion." This implies no less than that Kepler's later astronomical discoveries, so important to us, including his first two planetary laws,[5] are simply results of this preoccupation with world harmony! Admittedly, he discovered them in the course of the work entrusted to him by Tycho Brahe in Prague. However, we must correct here another all too common opinion. It was not primarily the famous astronomer Brahe who drew the young Kepler to him: the latter's plan was a completely different one. He tells us this at the point when he finally succeeds in determining the proof of world harmony, namely, in the fifth book of his *Harmonices Mundi*, in the prologue of which are the significant words:[6] "What induced me to devote the best part of my life to astronomical studies, to seek out Tycho Brahe and choose Prague for a residence, I have finally brought to light with God's help." In other words, Kepler sought out Tycho Brahe for the sake of proving world harmony, for the simple reason that he believed that he could obtain the best data for this proof from Brahe's outstanding observations. As would become apparent later, in *Mysterium Cosmographicum* he had already laid out a model, a hypothesis, and an approximate solution.

Another little-known fact is that Kepler's third planetary law can be found in the middle of that same fifth book of *Harmonices Mundi* that contains the proof of world harmony. It appears in chapter three as the eighth of thirteen major postulates of astronomy required for his proof.[7] So it was by no means a main premise of the work, but served Kepler merely as an aid toward proving world harmony! We even know that this third planetary law only occurred to Kepler shortly before the book's completion: it was inserted late and has little to do with the actual proof, but provided a final confirmation.[8]

After Kepler had furnished the proof of world harmony in the fifth book of *Harmonices Mundi*, he concluded with a prayer of thanksgiving to the Creator, in which we find the characteristic words: "You see that I have now accomplished the task to which I was called. I have applied to it all the powers of my spirit bestowed upon me by You. To those who will read my treatise I will have revealed the magnificence of Your works, or as much of their eternal wealth as my humble understanding could grasp."[9]

All these statements plainly show what Kepler perceived as his true life's task, and make it all the clearer that for him the "important scientific discoveries" were not the crucial ones. This surprising fact emerges from the content of *Harmonices Mundi*, to which we must now briefly turn. First, two facts must be established. One is known to us, namely, that Kepler had in the meantime (i.e., since *Mysterium Cosmographicum*) discovered the elliptical form of the planetary orbits. Secondly, he had been intensively occupied with music theory, and had acquired a solid knowledge of this field, mainly under the guidance of Sethus Calvisius. Like the Pythagoreans, he made use of the monochord, on which we have a very instructive report in a letter he wrote to Herwart von Hohenburg in April 1607: "In my harmonic researches, my best schoolmistress has been experimentation. Over a resonant chamber we stretch a metal string. With a movable bridge placed beneath it, we travel back and forth on the string—to the right, to the left—striking repeatedly the two segments of the string divided by the bridge, and then we remove the bridge and let the whole string resound. The rest we entrust to the judgment of our ear. When the latter assures us that both segments make a concord with the whole string, one draws a line at that point on the soundboard and measures the length of both sections of the string. Thus one discovers what proportions emerge. Sometimes the two sections are consonant with each other but not the whole string; at other times, one section will be consonant with the whole string, while the other creates a dissonance both with it and with the whole."[10]

In other words, Kepler worked out the interval ratios by his own experiments, i.e., the fact known since antiquity that the intervals of our music are inseparably linked to numerical ratios, usually very simple ones: ratios of string lengths as on the monochord, wavelengths, or, reciprocally, frequencies. The ratio 1:2 gives the octave, 2:3 the fifth, 3:4 the fourth, and so on. This theory of ratios, which also plays a role in geometry, now became the guide for Kepler's subsequent investigations, and with its help he finally succeeded in finding the proof of harmonic laws in the cosmos that he had sought since his youth, namely, the musical harmonies generated by the planets. This proof is given in the *Harmonices Mundi*, the "Five Books on World Harmony," to whose contents we now turn.

As the title states, the work consists of five parts, the last of which contains the actual proof, while the others simply supply the necessary foundations. But Kepler also has something else in mind here. He wants to demonstrate that in the most varied areas analogous sets of laws exist, which although they must be stated differently, still exhibit a clear relationship when viewed with a morphological mode of thought. The first two books deal with geometrical fact. The third book, the most comprehensive, incidentally, contains music theory (and few know that here Kepler was the first to use the terms "major" and "minor" in the modern sense);[11] and the fourth finally treats astrological problems. Naturally the fifth book has astronomical content, because it contains the presentation of the planetary orbits, but at the same time it is a synthesis of the problems broached in the previous four books, and refers most of all to the third book, since Kepler uses music theory to conduct his proof.

We have already stated that Kepler's third planetary law is also given in this fifth book. Although it is only employed as a means to an end, it deserves some consideration in view of its great scientific importance. In Kepler it reads as follows: ". . . it is a sure and established fact that the proportion between the orbital periods of any two planets is exactly one and a half times the proportion between their mean distances, i.e., between the orbits themselves."[12] This statement is different from the one we know today, and shows clearly that Kepler was operating within the doctrine of proportion and stating the problem in those terms, whereas he "utters no word of the physical deliberations that have led him . . . to the discovery of the third law," as Max Caspar explicitly remarks.[13] In this instance, then, Kepler is acting primarily

as a harmonicist rather than as a natural scientist. And now
to the actual content of the fifth book.

The book opens with a short presentation of the five Platonic solids, thus resuming at the precise point where Kepler
had attempted his first proof of world harmony in *Mysterium Cosmographicum*. Only here he immediately goes a
step further in alluding to the relationship between the harmonic proportions and these five regular solids. The thirteen
astronomical postulates follow, which include the third
planetary law, and the presentation of the musical harmonies in the planetary orbits begins in Chapter 4. Kepler examines many different data for the orbits, including their
distances from the sun, their durations, the daily arcs, etc.,
and transposes the astronomical measurements into interval
ratios that he tabulates and discusses. The results do not sat-
isfy him until he makes the most important discovery by
comparing the values of the angles as measured from the sun
and formed by the planets at their extreme points (aphelion
and perihelion) in the space of twenty-four hours. A whole
system of simple intervals emerges, sixteen in all, that with
two exceptions are all musical consonances, and generally
triadic ones.

Saturn	Aphelion	a	a:b	= 4:5	(major 3rd)
	Perihelion	b	a:d	= 1:3	(12th)
			c:d	= 5:6	(minor 3rd)
Jupiter	Aphelion	c	b:c	= 1:2	(octave)
	Perihelion	d	c:f	= 1:8	(3 octaves)
			e:f	= 2:3	(5th)
Mars	Aphelion	e	d:e	= 5:24	(minor 3rd + 2 octaves)
	Perihelion	f	e:h	= 5:12	(minor 3rd + octave)
Earth	Aphelion	g	g:h	= 15:16	(diatonic semitone)
	Perihelion	h	f:g	= 2:3	(5th)
			g:k	= 3:5	(major 6th)
Venus	Aphelion	i	i:k	= 24:25	(chromatic semitone)
	Perihelion	k	h:i	= 5:8	(minor 6th)
			i:m	= 1:4	(2 octaves)
Mercury	Aphelion	l	l:m	= 5:12	(minor 3rd + octave)
	Perihelion	m	k:l	= 3:5	(major 6th)

Of course, we cannot hear these harmonies directly, though we need only adapt the ratios to a monochord or another suitable instrument to let them sound. In other words, one must transpose these intervals into the audible range, which is quite a simple matter; and so Kepler naturally uses the standard interval designations for these ideal sounds. With equal success, he then investigates the orbit of the moon about the earth, and resumes his examination of the planetary orbits, using as a foundation the interval ratios established for the extreme points of the orbits. From the resulting planet-tones, he attempts to construct scales, largely major and minor, and also counterpoints, polyphonic phrases, and individual melodies to characterize the various planets. Finally he even formulates a hypothesis for how the harmony of all the planets together must have sounded on the first day of creation. This extends through the eighth chapter of the fifth book, followed in the ninth chapter by a conclusion and summary that is of particular interest to us. In this ninth chapter, the longest of the book, Kepler compares his line of reasoning with his first proposal in *Mysterium Cosmographicum*. Most important to us are the typically Keplerian expressions here. The heading for the whole fifth book already testified to this: "The most perfect Harmony in the Celestial Movements, and the remarkable generation therefrom of Eccentricities, Orbital Radii, and Cyclical Durations."[14] But what does this mean? Apparently that Kepler did indeed perceive the eccentricities, orbital radii, and cyclical durations—the actual scientific facts concerning the planetary orbits—as *consequences* of the musical harmonies. Or, even more clearly: the "generation of eccentricities," which is none other than the elliptical form of the orbits, and hence Kepler's greatest discovery, is for him a result of these musical laws! And the heading of the ninth chapter says exactly the same: "That the Eccentricities of the individual Planets have their Origin in the Concern for Harmonies between the Planets."[15] So here, too, the elliptical form is grounded in the musical harmonies.

Thus Kepler's thinking is precisely the opposite of the causal thinking of natural scientists, who in this case would consider the musical intervals as phenomena resulting from the elliptical form of the planetary orbits. Kepler argues to the contrary, stating that the elliptical form is necessary for the intervals to be generated at all, which would have been impossible with circular orbits. He is not thinking causally, but rather finally or teleologically. He does not perceive the event as an effectuating or efficient cause, but rather as a goal or final cause to be reached. He prefers this finalistic way of reasoning because of his unshakable conviction of the governance of a creator of the world: hence he conceives of the world's ascertainable laws as the creator's will. In this way his discoveries become thoroughly understandable for the first time, because at the outset neither the elliptical forms of the planetary orbits nor the musical laws that came to light at the same time made sense on their own.

The reason for this is that in Kepler's era the circle was considered the most perfect plane figure, while the ellipse was seen as imperfect and inferior. Under these circumstances his discovery of the elliptical orbits was unacceptable even to Galileo,[16] who obstinately stuck to the dogma of the circularity of the orbits of all heavenly bodies. Therefore Kepler was compelled to explain and almost excuse his great discovery, and he did this by reference to the creator. He stated that ". . . the Creator, source of all Wisdom, constant preserver of order, the eternal and absolute fountain of all geometry and harmonics, He, I say, this divine Artisan, His mighty self, has joined together the harmonic ratios that arose from the regular plane figures with the five regular solids in order to fashion from both classes of figures the most perfect Archetype of the Heavens: an Archetype, which on the one hand expresses the idea of the spheres that surround the six celestial bodies by means of the five solid figures, and on the other hand expresses by means of derivations from the plane figures and the harmonies the degrees of eccentricity of the individual orbits for the purpose of regulating the movements of those bodies. From these two component parts a unified, balanced system had to be made. The greater proportions of the orbits had to yield to a slight alteration in favor of the lesser proportions of the eccentricities required for the generation of the harmonies; and conversely, those of the harmonic ratios that exhibited the greatest congeniality with a solid figure at any given moment had to be fitted with the planets, insofar as was possible with these harmonies."[17]

This quotation most tellingly reveals Kepler's way of reasoning, for at its core are the words referring to the old model of the solar system with its circular orbits as depicted in *Mysterium Cosmographicum*: "The greater proportions of the orbits had to yield to a slight alteration in favor of the lesser proportions of the eccentricities *required for the generation of the harmonies.*" Kepler's opinion is clearly that God consciously rejected the ideal circular orbits, because he wished to achieve a musical harmony of the planets. It follows for Kepler that the musical harmonies must be more important for God the Creator than the geometric ones, otherwise he would not have sacrificed their ideal form, the circle. This Kepler implied in the following words: "That where a choice exists between various things that are not wholly compatible with one another, preference must be given to that which has priority, and that which is of inferior rank will yield as much as is necessary: this is clearly manifest in the word *cosmos*, which means 'ornament.' By the same token, however, insofar as life takes precedence over the body, and form over the material, the harmonious takes precedence over the simple geometrical ornament."[18]

This presentation of Kepler's fundamental concern, supported by his own statements, and the resulting correction of his image, invites reflections on this surprising and unique worldview. Of course the question immediately raised is that of the correctness of what he worked out. About thirty years ago the Frenchman Francis Warrain examined this question thoroughly and answered it with all the clarity one could desire.[19] He compared Kepler's measurements with current astronomical values and confirmed an extremely high degree of agreement, for example, in the table of aphelion and perihelion proportions that stands at the center of the fifth book of *Harmonices Mundi*. Only two of the ratios needed modifica-

tion, while on the other hand it was shown that the deviations from exact proportions[20] as discovered and discussed by
Kepler are far slighter: hence his computations have become
even more precise. Above all, Warrain also applied Kepler's
methods to the planets Uranus, Neptune, and Pluto, discovered in the interim, and confirmed in their orbits, too, a host
of interval proportions. Kepler's planetary harmonies, therefore, hold true to this day; they are a reality that belongs as
much to the eternal state of the cosmos as do his famous planetary laws.

The question of the correctness of Kepler's harmonic world
picture may also be posed in another way. Some skepticism
could be leveled at the universal validity of the musical laws
enunciated by him, laws that he regarded, incidentally, as dispositions of the human soul as well.[21] Today both are placed in
doubt and disavowed by avant-garde composers, so that we
must make a musicological digression based on recent research not widely known even in professional circles.

The most important point of departure for this question is
the so-called Husmann Theory of Consonance, first published by Heinrich Husmann in 1953[22] and in fact not quite
correctly named: for in truth we are not dealing here with a
theory or a hypothesis, but with the results of very careful experiments and their mathematical interpretation. At the core
of these is the discovery that, as a result of the nonlinearity of
human hearing, there are sounds that arise in the ear besides
those that reach the eardrum. These inner sounds are of two
different kinds. First there are *subjective overtones*: every incoming tone acquires an additional overtone row in the ear
with the same construction as that occurring objectively in
nature, so that these subjective (or auricular) overtones considerably amplify those already entering. Secondly, there
arise in the ear whenever two or more notes are sounded
(hence with every interval) so-called *combination tones*.
These either add or subtract the frequencies of the given
tones, hence we also speak of "summation" or "difference
tones." Certainly the latter phenomenon had been known
since the Baroque era, but it was Husmann who, besides dis-

covering the subjective overtones, pointed out that combination tones of a higher order also play a significant role in the ear. Put simply, they are the ones formed from the overtones of the incoming notes. With every interval, up to seventy-two combination tones may thus be produced.[23] Astonishing things are happening in our ears, which we are unaware of since they are so very quiet; but in effect these numerous sounds create a sort of net or, more precisely, a sieve, for that is how it works. When an interval sounds, two possibilities exist for every combination tone: either it will coincide with one of the overtones of the two fundamentals, thus minimally amplifying it, or else it will fall into the gaps in the overtone row, distorting it, blurring it, and hence altering its natural sound. Highly simplified, this is what can be proven experimentally on the basis of the anatomy of the ear.

Closer analysis of these complicated events in the ear now yields some very remarkable facts. First of all, it appears that the coincidence of overtones and combination tones will only be possible if the interval in question is made from a ratio of whole numbers. With other intervals, all the combination tones fall into the gaps of the overtone row. What this means is that intervals formed of whole-number ratios are preferred, insofar as their final effect is a purer sound. In other words, the interval proportions on which our musical system has been founded since antiquity have arisen neither by accident nor from speculation, but correspond exactly to a physiologically explicable disposition of our ear. In those days they were at least instinctively correct, and with these findings one can even demonstrate why they excluded certain notes from the tone system.[24]

Although intervals with simple numerical ratios are, in general, more suited to our ear, this does not apply to all equally. As the second important result, it has been shown that with any given interval a different number of combination tones coincides with the overtones. Comparing the numbers as computed, a table results in which the octave stands at the top, followed by the fifth, the fourth, etc., and at the end of the table stand the minor second and the tritone.[25]

COMBINATION TONES IDENTICAL WITH OVERTONES		INTERVAL	PROPORTIONS
Number	Percent		
72	100	octave	1:2
42	58	5th	2:3
28	39	4th	3:4
24	33	major 6th	3:5
18	25	major 3rd	4:5
14	19	minor 3rd	5:6
10	14	minor 6th	5:8
8	11	minor 7th	5:9
2	3	major 2nd	8:9
2	3	major 7th	8:15
0	0	minor 2nd	15:16
0	0	tritone	32:45 [or 1:√2]

This sequence corresponds exactly to the ordering that has determined the differentiation between consonance and dissonance ever since antiquity. The consonance-dissonance difference, one of the most important bases of our music, is therefore founded on facts.

The experiments initiated by Husmann lead to further astonishing results. From this consonance-dissonance table it is possible to deduce that the major and minor modes arose on the basis of this disposition of the sense of hearing, and further computations also lead to an explanation for the division of the octave into twelve semitones.[26] The proportions of intervals, the consonance-dissonance distinction, major and minor, and the twelvefold ordering of notes—all can be deduced from the disposition of the human ear. In fact, the most important foundations of our musical tradition may be traced to man's own structure. Though never aware of this as scientific axiom, composers quite obviously acted correctly out of intuition, and on the basis of their sure instincts wrote their music for man. This means, however, that traditional Western music is finalistically oriented, directed toward a goal, and that this goal has always been man himself. It is no wonder, incidentally, that from the time when this instinct was no longer trusted and doubt began to be cast on the traditional foundations of music, now called restrictive and conventional, increasingly newfangled, clever, intellectual schemes were produced, causally rather than teleologically generated, and music became more and more incomprehensible.[27]

Certainly not all phenomena can be satisfactorily explained by this complex yet also meaningful disposition of the sense of hearing. But with further research it appeared that a similar disposition had to be assumed in the psychological realm too. This analogous psychological disposition was even demonstrated by experiments with the deaf-and-dumb.[28] Only two of the facts need be given here: first, an exact qualitative correlation to the interval disposition in the physiological realm; second, a certain flexibility that makes it possible to correct imprecisions and deviations from the exact ratios, as for example in tempering. This corroborated a discovery made in the Baroque era by Leonhard Euler, who was the first to allude to so-called "corrective hearing": the ability of our hearing to correct itself.[29]

Having surveyed the results of modern research on the disposition of human hearing, we now return to Johannes Kepler. With this new information we may summarize the main features of his harmonic worldview, amplifying some details:

1   Kepler's world harmony consists of musical laws, in particular of simple, largely consonant intervals with a clear preference for major and minor.

2   As we know today, these intervals are in accord with the disposition of human hearing in both the physiological and, as Kepler assumed, the psychological domain.

3   Analogical thinking plays a considerable part in Kepler, insofar as analogies between various sciences are brought out, the analogy between cosmic and musical laws is established, and also the analogy to the human disposition

is asserted and later proven. All these analogies are constructed with the help of simple proportions.

4 Teleological or finalistic thinking is Kepler's second important method of reasoning, so that an additional analogy exists to traditional Western music, which is unconsciously formed in this way.

5 To sum up, it can be stated that Kepler's harmonic world picture rests upon scientifically provable laws and on methods that are in accordance with the nature of hearing and the foundations of music. The sense of hearing is included in our knowledge of nature, and psychological perceptions, such as those engendered by the intervals and other fundamentals of music, become essential elements of this worldview.

Thus Kepler's harmonic worldview differs markedly from that of the natural sciences which is characterized above all by causal thinking, a quantitative perception of the world, and a functionalistic procedure with mathematics at its core. Perhaps this harmonic worldview can provide the much-needed complement to the scientific one, long recognized as one-sided. Yet again doubts come to the surface: doubts about the universal validity of this worldview — for after all, it was only astronomical laws that were being discussed — and doubts, too, about the alien quality of this harmonic perspective. Scientists tend to consider the musical and psychological experience of the interval ratios simply as a side effect, an incidental by-product of no essential significance. We must take issue with that here.

In fact the occurrence of interval ratios as a law of nature is in no way restricted to astronomy. Without making any attempt at comprehensiveness, we will give several typical illustrations, whose proofs must of course be drawn from the appropriate professional literature. The best known must be the correlation between the crystal structure and musical laws, since the crystallographer Victor Goldschmidt emphasized it in many publications.[30] Consequently modern crystallography also refers to harmonic research.[31] A great number of proportional laws may be detected in this field by various methods. In *chemistry*, it has been determined that the law of multiple proportions yields harmonic results; countless chemical compounds have been examined and have proven that the ratios, without exception, have been those of musical consonances.[32] That the overtone row is a cornerstone of *acoustics*, i.e., a law of nature made up of interval proportions, is self-evident here. *Biology* can acknowledge a whole series of harmonic contributions. Almost invariably, simple intervals occur in the philotoxical laws;[33] numerical laws have been discovered in the cell division of algae that correspond to the major triad;[34] the Mendelian laws turn out to be identical with the simplest intervals.[35] Birdsong agrees completely with human music, so that an identical disposition must be assumed with birds, especially since it is certain that birds do not imitate human music, even though they are in a position to do so.[36] Interval laws appear particularly in *anthropology*, uncovered in part by medical research into the external structure of the human figure, which ever since antiquity has repeatedly been depicted as being made of aliquot parts. The most enlightening research of all, however, is that of Gunther Hildebrandt[37] on rhythmic ordering in the human organism, not only showing an almost perfect coordination in the simplest numerical ratios in the long waveband, but also finding intervallic proportions governing the circulation of the blood, breathing, pulse, blood pressure, etc. Hence Hildebrandt refers explicitly in his dissertation and elsewhere to harmonics.[38] Naturally the disposition of the aural sense, as already mentioned, belongs in the field of anthropology.

This enumeration, which includes only the most important results, must suffice at this point. We must add, however, that these musical laws appear almost exclusively at essential places, and that we are hardly ever dealing with any arbitrary proportions, but with those that have a characteristic musical significance: we mentioned the overtone row, the major triad, and consonances. The facts given here in summary form certainly make it impossible to try to devalue these findings to mere side effects; indeed we must say that to overlook or to trivialize these conspicuous harmonies would be to act in a thoroughly unscientific fashion!

In one case, the analogies between the various fields characterized by intervallic laws go much further. A square table of numbers exists that was reconstructed about a hundred years ago and must have played an important role in ancient Pythagoreanism.[39] This table, which we call the Lambdoma because it was originally developed in the form of the Greek letter Lambda, consists of numerous overtone rows and contains a wealth of highly interesting properties. The most amazing thing is the fact that this Lambdoma in its totality is applicable to arithmetic, geometry, acoustics, crystallography, and cybernetics, and that furthermore it can also be interpreted theologically and philosophically.[40] It is particularly ironic that crystallography[41] and cybernetics[42] stumbled on this numerical table in the course of their own scientific work, without any previous knowledge of its existence, to say nothing of its antiquity. This Lambdoma most probably was at the actual core of the Pythagorean doctrine of world harmony. Kepler devoted his entire life to the proof of this harmony, kept in those days in strict secrecy and therefore only transmitted in legendary form.

Our conclusion is not only that Kepler's harmonic world image is correct in every detail, but also that further pursuit and elaboration of his methods and perspectives permit a truly all-encompassing worldview to emerge, whose existence can no longer be doubted. It concerns principally a different perspective on the world and the use of different categories for its interpretation. It is the same real world as described by the natural scientists, whose insights and achievements we do not wish to belittle, but each of these worldviews is only a partial one and requires completion. This alternative perspective of the harmonic worldview was put very tellingly in an essay on Kepler by Walter Harburger: "When we happen upon the basic musical elements, consonances as well as dissonances defined mathematically or

physically, it is not so much the music that is mathematically or physically determined, but much more the mathematics or physics that is permeated by music."[43]

For Kepler there was as yet no separation between the two
modes of observation, though as we have seen in his holistic
world picture, the harmonic components clearly had priority. The case must have been the same in ancient Pythagoreanism, otherwise the harmonic theorems would not have
been kept so strictly secret. And today, since we possess a
new science of "research in harmonic principles,"[44] in which
these traditions are united with modern scientific knowledge, the harmonic components of the world become more
visible than ever. We might even suggest that the purely
quantitative, scientific observation of nature is perhaps a
side effect of *this* worldview! In any event, this is how Kepler
thought when he subordinated his scientific discoveries to
harmonic laws. Since those times, the quantitative view of
nature has predominated, and the thought of a harmony of
the world appears more distant than ever, however urgently
we need it. But this harmony can return for us, too; for it requires only another perspective on the world, the harmonic
one, attainable at any time and perhaps more easily today
than yesterday. Johannes Kepler sought and found the world
harmony, and thereby became a pioneer of natural science.
We modern people should turn to his *World Harmony* and
learn to interpret the great achievements of natural science
in its light, and thereby find our way back to the Harmony of
the World.

Notes

1. J. Kepler, *Weltharmonik*, trans. M. Caspar, Darmstadt, 1967.
2. G. Náder, "Die heuristische Rolle des Harmoniebegriffs bei Kepler," in *Studium Generale*, Jg. 19, no. 9 (Berlin, 1966).
3. M. Caspar and W. v. Dyck, *J. Kepler in seinen Briefen*, Munich, 1930, vol. I, pp. 187 ff.
4. J. Kepler, *Mysterium Cosmographicum—Das Weltgeheimnis*, trans. M. Caspar, Augsburg, 1923. [See extract in the appendix. Ed.]

5. J. Kepler, *Astronomia nova*, Heidelberg, 1609.

6. Kepler, *Weltharmonik* (see n. 1), p. 279.

7. *Ibid.*, p. 291.

8. Haase, "Marginalien zum 3. Keplerschen Gesetz," in *Kepler Festschrift*, Regensburg, 1971. [Also in Haase's *Aufsätze zur harmonikalen Naturphilosophie*, Graz, Akademische Druck-u. Verlagsanstalt, 1974, pp. 117–125. Ed.]

9. Kepler, *Weltharmonik*, p. 350.

10. M. Caspar and W. v. Dyck, *op. cit.*, vol. I, p. 276.

11. P. Beyer, *Studien zur Vorgeschichte des Dur-Moll*, Kassel, 1958, p. 68.

12. Kepler, *Weltharmonik*, p. 291.

13. *Ibid.*, p. 386.

14. *Ibid.*, p. 277.

15. *Ibid.*, p. 316.

16. G. Galilei, *Sidereus Nuncius etc.*, ed. H. Blumenberg, Frankfurt/M., 1965, pp. 13, 251.

17. Kepler, *Weltharmonik*, p. 317.

18. *Ibid.*, p. 348.

19. F. Warrain, *Essai sur l'Harmonices Mundi ou Musique du Monde de Johann Kepler*, 2 vols., Paris, 1942.

20. *Ibid.*, vol. 2, p. 135.

21. Kepler, *Weltharmonik*, p. 206.

22. H. Husman, *Vom Wesen der Konsonanz*, Heidelberg, 1953.

23. R. Haase, *Grundlagen der harmonikalen Symbolik*, Munich, 1966, p. 79.

24. *Ibid.*, p. 78.

25. *Ibid.*, p. 79.

26. R. Haase, *Die harmonikalen Wurzeln der Musik*, Vienna, 1969, pp. 52 f., 56.

27. *Ibid.*, pp. 67 f.

28. A. von Uden, "Möglichkeit und Verwertung der Lautempfindung bei taubstummen Kindern," in *Neue Blätter für Taubstummenbildung*, Jg. 9, nos. 5–6, Heidelberg, 1955.

29. Haase, *Grundlagen* (see n. 23), p. 87.

30. V. Goldschmidt, *Über Harmonie und Complication*, Berlin, 1901; "Über Harmonie im Weltenraum," in *Annalen der Naturphilosophie*, vol. 5 (1906); "Über das Wesen der Kristalle," in *ibid.*, vol. 9 (1910); *Über Complication und Displication*, Heidelberg, 1921.

31. G. C. Amstutz, "Symmetrie in Natur and Kunst," in *Der Aufschluss*, Jg. 16, no. 6 (1966).

32. L. Wolf, "Symmetrie, Harmonie und Bauplan in Mathematik und Naturwissenschaft," in *Beiträge zur christlichen Philosophie*, no. 3, Mainz, 1948.

33. H. Kayser, *Harmonia Plantarum*, Basel, 1943, pp. 141 ff.

34. F. Moewus, "Zur Genetik und Physiologie der Kern- und Zellteilung," in *Forschungen und Fortschritte*, Jg. 25, no. 5/6, Berlin, 1949.

35. R. Haase, "Die harmonikale Struktur der Mendelschen Gesetze," in *Zeitschrift für Ganzheitsforschung*, Jg. 9, no. 4, Vienna, 1965. [Also in Haase's *Aufsätze* . . . (see n. 8), pp. 29–35. Ed.]

36. W. Neuhaus, "Sinnesphysiologie und Neurologie der Tiere in ihrer Bedeutung für die Verhaltensforschung am Menschen," in F. Keiter,
Verhaltensforschung vom Menschen, n.d.

37. G. Hildebrandt, "Physiologische Grundlagen für eine tageszeitliche
Ordnung der Schwitzprozeduren," in *Zeitschrift für klinische Medi-
zin*, vol. 152 (1954); "Grundlagen einer angewandten medizinischen
Rhythmusforschung," in *Die Heilkunst*, Jg. 71, no. 4, Munich, 1958; *Die
rhythmische Funktionsordnung von Puls und Atmung*, Stuttgart,
1960; "Rhythmus und Regulation," in *Die medizinische Welt*, no. 2,
Stuttgart, 1961; "Die Koordination rhythmischer Funktionen beim
Menschen," in *Verhandlungen der deutschen Gesellschaft für innere
Medizin*, 73rd Congress, Munich, 1967.

38. *Die rhythmische Funktionsordnung* . . . (see n. 37).

39. A. von Thimus, *Die harmonikale Symbolik des Alterthums*, 2 vols.,
Cologne, 1868, 1876, reprinted Hildesheim and New York, G. Olms,
1972.

40. H. Kayser, *Lehrbuch der Harmonik*, Zürich, Schwabe, 1950, pp. 56 ff.

41. V. Goldschmidt, *Über Harmonie* . . . (see n. 30), p. 34.

42. G. Günther, *Das Bewusstsein der Maschinen*, Baden-Baden, 1963, Appendix III.

43. W. Harburger, "Johannes Keplers mystiche Sendung," in *Festschrift für
H. L. Held*, Munich, 1951.

44. R. Haase, "Harmonikale Grundlagenforschung—eine neue Wissen-
schaft," in *Musikerziehung*, Jg. 22, nos. 3–4, Vienna, 1969. [Also in
Haase's *Aufsätze* . . . (see n. 8), pp. 9–18. Ed.]

The Sequel to
Kepler's World Harmony

AFTER several centuries in which the life work of Johannes Kepler has been misrepresented, and his real self-imposed mission, namely the proof of the legendary Pythagorean world harmony, has been suppressed, discredited, and demeaned, Max Caspar[1] and Hans Kayser[2] have at last set matters right. In the light of present knowledge, the various past accounts of Kepler's world harmony appear grotesque; they would be comic if the background were not so tragic. Three tasks remain today: to expose the errors of past historians;[3] to justify the Keplerian proof of an acoustic and musical world harmony,[4] and to make known the research that continues Kepler's cosmic harmony, thereby confirming, at least in part, the correctness of his method. The third task has so far been neglected, and it is this that we undertake here.

Kepler's proof of a comprehensive harmony of the planets of our solar system was reached with the help of interval ratios. Its centerpiece is the table in *Harmonices Mundi*, Book V, in which he relates the aphelion and perihelion arcs of the planets to one another.[5] These are the angles, measured from the sun, that are formed in twenty-four hours by the planets while moving at the two extremes of their orbits: their closest and furthest points from the sun. Kepler discovered that comparison of these pairs of values yields simple proportions that are without exception identical to well-known musical intervals. Simply put, the data are as follows:

Saturn	Aphelion	a	a:b	=	4:5	c	e		
	Perihelion	b	a:d	=	1:3	c		g	
			c:d	=	5:6		e	g	
Jupiter	Aphelion	c	b:c	=	1:2	c			c′
	Perihelion	d	c:f	=	1:8	c			c′
			e:f	=	2:3	c		g	
Mars	Aphelion	e	d:e	=	5:24		e	g	
	Perihelion	f	e:h	=	5:12		e	g	
Earth	Aphelion	g	g:h	=	15:16			b	c′
	Perihelion	h	f:g	=	2:3	c		g	
			g:k	=	3:5		e	g	
Venus	Aphelion	i	i:k	=	24:25		g g#		
	Perihelion	k	h:i	=	5:8		e		c′
			i:m	=	1:4	c			c′
Mercury	Aphelion	l	l:m	=	5:12		e	g	
	Perihelion	m	k:l	=	3:5		e	g	

One can interpret the musical meaning of this table in various ways; the simplest is to correlate the given proportions with the appropriate interval names, that is (from the top), major third, twelfth, minor third, octave, triple octave, fifth, etc. Kepler himself attempted to combine the individual intervals into scales. His main concern was to obtain major and minor modes[6] (a designation, incidentally, which Kepler was the first to use in the modern sense[7]). We have undertaken on the other hand to seek the intervals where they occur in nature, namely in the overtone series, which as a natural law represents one of the most important foundations of acoustics and music. (The overtone series was only discovered after Kepler's time by Marin Mersenne, which explains why Kepler could not avail himself of this data.)

The regular construction of the overtone series resides in the fact that the individual partial tones are whole-number multiples of the fundamental frequency (or their reciprocals, in the case of wave and string lengths). If we proceed from the overtone series of the note c, designated by 1, then its partials bear the relative frequencies of the numbers given above them, and the combinations of numbers provide the interval proportions belonging to the notes beneath them — a principle also valid when skipping one or more notes or numbers:

1	:	2	:	3	:	4	:	5	:	6	:	7	:	8, etc.
c		c′		g′		c″		e″		g″		b♭‴		c‴, etc.

Returning to Kepler, if we look for the proportions provided by the table in one overtone row, and refer them all to one common fundamental (whereby for simplicity we choose c, though any other note would have been possible, since we are dealing with relative proportions), we obtain those notes that stand to the right of the Keplerian table, notes that for the sake of clarity we have transposed into one octave. The result is amazing: of the 32 given notes, 30 are those of the major triad, namely C, E and G, and only the two notes G# and B appear as exceptions. Our method of interpretation, therefore, provides an excellent overview, and gives a musical meaning that considerably simplifies the table, which is at first glance somewhat impenetrable. For the same reasons it will serve as well in what follows.

To the best of our knowledge, the first person to adopt Kepler's reconstructed table was Ludwig Günther,[8] who used Kepler's procedure to investigate the planets, discovered after Kepler's time. He tested its applicability to Uranus, and also examined the asteroids, of which Ceres, Vesta, Pallas, and Juno share the halftone C# in common, albeit with some deviations. Why no values were given for Neptune remains unexplained.

Keplerian world harmonics were then taken up comprehensively by Francis Warrain,[9] who in his two-volume work of 1942 not only made Kepler's research available to French speakers, but also wrote the definitive modern book on world harmony that also treated the earliest work of Hans Kayser.[10] Warrain compares Kepler's measurements with today's results, and also refers to the planets discovered since Kepler, including Pluto. It is impossible here to do full justice to this excellent work: we must confine ourselves to those data of Warrain's that have direct bearing on the matter at hand. We will borrow one of his large tables (see below) containing all relevant information.[11]

First, it becomes apparent from this table that, almost without exception, Kepler's measurements were very precise. Of all his intevals, only three had to be altered because of a revised measurement. These are the ratios: c:f = 12:25, l:m = 9:20, and k:l = 16:27. In many instances, the modern measurements even make Kepler's suggested intervals more exact. In any event, it is clear that Kepler's methodology and its general results are still valid today.

Warrain also established other ratios that were not contained in Kepler's chart, comparing the aphelion and perihelion of neighboring planets, and including Uranus (with the same results as Günther), Neptune, and Pluto. We will now summarize all of Warrain's data in the same form as Kepler's table, to which actually it constitutes the sequel. For simplicity we will put the new planets at the end, taking the disturbance of their sequence into account.

Saturn	Aphelion	a	a:b	=	4:5	c	e		
	Perihelion	b	a:d	=	1:3	c		g	
			a:c	=	2:5	c	e		
			b:d	=	5:12		e	g	
			c:d	=	5:6		e	g	
			b:c	=	1:2	c			c′
Jupiter	Aphelion	c	c:d	=	9:50	d		g#	
	Perihelion	d	c:f	=	12:25			g g#	
			d:f	=	4:27	c			a
			d:e	=	5:24		e	g	
Mars	Aphelion	e	e:f	=	2:3	c		g	
	Perihelion	f	e:g	=	9:20	d	e		
			e:h	=	5:12		e	g	
			f:h	=	3:5		e	g	
Earth	Aphelion	g	g:h	=	15:16				b c′
	Perihelion	h	f:g	=	2:3	c		g	
			g:i	=	3:5		e	g	
			g:k	=	3:5		e	g	
			h:i	=	5:8		e		c′

Planet	Point		Ratio		Value	c	d	e	g	g#	a	b	c'
Venus	Aphelion	i	i:k	=	24:25				g	g#			
	Perihelion	k	h:k	=	5:8			e					c'
			i:l	=	5:9		d	e					
			i:m	=	1:4	c							c'
Mercury	Aphelion	l	k:l	=	16:27	c					a		
	Perihelion	m	l:m	=	9:20		d	e					
			k:m	=	81:320			e e^{+1}					
Uranus	Aphelion	n	n:o	=	5:6			e	g				
	Perihelion	o	n:b	=	3:5			e	g				
			o:a	=	5:6			e	g				
			n:p	=	5:9		d	e					
Neptune	Aphelion	p	p:q	=	80:81			e e^{+1}					
	Perihelion	q	n:q	=	5:9		d	e					
			o:p	=	9:20		d	e					
			o:q	=	15:32							b	c'
			p:s	=	$(80:81)^2$								
Pluto	Aphelion	r	r:s	=	9:25		d			g#			
	Perihelion	s	p:r	=	5:24			e	g				
			q:s	=	8:9	c	d						
			q:r	=	8:18	c	d						

The 39 proportions of this table show that we are dealing without exception with familiar elements of musical acoustics. They appear unusual only when they involve intervals greater than the octave, but to eliminate octaves one need only multiply or divide one of the numbers by two (for example, 5:24 may be reduced to 5:6, the minor third, 5:24 being a minor third plus two octaves), so that the result is simpler than it seems. Only the ratio p:s is musically unusable, giving a double syntonic comma that cannot be employed in music as it stands. Yet even this value is acoustically significant, since the syntonic comma 80:81 is a most important constant in acoustics. It is formed in the overtone row from the partials 80 and 81, both legitimately called E (when the fundamental is C), and in effect creates a unison (the E numbered 81 is given as E^{+1} Thus we retain the two single syntonic commas p:q and k:m (the latter extended by two octaves) as unisons or primes.

If after transposing all the intervals within a single octave

we tabulate the occurrence of intervals, the following picture
emerges:

Unison			
(syntonic comma)	2	Fifth	3
Minor second	4	Minor sixth	2
Major second	6	Major sixth	6
Minor third	7	Minor seventh	2
Major third	2	Major seventh	—
Fourth	—	Octave	2
Tritone	2		

With the exception of the fourth and the major seventh, all
our common musical intervals are represented, albeit with
differing frequency. Kepler acted very reasonably, therefore,
when he attempted with a far more modest reserve of notes to
build scales and melodies from these intervals.[12]

Another picture emerges when we relate all these intervals,
considered statistically before, to a common tonality, once
again assuming them to be the overtones of a fundamental C.
We have set out the resultant tones as they appear on the right
of the table, and find the following occurrences when transposed within an octave:

C	D	E	G	G#	A	B
17	10	25	16	4	2	2

Of these 76 notes, 72 belong to the major scale of C, though
the same notes would belong to the minor scale if A were considered the fundamental; accordingly, the four G#'s appear as
exceptions in terms of music theory. This picture, then, is not
quite so homogeneous as Kepler's original table, though with
more than twice the number of notes this could hardly have
been expected. If we search here for the underlying criterion
of Kepler's table, that is, the major triad, however, it appears
that 58 notes fall on either C, E, or G, which is of course remarkable enough. We can thus speak without hesitation of

the dominance of the major triad or of the major mode. The minor triad A, C, E, is by contrast only represented by 44 notes.

It is clear, then, that revisions, corrections, and supplements to the cornerstone of Kepler's world harmony can still lead to significant results, and, indeed, that the main criteria have remained intact. In Kepler's *Mysterium Cosmographicum*,[13] his first attempt at describing a world harmony, where he believed he could explain the geometric principles behind the planetary spheres by way of the Platonic solids, Warrain perceives an infrastructure for the interval system he discovered later:[14] an approximate solution, in other words, to the musical world harmony revealed in the *Harmonices Mundi*, Book V. One could pursue this line of thought and consider the table of intervals constructed by Warrain as a further improvement and elaboration of Kepler's solution to the problem, not forgetting that Kepler's discoveries have almost invariably remained valid and require only slight correction and elaboration, by applying — and this is most important — Kepler's own methodology.

Günther's and Warrain's additions are not the only supplements to Kepler's *World Harmonics*. Indeed in the fifth book of this work Kepler himself made several attempts to demonstrate interval proportions within the planetary orbits, but with less success than in the case of the aphelion and perihelion arcs. Among other things, he investigated the distances of the planets,[15] but as he was not satisfied with the outcome we will omit his presentation here. Two important astronomers, Titius (1729–1796), and Bode (1747–1826) used this part of Kepler's research as a point of departure and ultimately developed what is now called the Titius-Bode law of the distance of the planets from the sun. In this the distance Sun–Earth is given as 10. The resultant series of laws (later completed to include the newly discovered planets) can be expressed in a twofold manner, and is given in the first two columns of the following table:

PLANET	DISTANCE AFTER TITIUS-BODE		ROOKES' PROPOSAL	
Mercury	$0 + 4 = 4$	or $4 + 0 .3$	1/16 P and	1/10 A
Venus	$3 + 4 = 7$	or $4 + 1 .3$	1/7	
Earth	$6 + 4 = 10$	or $4 + 2^1 .3$	1/5	
Mars	$12 + 4 = 16$	or $4 + 2^2 .3$	1/3	
Asteroids	$24 + 4 = 28$	or $4 + 2^3 .3$		
Jupiter	$48 + 4 = 52$	or $4 + 2^4 .3$	1	
Saturn	$96 + 4 = 100$	or $4 + 2^5 .3$	2	
Uranus	$192 + 4 = 196$	or $4 + 2^6 .3$	4	
Neptune	301		6	
Pluto	$384 + 4 = 388$	or $4 + 2^7 .3$	6P and	10A

Both forms of the Titius-Bode sequence actually contain the same harmonic core, namely a series of octaves of the twelfth of a given fundamental. In the first case, this series is immediately identifiable in the number sequence 3, 6, 12, 24, etc., the doubling implying octave transposition. In the second case, the octave transposition is recognizable in the indices (power of 2), but because these are then multiplied by 3, the same values as in the first case are produced. This multiplication by 3 is what gives the twelfth, for the series of powers of 2 beginning with 1 $(2°)$ would only furnish octaves of a fundamental C, whereas multiplication by 3 would lead to its twelfth g′ (third partial), and thereafter one is dealing with higher octaves of g′ (6th, 12th, 24th partials, etc.).

Nevertheless, this development of the series only approximately resembles an acoustical and musical structure; for the more distant planets it becomes increasingly imprecise. Hence Rookes[16] suggested taking as a referential measurement not the distance Sun–Earth, but rather that of Jupiter's perihelion to the sun (= 1). This yields the more exact value reproduced in the third column of our table; in the cases of Mercury and Pluto, owing to their wide eccentricities, Rookes felt obliged to provide both the perihelion and aphelion values. Once again, though, the outcome is harmonic, since beginning with c = 1 all the values may be given exactly as tones:

1/16	1/10	1/7	1/5	1/3	1	2	4	6	10
$C_{\prime\prime\prime}$	$A^{b}_{\prime\prime\prime}$	$D_{\prime\prime}$	$A^{b}_{\prime\prime}$	F,	c	c′	c″	g″	e‴

Musically speaking, this sequence is of particular interest, because those tones *beneath* the fundamental C constitute predominantly a minor triad (F, A^{b}, C), whereas those *above* the fundamental represent exclusively a major triad (C, E, G). In other words, this result closely resembles in principle the Kepler-Warrain analysis of the aphelion and perihelion angles of the planets.

While the Titius-Bode sequence is a familiar astronomical law, a far less known fact is that the mean distances of the planets have been investigated by means of another admittedly approximate process. It involves the "method of complication"[17] proposed by the crystallographer Victor Goldschmidt. This method, for which he has become famous, applied not only to crystals, among other things, but also to the planets.[18] By this process Goldschmidt believed that he had discovered a universal law of nature, and in fact he attempted to demonstrate it, with amazing success in various fields. The resulting set of laws is also a harmonic one, since numbers and fractions consistently emerge that can be regarded in terms of intervals. Goldschmidt clearly recognized this. Like Kepler, he thought in harmonic terms, and in his writings he was one of the forerunners of Hans Kayser.[19] It is interesting that as a scientist he undertook to write a two-volume music theory,[20] although it contains a few questionable items.

The method of complication consists in referring the natural values (z) of a system marked by distinctive limits (z_1 and z_2) to one another by way of a formula, whereby new values are acquired (p) that can then be arranged in a mathematical equation. The formula reads:

$$p = \frac{z - z_1}{z_2 - z}$$

In his various writings,[21] Goldschmidt applied this formula

to the planets, their satellites, and the asteroids, and shortly
before his death he included the newly discovered Pluto.[22] In
so doing he applied his complication formula in various ways,
taking different systems of reference in which the sun nearly
always constituted one limit. The other limit was sometimes
the universe (∞), sometimes other points. Thus, he obtains,
for example, the p-values for the smaller planets from a system   bounded   by   the   sun   and   Jupiter,   investigates the asteroids in three different ways (between Sun–
Jupiter, Mars–Jupiter, and Earth–Jupiter). His reasons for doing
so are not our concern here, since it is enough to list the results,
that is, the p-values.

For the mean distances of the larger planets, these are:

	Sun	Jupiter	Saturn	Uranus	Neptune	Pluto	Universe
p	0	1/2	1	2	3	4	∞

For the mean distances of the smaller planets:

	Sun	Mercury	Venus	Earth	Mars	Jupiter
p	0	1/2	1	3/2	3	∞

The first series corresponds to the tones C c c' g' c", the second
to the tones (transposed) C c g g'. Without further discussion of
the individual procedures and tones, we will now give the other
results in tabular form, since this is the best way of exhibiting
the regularity of relationships:

Larger planets		1/2		1		2	3	4	
Smaller planets	1/3		2/3	1		2			
Asteroids (Sun–Jupiter)	1/3		2/3	1		2	3	4	5 6
Asteroids (Mars–Jupiter)		1/2	2/3	1		2			
Asteroids (Earth–Jupiter)		1/2	2/3	1					
Jupiter's moons		1/2	2/3	1		2			
Uranus's moons		1/2	2/3	1	3/2				
Saturn, inner moons		1/2	2/3	1	3/2	2			
Saturn, outer moons				1	6/5	3			
Earth's moon				1					

(The limiting values of 0 and ∞ are omitted in all cases.)

The resemblance between the rows is plain to see, and it is evident that these are all interval proportions. But in this case we cannot associate the rows with equivalent tones, for despite similar numbers we must keep in mind that each row is based upon a different system of reference; it possesses, so to speak, its own "tonality" or "key." Only for didactic reasons could one refer the given values to a fictitious common fundamental, in order to illustrate the musical connection. It would look like this:

1/3	1/2	2/3	1	6/5	3/2	2	3	4	5	6
F,	C	F	c	e^b	g	c′	g′	c″	e″	g″

It is remarkable, nonetheless, that even with the change in the system of reference, the same simple ratios appear again and again. This must surely be attributed to a deep natural connection, which in fact is what Goldschmidt assumes. And this is what Kepler finally proved by his discovery of the acoustic and musical laws behind the solar system's structure. Its musical nature is so comprehensive that, whatever points of reference one takes, simple musical factors repeatedly come to light.

Even with this wealth of evidence corroborating the harmonic laws shown by Kepler to be inherent in the solar system, we must meet a frequently raised objection. It is often pointed out that the planetary intervals are not quite exact, and that strictly speaking the orbits of the planets are not ellipses at all; that all fundamental laws are only idealized conceptions; and that in reality there are considerable and ever changing deviations as a result of mutual disturbances by the planets. Of course this is true; as we pointed out with Titius-Bode, Rookes, and Goldschmidt, we are dealing with approximations. But on the other hand, Warrain made it clear in 1942 that since Kepler's time, changes in the aphelion and perihelion angles were so slight that corrections were barely necessary, not to mention the fact that the revised values made it possible to greatly expand Kepler's interval system. Kepler himself was well aware of the fact that his interval ratios were by no means always exact,[23] and he discusses these deviations quite openly at the end of the table that we have shown as the core of his fifth book.

A general comment must be made on all these imprecisions, deviations, and alterations. Let us begin with a thought-experiment. We drop an iron ball and a sheet of paper simultaneously and from the same height and see that the sheet of paper reaches the ground a good deal later than the iron ball. How is this possible, since all bodies must fall equally fast according to the law of gravity? The answer is obvious: the time difference is due to the resistance of air and the particularly adapted shape of the sheet of paper. Yet the law of gravity has not been contravened by the sheet of paper; only its effect is not as easily recognizable as in the case of the iron ball. The law of gravity was influenced by other laws, and the descent of the sheet was a result of all the participating laws, including that of gravity. What we show by this is that the appearance of additional influences or interferences does not automatically invalidate or replace a previously established law, but brings about modifications and variables that, were they subtracted, would reveal the original law in all its purity. In such cases, Kayser proposed the distinction between *norm* and *law*, and included them in his harmonic considerations.[24] Norms are the underlying principles, and laws the manifest laws of nature that modify norms. The elliptical forms of the planetary orbits, therefore, are norms that the mutual disturbances of the planets continuously alter, without thereby eliminating the basic fact of the underlying norm. The interval laws discovered by Kepler could also be interpreted in this fashion, although Warrain's data suggest that this is hardly necessary yet, since after the approximately 320 years since the *Harmonices Mundi* appeared in Linz (1619), only minute changes have been registered.

It is a different matter with the obvious and basic phenomenon of deviation from exact proportions, openly discussed in both Kepler and Warrain. The scientific line of approach to such deviations is to summarize, substantiate, and discuss them as precisely as possible. Since in Nature there are no pure norms, but rather an abundance of dynamic variables, this "quest for error" is awarded so much space that natural scientists often lose sight of the norm itself or consider it so self-evident that it is hardly ever mentioned. Thus the planetary laws, interval ratios, etc., are called "purely ideal."

At this point it is appropriate to consider a property of our hearing that indeed concerns audible laws — or rather, laws made audible by transposition into the audible range. (Cases of distortion at the edge of the aural spectrum such as the "mel-effect" can be disregarded as they are based on the non-linearity of hearing.) Recent research[25] shows that human hearing is not only attuned significantly to our familiar foundations of music (interval proportions, distinction of consonance and dissonance, twelvefold gradation, major-minor, etc.), but, most importantly, that the psychological and unconscious realm complements this disposition of the ear. This unconscious realm *knows* something of the interval proportions, and takes a decisive part in the multilayered and complex process of musical hearing.[26] Principally, however, this psychological disposition — and here we come to the crux of it — is capable of unconsciously correcting all deviations that occur (notably those of mistuning). Since the time of Euler, who discovered it, this property has been called "correctional hearing," and more recent studies in information theory have found that this unconscious compensation can account for up to 40 percent of a semitone.[27]

If we apply this to the problem of cosmic deviations, then we should also include this correctional hearing in the contemplation of the world by *listening*, which, in the final analysis, is the harmonic attitude. This suggests that the "mistunings" of the planetary intervals given by Kepler and Warrain would immediately be corrected unconsciously by our hearing, so that they would not even enter our consciousness as deviations! On a harmonic basis, then, their discussion is superfluous.

Notes

1. J. Kepler, *Weltharmonik*, trans. with notes by M. Caspar, Darmstadt, 1967.
2. H. Kayser, *Der hörende Mensch*, Berlin, 1932; "J. Kepler und die Sphärenharmonie," in *Schweizer Rundschau*, vols. 7–8 (1946–47), also in *Die Harmonie der Welt*, Vienna, 1968.
3. R. Haase, *Geschichte des harmonikalen Pythagoreismus*, Vienna, 1969, pp. 88, 108 f.
4. R. Haase, "Harmonikale Gesetze in der Natur," in *Zeitschrift für Ganzheitsforschung*, Jg. 14, no. 2, Vienna, 1970.
5. Kepler, *op. cit.*, p. 301.
6. *Ibid.*, pp. 305 ff.
7. *Ibid.*, p. 127.
8. L. Günther, *Die Mechanik des Weltalls*, Leipzig, 1909, pp. 142 f.
9. F. Warrain, *Essai sur l'Harmonices Mundi ou Musique du Monde de Johann Kepler*, 2 vols., Paris, 1942.
10. *Ibid.*, vol. 2, pp. 110 ff.
11. *Ibid.*, vol. 2, p. 79.
12. Kepler, *op. cit.*, pp. 309 ff.
13. J. Kepler, *Mysterium Cosmographicum—Das Weltgeheimnis*, trans. with notes by M. Caspar, Augsburg, 1923.
14. Warrain, *op. cit.*, vol. 2, p. 135.
15. Kepler, *Weltharmonik*, p. 297.
16. D. Rookes, Reader's letter in *Nature*, vol. 227 (29 August 1970). The author thanks Prof. L. Jaenicke of Cologne for this information. [The suggestion is already present in Goldschmidt, 1906 (see note 21), p. 66, where the right-hand column is given exactly, with the exception of Pluto's values and the double value of Mercury. Ed.]
17. V. Goldschmidt, *Über Harmonie und Complication*, Berlin, 1901.
18. V. Goldschmidt, in *Brockhaus Enzyklopädie*, vol. 7, Wiesbaden, 1969, p. 455.
19. R. Haase, *Hans Kayser—ein Leben für die Harmonik der Welt*, Basel, 1968, pp. 53 ff.
20. V. Goldschmidt, *Materialen zur Musiklehre*, Heidelberg, 1925.
21. V. Goldschmidt, "Über Harmonie im Weltenraum," in *Annalen der Naturphilosophie*, vol. 5 (1906); "Über Harmonie im Reich der Planetoiden," in *Ibid.*, vol. 11 (1912).
22. V. Goldschmidt, *Der Planet Pluto und die Harmonie der Sphären*, Heidelberg, 1932 (vol. 18 of Heidelberger Akten der von-Portheim-Stiftung).
23. Kepler, *op. cit.*, p. 301.
24. H. Kayser, *Lehrbuch der Harmonik*, Zürich, 1950, p. 266.
25. R. Haase, *Die Harmonikale Wurzeln der Musik*, Vienna, 1969. [See also Haase's *Über das disponierte Gehör*, Vienna, Doblinger, 1977 (*Fragmente als Beiträge zur Musiksoziologie*, no. 4). Ed]
26. *Ibid.*, p. 41.
27. H. Eggeling, "Kriterien semantischer und ästhetischer Information bei absoluter Musik," in *Praxis und Perspektiven des programmierten Unterrichts*, vol. 2, Quickborn, 1967.

HANS
ERHARD
LAUER

HANS ERHARD LAUER was born July 17, 1899 in Schwenningen in the Black Forest and spent his formative years in Basel, where his father was manager of a clock factory. His first ambition was to be a composer and conductor, but in 1916, after hearing Rudolf Steiner lecture, he became committed to the anthroposophical movement, especially in its political aspect as proponent of the Threefold Social Order. After war service his scene of activity shifted to Stuttgart, the center of the anthroposophical movement in Germany. In 1919, while enrolled at the University of Tübingen, he gave his first lectures in Anthroposophy to an informal student group. In 1922 his doctoral dissertation on the Swiss philosopher I.P.V. Troxler was accepted by the University of Vienna, having been rejected the previous year by Karl Jaspers at Heidelberg. Lauer now moved to Vienna, working there until the Anschluss as journal editor and manager, writer, and guest lecturer throughout Eastern Europe. In this period he also composed a volume of songs (*Jugendlieder aus den zwanziger Jahren*, Stuttgart, Novalis Verlag, 1980), and in 1930 married Marta von Stefanovic. During his Vienna period he was also constantly in touch with developments at the anthroposophical headquarters at Dornach, near Basel, playing an important role in the changes that followed the death of Rudolf Steiner (1925).

With the Nazi occupation of Austria, Anthroposophy was banned and Lauer underwent a difficult period of homelessness in Prague, Belgrade, and other centers of anthroposophical activity. Finally he was able to settle in Switzerland as a teacher (until 1964) in the Rudolf Steiner schools of Basel and Zürich, and as Dozent at the Freie Hochschule für Geisteswissenschaft at the Goetheanum in Dornach. He founded a new periodical, *Blätter für Anthroposophie* (1949–67, thereafter called *Mensch und Welt*), and edited it until his death on June 17, 1979.

Lauer published more than forty books and about 500 articles, covering the whole range of anthroposophic thought but especially its applications to history, epistemology, and the problems of the twentieth century. His work is distributed by Marta Lauer, Sempacherstrasse 61, CH-4053 Basel, Switzerland. [Source and Bibliography: Lauer's autobiography, *Ein Leben im Frühlicht des Geistes: Erinnerungen und Gedänken eines Schulers Rudolf Steiners* (Freiburg i. Br., Verlag die Kommenden, 1982), and *In memoriam Hans Erhard Lauer: Ein Leben als Zeugnis und Aufruf* (ibid., 1977).]

"Mozart und Beethoven in the Development of Western Culture" was first published as *Mozart und Beethoven im Entwicklungsgang der abendländischen Kultur* (Basel, R. G. Zbinden, 1956, 2nd ed. 1961). "The Evolution of Music through changes in Tone Systems" was first published as *Die Entwicklung der Musik im Wandel der Tonsysteme* (1935, 2nd revised ed., 1960, reissued Basel, Verlag die Pforte, 1976).

Mozart and Beethoven in the Development of Western Culture

A MEDITATION

ON CULTURAL HISTORY

FOR MOZART'S 200TH BIRTHDAY

The conversation turned to the great men who lived before Christ among the Chinese, Indians, Persians, and Greeks, and that the power of God was as active in them as in some of the great Jews of the Old Testament. We also touched on the question: How does God's activity manifest in the great natures of the present-day world in which we live?

"If you hear people talk," said Goethe, "you'd almost think that they believe that God has retreated into silence completely since that time, and that man now stands entirely on his own feet and must see how to succeed without God and His daily invisible inspiration. Man still admits a divine influence in religious and moral affairs, but in matters of science and the arts he thinks that they are purely earthly and nothing more than a product of mere human power.

"Let someone try, however, to bring forth with human will and human powers something to rank with the creations that bear the names of Mozart, Raphael, or Shakespeare. I know very well that these three are by no means the only ones, and that in all realms of art innumerable worthy spirits have worked who have created things just as great as those named. But if they were as great as those, they exceeded ordinary human nature to the same extent, and were just as gifted by the gods.

"But what is all this, and what should we make of it? God has certainly not been resting ever since those commonly imagined six days of Creation: rather, He is continually working as much as at the beginning. To have put together this gross world out of simple elements and set it rolling year in, year out, in the sun's rays would certainly

150

have given Him little pleasure if He hadn't had the plan to found a nursery for a world of spirits on this material basis. So He is now continually active in higher natures, in order to lead the lesser ones forward."

ECKERMANN ON MARCH II, 1832, ELEVEN
DAYS BEFORE GOETHE'S DEATH

L IKE beneficent gods, the great geniuses of art have accompanied the life of historical mankind. From the cornucopias of creative powers far surpassing the human scale, they distribute, in their brief periods on earth, an abundance of gifts that serve mankind as spiritual nourishment for hundreds, even thousands of years. One could say that they fulfill the same role in historic times as those heroes in the prehistoric past who acted as leaders of mankind and cultural founders and were revered by ancient peoples as semidivine beings. After all, the Greeks also considered their gods as semihuman beings, not only representing them sculpturally in human form, but also assigning them a variety of human, indeed, all-too-human traits alongside their divine powers.

More than in any other art, it is permissible in music to use such mythological notions to characterize its greatest geniuses. This is not only because, as the purest of all arts, music has received its name directly from the goddesses who inspire all artistic creation. For historical times, and especially for our own, in which it has become an autonomous art, music's creations mean the same as mythologies meant to older epochs. Just as the imagery of the latter hid a revealed wisdom, impermeable to conceptual thinking but opening its meaning to the feeling of the heart, so too do the genuine creations of music refuse a rational explanation. Yet they comprise (in the words of Beethoven) a "higher revelation than all wisdom and philosophy," which only unlocks itself, to be sure, for the sensitive nature. The great works of modern music constitute the mythological world of our times. Richard Wagner rightly endowed his "music dramas" with mythic content: stage works born from the womb of music. Other dramas too, whose settings have been thoroughly imbued with the spirit of music, attain the realm of the mythical, such as *Don Giovanni, The Magic Flute, Fidelio, Meistersinger,* and others. Myth, therefore, is the only adequate language in which to speak of the great masters of music.

In what follows, prompted by the bicentenary of Mozart's birth, an attempt will be made to speak in this mythic language both of him and of Beethoven, his successor to the throne of music's realm. We will proceed with the assumption that creative geniuses of their caliber never incarnate haphazardly. In order to fulfill the tasks that they have to accomplish, there must have been a preparatory development in their area of activity. They enter historical activity only when their field has attained maturity, so that it can become both foundation and point of departure for their creation. They also require a certain general cultural environment in harmony with the character of their mission. Mozart and Beethoven are to be understood as the musical representatives of that apex of spiritual flowering that middle European culture had attained around the turn of the eighteenth and nineteenth centuries. It was then that the greatest spirits in the fields of poetry and philosophy that central Europe has ever produced, including the poets Lessing, Goethe, Schiller, Hölderlin, Novalis, and Kleist, and the thinkers Kant, Fichte, Schelling, and Hegel, appeared. As contemporaries on the musical plane the greatest creative geniuses were also to be found in Viennese classicism: Haydn, Mozart, Beethoven, Schubert, and others. Among these Mozart and Beethoven indisputably stand out as the greatest. And the spirit that expresses itself in their works is the very same spirit that also permeates the literature of the Weimar classicists and the thought of those philosophers. Even if Mozart, for example, was hardly acquainted with these works of poetry and philosophy, it is no coincidence that the year of his birth should fall between those of Goethe and Schiller, just as Beethoven's coincides with that of Hegel and Hölderlin.

This Golden Age of middle European spiritual life bears a unique relationship to the ancient Greek culture that was still nourished by the image-forming forces of myth. It is not simply an elaboration or imitation of the latter, like the Italian Renaissance or French classicism. Rather the ancient Greek culture itself reemerged in this era, as it were from the depths of historical evolution, in a shape transformed according to the conditions imposed by the interim development of mankind. In external form it is a new metamorphosis; in its inner being it is the same, just as single human individualities are the same in the sequence of their incarnations.

This Greek culture was still part of the phase of the "descent" of human consciousness from an earlier God-revelation into the sphere of physical-sensible experience, and had unfolded mainly on the path of thought, as Rudolf Steiner says (albeit of thought still inculcated with the leftovers of mythic pictoriality). In its modern manifestation, it was part of the phase of "re-ascent" to the superphysical or spiritual, and its center of gravity had shifted to the opposite pole of human soul-life, the element of will. Just as the spiritual view of the ideas still underlies the Platonic-Aristotelian philosophy, so too the thought systems of classical German philosophy are marked by self-elevation by means of the will to the experience of the spirit.

Applying this to the arts, we may say that formerly it was the unfolding of the plastic arts—which according to Schopenhauer bring the ideas of things before the eye—that had lent their stamp to this culture. Greek sculpture and Greek temple architecture will forever remain the most characteristic symbols of the old Hellenic culture. Now in its new incarnation it received its most characteristic expression in the development of music, in which (continuing with Schopenhauer) the world-will comes to the fore. And even more than classical German literature or philosophy, classical German music has achieved the broadest international recognition.

Stated in yet another way: if during the earlier phase of human "incarnation" the concern was to feel out and depict the essentially human in the symbol of the bodily form, now, during the phase of "spiritualization," the concern is to grasp it in the structure and activity of the soul-spiritual inner being. For in both cases the central premise was man: his knowledge, his development, and his realization. Both eras, despite their characteristic differences, were stamped with the ideal of "humanity." Then, as now, the secret of the human being was perceived in the harmonic proportioning of his various organs, limbs, and essential faculties: then, in the harmony of his bodily members; now, in the harmonic consonance of his soul forces. And in addition, both of these high points of creativity were essentially concerned with the realization of beauty, pure and complete. Then, it was with the formation or representation of the beautiful body; now, with that of the "beautiful soul." For how else will beauty be obtained if not through the overcoming of all contradiction and disproportion, all excess and deficiency between the individual parts or moments of a whole? Those same balanced ratios, the same symmetry that we encounter in the formation and organization of the columns and pediments of Greek temples, or in the anatomical proportions of the "canon" of sculptural human representation, we find once again in the proportional and symmetrical relationships of musical motives, themes, periods, movements, etc., in the creations of the modern classical composers. The greater the time lapse separating us from the latter era, the more obvious it seems that a new Hellenism appears interwoven there in the musical element.

Of course the ancient Greeks were also aware not only of a prenatal celestial spirit world in which the human soul originated, but also of the world of earthly matter into which the soul, incarnating in a bodily shell, had to descend in order to discover itself in the overcoming of earthly matter. To them, all human life and striving appeared to be fixed between these two poles; from both sides they saw flowing toward them the knowledge they had to acquire and the faculties they had to apply. In that upper world they beheld the light realm of divine ideas, of the archetypes of all order and formation to which, according to Plato's doctrine of anamnesis, the thoughts kindled in the soul refer as if to images of memory. From there too they became aware of the sound of Apollo's lyre that, together with the song of the Muses whose dances surround the god of light, impels and inspires all human artistic productivity. According to the teachings of Pythagoras, the movements of the stellar spheres sound to the open ear of the spirit as a heavenly music. They were aware, however, that they owed to the forces of this lower world the faculties that had to prove themselves in the mastery of earthly matter. This mastery manifested itself to them in the continuous conquering of formlessness and chaos, into which matter always seeks to fall by its very nature.

They saw these two origins of their cultural life as represented by two mythical figures, whom they revered as the most special teachers of mankind and founders of culture.

One of these was the singer Orpheus, the archetype of all artistic, "musal" creativity: the son of a Muse and the favorite and protégé of Apollo, who made him the gift of a golden lyre and instructed him in divine wisdom. What rang out in his song, accompanied by the sounds of this lyre, was the wisdom by which the universe had come to be, and by which, after the generation of the gods, the kingdoms of nature had been added to the cosmic hierarchy. Because the laws inherent in nature revealed themselves in his song, the music possessed the magic power to move stones and rocks, to make flowers and trees bow down before the singer, and to tame wild animals so that they would docilely follow in his steps. He awakened in the people who heard him a deep longing for their spiritual world of origin. Thus the singer journeyed through the lands as a teacher of wisdom and messenger of the world's secrets. His disciples and successors, assembled in the Orphic mystery communities, transmitted for many centuries the knowledge of the luminous origin of the human soul and its recurrent temporary imprisonment in an earthly body. A later echo of this Orphic wisdom still permeates Platonic philosophy. Of Orpheus himself, however, the legend states that although he penetrated to the World of the Dead, he was unable to bring his spouse, who had died from the bite of an ad-der, back to life. He was unable to do so because he had violated the command not to look back at her after she had been granted permission by the God of the Dead to follow him. Finally it reports that he was slain by crazed Bacchantes, handmaids of Dionysus, the lord of the earthly and subterranean forces of nature, because they felt rejected by him.

The Greeks discerned the other founder of human culture in Prometheus, one of the race of Titans, sons of Uranos and Gaia. Indeed to them he was not only the founder of a culture, but the creator of their own corporeal-natural existence. According to the legend, he had shaped the bodies of the first humans from earthly clay and endowed them with earthly souls by mixing both good and evil from the soul forces of the animals, to which Athena, the daughter of heavenly Zeus, then added a breath of divine spirit. When Zeus, out of fear of the new race, withdrew his goodwill and refused the gifts first granted, Prometheus stole fire from the gods, brought it to man, and taught him how to use it for working clay and ore into products of the arts and crafts and for tools and weapons. Hence they learned the command of the material world from him and fulfilled and perfected their cultural creativity in this direction. The fate of Prometheus was a tragic one, albeit in a different way from that of the singer Orpheus. As punishment for stealing the fire, he was chained to a rock in the Caucasus by Zeus' order and then, because he would not reveal the secret of the end of the gods' reign, was cast by Zeus into Tartarus where he awaited his destined deliverance at the hand of Herakles. For mankind Zeus had Hephaistos fashion the maid Pandora, out of whose box all the evils of the world poured forth when it was opened by Epimetheus, the brother of Prometheus. When he shut the cover again, only Hope remained in it, the sole good offered as comfort to mortals.

Just as the wisdom of Orpheus, the magic power of his song, and the signature of his fate point to the past, so the stealing of fire, the "technology" thereby obtained, and the tragic fate of Prometheus indicate the future. Indeed the latter only finds resolution in a future event. Even if both impulses were blended together in Greek culture, taken as a whole it was most influenced by Apollonic forces. It emphasized sculptured bodily representation born from the formative forces of the archetypal ideas. Certainly the origin of this representation was conceived in musical terms, marked in the Hellenic era by imbuing all artistic creations — architectural and sculptural as well as verbal and poetic — with measures, rhythms, and proportions. For that very reason music did not yet emerge as an independent art. For the Greeks, "music" still consisted basically of a wisdom permeated by the spirit of the "musal-musical," or of a musical experience woven into the element of a wisdom-filled knowledge. The most noble and exalted form of musical culture appeared to be music theory (the concern with rhythms, numerical interval ratios, etc.), whereas practical music making with external instruments appeared as an inferior artistic occupation.

Let us now look at the transformed renascence of this ancient Greek culture in the spiritual life of German classicism. That the latter is stamped by the predominance of Promethean will forces has already been mentioned in relation to its philosophy. This also suggests, among other things, that its world image is basically an historical picture, whereas that of Greek antiquity was a picture of nature. And within the context of this historical picture, the figure of Prometheus again takes a leading position as the archetypal representative of mankind striding through history. It is notable that this Golden Age of German culture displays no cogent or original creativity in the realms of architecture and sculpture, reverting to a more or less sterile imitation of Greek antiquity whenever anything at all was produced in this field. The energies of original creativity shifted entirely to music, the opposite pole. Since the beginning of the modern era, instrumental music had been freeing itself from language to create an autonomous art form. With the appearance of an unprecedented series of creative geniuses, especially in the era of Viennese classicism, this musical form underwent a progressive flowering of its various elements and expressive means that can only be compared to those that permeated the plastic arts during Greek antiquity in the times of Myron, Polyclitus, Phidias, Praxiteles, and Lysippus. (See in this context Carl Hinrichs, *Ranke und die Geschichtstheologie der Goethezeit*, Göttingen, 1954.) As an individual art form, music experienced a profound change not only in its external autonomy, but also in its essence; and the former is after all only an expression of the latter. Now it no longer means, as it once did, a contemplation (*theoria*) steeped in a musal-musical wisdom, but an activity (*praxis*) living fully in musical creativity. Music's tonal figures no longer reveal those laws that formed the beings of the external kingdom of nature, or even the human body, as they once did in the song of Orpheus. They are now transformed into the purest language of the human soul, giving artistic expression to the whole gamut of the soul's own emotions, feelings, and willful impulses, to all the stages of its development, even (which is most important) to all the phases of the birth of the "I" occurring in its innermost self. Then in Romanticism the expressive ability of this language is carried to its highest point of refinement and differentiation. Nevertheless, this complete evolution shifts repeatedly between two poles, whose purest and highest representatives are Mozart and Beethoven.

Mozart, the quintessential musical prodigy, brought by his birth a musical genius into earthly being from the regions of celestial light. From his earliest childhood it burst forth in powerful streams and continued to gush with unabated creative force throughout his whole life, albeit for only half a normal lifespan. He was carefully trained and led into adolescence by his father, an excellent musician and teacher who was fully aware of his responsibility toward his son's miraculous gift. As a child Mozart was taken on long journeys to aristocratic courts and to the most important centers of contemporary musical culture, where he absorbed all the musical achievements of his day: the art of Italian opera as well as that of orchestral music then blooming in Germany. His own music, maturing rapidly from budlike tenderness to full bloom, maintained a heavenly purity and a childlike inno-

cence nevertheless in all its stages and phases of development. It was as if it were woven of Apollonic light, free from
all earthly weight and living in spotless beauty.

By his own account, he saw his musical creations as a composer as an audible vision or as images entirely complete in
the spirit. His work consisted only in putting them down on
paper, which he often succeeded in doing with incredible
speed. They emerged from his spirit articulated and constructed, formed and polished, betraying no effort at all in
their production. What best characterizes them is the inex-
haustibility of Mozart's melodic fantasy, and the way he
molded the emanating melodic forms that he treated mainly
as leading voices, even in symphonic and chamber music. On
the other hand there is the dimension of form, never dispro-
portionate or excessive, and the absolute objectivity of the artistic shaping. Giving himself boundlessly to his human
environment, entering and immersing himself in it with the
greatest sensitivity to all its manifestations, he knew how to
extract melodies and harmonies from it that express its inmost being. In his operas he thus became the most comprehensive musical creator of characters and soul experiences,
and here again, what lends these works their incomparable
magic is the unique plasticity of the musical portrayals of
those characters and experiences. Be it Don Giovanni or Le-
porello, Figaro or Cherubino, Sarastro or the Queen of the
Night, Tamino or Papageno, Pamina or Monostatos, they
stand before us in all their dissimilarity as figures made
equally of three-dimensional musical substance. Though in
the course of his life Mozart entered ever more deeply into
earthly spheres with their obscurities and entanglements, at
the same time he always remained above them, painting
everything, good and evil, with equal affection, and all still
gilded with the radiant light of a primordial paradise. He was
truly a modern Orpheus, playing on a golden lyre, who
awakens in our soul a rapturous memory of our origin in a
higher world!

In contrast to Mozart there is Beethoven. Surviving a difficult, joyless youth, forced to become a piano virtuoso by an

alcoholic father, he was left to his own devices early on. He became aware of his slowly ripening genius as it began gradually to unfold its wings. Imbued with the highest degree of self-awareness he entered the big world, meeting its desires and moods with intractable defiance, serving no lord but his own genius and its artistic mission. The autonomy and equality into which music had matured in relation to its older sister arts found for the first time a human representative in him. By his achievement he wrested from the world the right to live independently for composition alone, in order to shape and construct, to pour and hew, and to fashion and transform what was volcanically glowing inside of him and striving toward the light. For this was the fire of the will, fetched down from heaven, which, transmuted into sound, will also ignite the listener and strike fire from his spirit. A colossal struggle began with, and for, form. That which originated in the heavens and transformed itself into the essential forces of earthly man opposed vigorously any formation that seemed to express the experiences and adventures of the *inner* man, indeed of what first comes to birth thereby as man's inner essence. And frequently enough in Beethoven's works we hear the hammerblows of the colossal will that had forged itself into a sounding form.

Thus in the *Eroica*, in which for the first time his most personal and inmost being appears before the world, Beethoven portrays the life and tragedy of a hero. For a finale he characteristically appends a theme and variations based on a theme first used in the ballet *The Creatures of Prometheus*. Beginning with the sound of a simple bass accompaniment, followed by gropings and stirrings that symbolize the barely animated human shapes, ensoulment first occurs with the onset of the actual melody. Then there is the Fifth Symphony, at whose opening we hear the blows with which "Fate knocks at the door," which leads the way through the deepest dark of night to the light . . .

For just as Mozart's fate ended in tragedy, Beethoven's passed through tragedy in another way.

Just as once upon a time the singer of Apollo succumbed to

the forces of the nether world, Mozart's life also ended at the point where man in his mid-thirties enters into the sphere of the chthonic forces that bring about aging and death. Poverty-stricken, abandoned and misunderstood, his luminous spirit vanished into the dark, his body lowered into a mass grave: a shocking image of how alien such a heavenly spirit had remained or become in our time, and of the extent to which it had lost the ability to ensure itself an understanding reception and a dwelling. And yet the tragedy of the original Orpheus appears deeper, since Mozart was able in another respect to overcome it. The singer of antiquity, despite his entrance into the nether world, was not able to recover the departed soul of his spouse. In the last years of his life Mozart joined and embraced the ideals of the Freemasons, who revived ancient mystery customs and initiation rites in their ceremonies. In *The Magic Flute*, at the zenith of his artistic career, he depicted an initiation ritual that appears to be a positive version of the Orpheus tragedy. Tamino overcomes all the dangers through which the path of initiation has led him, by resolutely passing the test of not speaking prematurely to his spouse Pamina. He frees her from the "captivity" in which she has been guarded and kept for him by Sarastro, after being seized from the power of her mother, the Queen of the Night. United with her he enters the Temple of the Sun. He is helped on the way by the magic flute—a transmuted lyre of Orpheus—and even the animals are there, approaching and listening to its sounds.

We travelled through the fiery glow,
Bravely fighting off its peril.
May your music be a shield,
In flood as it was in fire.

The union of the lovers has succeeded, and the luminous world of the sun is once again attained. Aside from Tamino, of course, there is also Papageno, representing the type of man who strives only for sensual pleasure and is entirely given to natural procreative love. The prince, however, on his evolu-

tionary path, has become a person in the complete, exalted
sense of the word. The message contained by this work culminates in the gospel of true humanity proclaimed by Sarastro.

In another way, Beethoven, the "Prometheus of the modern
world," as Rudolf Steiner first acknowledged and called him,
also had to struggle for the path through darkness to light. As
already mentioned, this road actually began with the Fifty
Symphony. For if Beethoven's artistic spirit appeared as it
were chained to the Caucasus Rock of the earthly by its incarnation in a body of robust constitution, with an unusually
thick-boned skull, he was cast into the nightclad depths of
Tartarus in the middle of his life by the onset of deafness. The
light of the external realm of tone was extinguished, the
world became silent for him. He was excluded precisely from
that element that was his world, and, as it were, imprisoned
in his own inner being. If Mozart was predestined to be an operatic composer by virtue of his almost feminine quality of
dedication to the personalities of his human environment
and by his ability to make them come alive in a finished musical sculpture before our hearing eye and our seeing ear, then
the quintessentially virile being of Beethoven, who was only
able to create what had been experienced in his own self, was
best represented by symphonic creation, in which the individual inner being could freely flow forth and be molded according to the drama within himself, unrestrained by
external figures and events. The setting to music of dramatic
material was only possible for him if its content agreed with
his inner experiences. Therefore *Fidelio* remains his only opera. Why *Fidelio* in particular? Because in Florestan's lan-
guishing in the dungeon he perceived a symbol of the
condition of his own soul, and its liberation by Leonore, who
leads Florestan up to the light of day, gave expression to his
own longings and strivings. It is also important to note, for
this notion of harmony between outer and inner, that
Beethoven not only set the Florestan-Leonore drama as a stage
work, but also gave it symphonic form three times in the
Leonore Overtures, granting its inner drama a purely musical
depiction. In all three overtures, in increasingly obvious and

eloquent musical pictures, he leads us to the central point of
the drama: the scene of the dungeon, in whose sepulchral
gloom nothing is left for the prisoner but hope, enchanting
his soul with the comforting dream image of deliverance: a
hope that Beethoven as a composer of Lieder had also set mov-
ingly. But the deliverance and re-ascent to the light of day are
also celebrated with increasing radiance in the sequence of
these overtures, and above all in the finale of the opera itself,
in which the concluding chorus of the Ninth Symphony is already foreshadowed. The last movement of the Fifth swells to
even greater Bacchanalian jubilation. In the Ninth, at the
summit of his artistic creativity, after one final struggle with
destiny in the course of which another dream shows itself to
the spiritual eye, a balm of hope distilled from the heavens is
poured into the soul. The victory over darkness is won, and a
song of jubilation is struck there over the full humanity for
whom a dear Father of Mankind lives above the firmament.
For just as at an earlier stage the outward human form was
vivified and ensouled, so now, with the struggle of the human
voice out of the wordless sounds of the instruments, man is
elevated to a higher state of being: that thorough spiritualization and complete individuation [*Ichwerdung*] of souls,
whereby they can join, for the first time, with the universal
human brotherhood. Thus this work culminates in the gospel
of man who finds himself a human being within humanity.

If victory over death and darkness could thus be achieved by
both masters, it was because both were born in the Christian
era, and hence a link had begun to form between their souls
and the influence of Him who had overcome death on the
cross. An external expression of this link is to be seen in the
two sister works whose genesis accompanies their two mas-
terpieces: Mozart's *Requiem* and Beethoven's *Missa Solem-
nis*.

In Greek antiquity, Orpheus as a singer was still considered
the archetype of all musal-musical creation, despite the fact
that his Apollonic wisdom manifested itself mainly in the
arts of architecture and sculpture, or spatial and bodily formation. Prometheus, on the other hand, who built bodies out

of clay and who founded the art of smithery by stealing fire, was not yet associated with the world of music.

In our own era, however, Beethoven the Promethean genius became the purest representative of music, insofar as it had become an autonomous art and acquired its characteristic stamp in "absolute" music, that is, in music produced by external instruments. In the meantime, the generation of a sonorous world in which the secrets of the inner man could be artistically revealed was wrung from earthly substantiality. Thus on the continuum from the Greek to the modern era, a singular crossing of the lines of evolution occurs.

In the dawn of modern musical development, the great masters of opera, from Monteverdi to Gluck, looked back toward ancient Greece and repeatedly used the fate of Orpheus as an underlying theme for new operatic compositions. When the Orpheus of modern composers appeared in Mozart, however, his music outshone all that had previously been written to such an extent that his works became the model from which all musical aesthetic concepts and judgments took their standard. The "demonic" quality of his works, the elemental-primordial way in which his music flowed forth from his spirit, appeared.as the purest revelation of the spirit of music. Only this evaluation did not last long. After Mozart's early death, as the figure of Beethoven grew increasingly strong on the horizon of his contemporaries through his symphonies, sonatas, and chamber works, *he* was soon considered the purest type of musician, particularly in the incipient Romantic era. "Beethoven . . . a Romantic and hence a purely musical composer," was the opinion of E.T.A. Hoffmann after the publication of the score of the Fifth Symphony. And so, too, it was Beethoven's compositions that became the foundation and point of departure for the musical developments of the nineteenth century (e.g., Berlioz, Liszt, and Wagner). The formally sculptured, graceful figures of Mozart seemed now to express a playful creativity of a lighter, more pleasing form that did not penetrate the depths of the human soul, but remained on its surface. Only a subsequent era acknowledged these creations as equal in significance to Beethoven's, as an art still filled with the primal forces of paradise: an art that, to quote Schiller, looks back to the Golden Age of Arcadia, just as that of Beethoven represents man's striving on the way to Elysium. It is significant that Goethe named Mozart as the only one who could have set to music that scene in the second part of *Faust* where he has his hero partake once more of the ecstasy of the Golden Age, after his marriage to Helen in the fields of Arcadia. On the other hand, it is typical that Schiller's Dionysian Ode to Joy, "Daughter of Elysium," should now be forged into an inseparable unity with Beethoven's melody.

In conclusion, we must still answer the question of why we have made this connection, admittedly unusual, between the two great masters of modern classical music and the mythical founders of culture and teachers of mankind from Greek antiquity. In the last centuries, composition has achieved a significance for mankind similar to that which the heroes and founders of mysteries had for the guidance and stimulus of human culture in ancient times. In our present era of internalization and individuation of the human soul, music, as the most direct language of the soul, has become the medium for the most exact and differentiated revelation of those evolutionary processes that the human soul goes through, or will go through. It is this medium, therefore, that empowers those who are called to contribute to or stimulate these evolutionary processes. With the sound images of modern music, the stimuli of evolution flow into the human soul of our day.

One more thing must be added. As the purest of the arts, in that it is sheer form and contains absolutely nothing material, music has a great responsibility at a time in which mankind is committed as never before to the world of substantiality and matter. Schiller suggested in his *Aesthetische Briefe* that all artistic activity is "play" in the higher sense of the word, insofar as it flows from that playful activity in which the spiritual and sensual natures of man are blended into a whole and in whose development he first becomes a whole person. At the end of this he states, "finally speaking freely," that "Man only plays in the sense implied when he is human in the fullest meaning of the word; and he is only fully human when he plays in this sense." This aimless play appears in no other art as purely as in music: hence we designate music making with an instrument as "playing" the piano, organ, violin, etc. And by dwelling in the element of form free of all materiality, it becomes the great healing counterbalance to the continual satiation of our spirit with material subjects, and to its restless hunt for material gain into which modern civilization has fallen as none other before it. Hence modern man's intense need to immerse himself again and again in this insubstantial form, this purposeless playing: the need that seeks and finds its fulfillment in the widespread musical activity of our time. If musical activity had been barred from our civilization, it would have been swallowed up by utilitarianism and materialistic thinking long ago. Of course one cannot ignore that the characteristic healing power of music has been increasingly crippled in recent times, and that modern musical activity itself has become quite degraded, in part to an industry and business, in part to a purely sensuous pleasure, and in part, thanks to modern technology, to mere background music for everyday activity. That, however, is entirely another matter.

If we look back on the development of modern music, Viennese classicism takes on a unique meaning for mankind. It came after music had served as just a part of worship in the times of Palestrina and Bach—or, stated differently, when it was wholly linked to the religious experience of the supramundane—yet before it sank in the nineteenth century into the personal-subjective realm, into the region of the sensual passionate element, or into the divisive forces of nationalism. During the Classic epoch music attained precisely that middle ground of the purely human, described by Schiller as playful activity, through which it could become the most widespread common spiritual property of modern mankind, independent of every specific form of religious denomination and rising above all national boundaries. Upon this human middle ground that music represents with the combination of grace, dignity, cheerfulness, and gravity that Schiller indicated as the fundamental features of genuine artistic play, there also rests the great humanizing effect that still radiates from their works and will be called upon to radiate for a long time yet.

The Evolution
of Music Through
Changes in Tone-Systems

Music is a higher revelation than all wisdom and philosophy. It is the only incorporeal entry into a higher world of knowledge, which surrounds [umfasst] one, to be sure, but which one cannot grasp [fassen]. The rhythm of the spirit has the property of grasping the essence of music: it gives presentiments and the inspiration of celestial science, and what the spirit receives from it through the senses is the embodiment of spiritual knowledge. Although the spirits live on it, as we live on air, it is another matter to comprehend it with the spirit; but the more the soul creates its sensible nourishment out of it, the more the spirit ripens toward a blissful accord with it. But few succeed, for just as thousands marry for love's sake, without love once being revealed in these thousands, though they all carry on the business of love, so thousands have dealings with music, but no revelation of it.   BEETHOVEN TO BETTINA BRENTANO
                                                                    1810

1   Man and Music

Anyone who has learned to play a musical instrument, or become somewhat familiar with music through singing lessons, is also aware of the fact that the notes, the raw material of the musical art, are not arranged by high and low pitches alone. They also appear in recurring spirals; the various octaves rise from "below" to "above"; the steps between the notes within the scale are not all the same, but alternate regularly between whole tones and semitones; and even that differs, depending on whether we are dealing with a major or a minor scale. They will also have learned about the twelve keys that are organized in the circle of fifths and distinguished from one another by the different number of notes that are sharped or flatted. In short, they have learned that the tonal material with which we make music is an organized system.

As a modern man, such a connoisseur of music certainly knows more: the system of notes and tone relationships referred to above has become familiar and self-evident to recent mankind—after all, are not all the classic works of the great masters of modern music written in that idiom?—in a way unknown to earlier stages of musical development. It is precisely our twentieth century that is about to overthrow the dominance of the tonal system and install another in its place. Not that the basic tonal material is to be rejected as such (although the most extreme tendencies do not shrink before the thought), but the heptatonic scales, the distinction between major and minor, and the various keys and their signatures are being scrapped by so-called "atonal" music; indeed, even the basic material itself is being expanded by the introduction of intervals smaller than the semitone: quartertones, sixth-tones, etc. The beginning of our century was marked by a search for new harmonies and experimentation with new note sequences, all of which has aroused resistance and rejection, and thrown into confusion and perplexity those whose ears are accustomed to the musical configurations of the great past masters. Even if in the course of his creative career one of the new composers steers back onto an older track, generally the new breaks through with such force that one hears it whether one wants to or not. Where will this development lead? How can we gain any insight into the confusion and contradiction of these experiments?

One way is to study the history of the tonal system and what it serves to express. Perhaps one must turn to acoustics in order to learn this. It teaches us that when a note is produced by a vibrating string, and when only half the string is permitted to vibrate, that same note sounds an octave higher. If two thirds of its length vibrates, then a fifth above the original note sounds; at 3/4 it is the fourth, at 4/5 the major third, etc. The vibrating segments of a string at the fundamental, the octave, the fifth, the fourth, and the third are in the following ratios to one another: 1, 1/2, 2/3, 3/4, 4/5. Acoustics refers to these as the system of overtones. When a string vibrates, its various other fractional lengths are also set in motion. These generate overtones that sound together with the key note (fundamental). Their number, varying according to the means of production, lends to particular tones their tone color.

The physical-acoustical data open up perspectives on the origins of tonal systems — as for example by H. Helmholtz in *On the Sensations of Tone*. They explain the basic position that the series of octaves occupies in the structure of our tone material; namely, that with respect to corresponding lengths of string, the series of octaves from low to high is in the following proportion: 1, 1/2, 1/4, 1/8, 1/16, etc. One can also understand the significance ascribed to the fifth within our tonal system (fifth as dominant, the circle of fifths, the intervals of a fifth separating the strings of stringed instruments), because it is based on the division of the vibrating string into three.

These mathematical regularities in intervals should not be underestimated. They are by no means accidental, but are a particular expression of the nature and character of the intervals. In order to see this connection, one must first understand something of the intervals' inner nature, independently of these numbers; then one needs to understand the numbers themselves not only as quantity but also as the expression of various qualities. Qualitative mathematics, still known in earlier days, is of course totally foreign to modern man. It requires a fundamental shift in outlook for him to become aware of the qualitative nature of numbers, which gives access to a deeper understanding of the facts. In his important work *Die Zahlengrundlagen der Musik* ("The Numerical Foundations of Music," 2 vols., Stuttgart, 1950/51), Ernst Bindel provides profound insights into the genesis of tone systems on the basis of just such a numerical recognition of the mathematical regularity of tonal relationships. His work rests on yet another basis, however, which brings us back to acoustics.

Today it is not only number that is considered in purely quantitative terms. In acoustics this concept is linked to the theory that only the vibrations of the air have objective reality: whereas, on the contrary, tone first arises in the human soul, i.e., it exists as a perception only in human consciousness. The musical element itself is entirely bypassed when one tries to explain tone systems by the usual numerical conceptions of the mathematical relationships between the string lengths or the numbers of vibrations. For in musical experience we do not live in the world of vibrating air, but in the world of tones and of intervals. We only discover their correspondence with numbers when we begin scientific experimentation. But this has nothing directly to do with our musical experience, nor for that matter with the artistic organization of the tone world. We do not tune our musical instruments with scientific apparatus, but with our empirical ears. And when we ourselves bring forth tones by singing, we produce the correct air vibrations by direct experience of the notes and intervals in question, without knowing about their numerical relationships. The tone world is not a mere epiphenomenon of air vibrations, a mere effect of which these are the cause, but its own independent world. And the air vibrations with their numerical relationships that we generate by means of any instrument, including our own larynx, are only the means by which we bring the world of tone to reveal itself physically. Of course only man can do this, but it is absurd to think that the tone world exists only in the human soul. Even if one understands how this concept arose and became dominant through modern physics, it remains no less absurd. It would be like saying that the world of speech does not exist as an external reality, but is located only in the human soul, and only occurs outside as the corresponding vibrations of air. The only particle of truth in this view is in the fact that the tone world, like that of speech, is brought into manifestation by man alone. For what resounds in nature without man (running water, the blowing of the wind, the bellowing of animals, the twittering of birds) is only a closer or more distant echo of this tone world. Physically sounding music exists in the world only through man. Hence, like speech, it must have a special relationship with man's inner nature, fulfilling a specific function within human existence and revealing a particular aspect of his inner being.

Yet how can this meaning be ascertained? Conventional psychology does not suffice here. An inner contemplation of the human soul-nature is required, one that is not provided by our normal consciousness (which includes that of psychological research). Our soul-nature lives in this everyday consciousness, and for precisely this reason it cannot simultaneously be the object of observation. Such an observation can only be made when the step has been taken from this ordinary consciousness to a higher one, whose vehicle is no longer the soul, but the spirit, i.e., man's innermost nature. The methods for this step have been developed in modern times in Anthroposophy or Spiritual Science, founded by Rudolf Steiner. It is made possible by an inner contemplation of the human soul-being, though accepting its results is very difficult for many people owing to traditional habits of thought and prejudices. But just as it contains the answers to many other enigmas of human existence, so it is with the question of the meaning of music. Here we will draw from it only what is relevant to the present problem. For this kind of contemplation it appears that what we perceive in the most fundamental sense as the life of the human soul consists of a polymorphic swaying back and forth between the states of "being given over to the world" and "being within oneself." Three principal forms of this emerge, operating at different levels and at different rates of time—somewhat comparable to the different speeds at which the hour, minute, and second hands circle the face of a clock.

The smallest or shortest of these pendular swings of the

soul-life takes place during the daily rhythm of sleeping and waking and belongs to the sphere of personal life. In the waking state the soul is "within itself," therefore aware of itself. In contrast, during sleep (according to the findings of this type of perception) it is so "given over to the world" that all awareness of itself is extinguished. Apparently this state of being given over to the world during sleep involves the soul being drawn from the body and "poured out" into a world of superphysical, supersensible reality. Conversely, its state of being with itself during wakefulness involves being "pulled together" in its corporeality. The soul's consciousness and unconsciousness rest essentially on its attachment to and freedom from the body.

The second type of pendular swing takes place during the course of a single complete human life, that is, the sequence of birth and youth on one hand, aging and death on the other. During birth and bodily growth up to the middle of life, the soul is proceeding step by step from a state of diffusion over a world of superphysical spiritual spheres to attachment with (or incarnation in) a body prepared for it out of the genetic current on earth. Here too the soul's gradual entry into itself is linked with its becoming aware of itself. From about the middle of life, however, it begins, at first hardly noticeably, to separate itself from the body until it departs completely to rejoin the wide spaces of a superphysical cosmos. The fact that after a certain time the soul can once again return from this phase to connection with a new body through a new birth, is due to its indwelling spirit that forms the immutable core of man and his true individuality. It is the spirit that ensures the continuation of this median rhythm of the soul in the form of repeated human lives on earth or reincarnations. This vibration is therefore grounded in the actual life of the human individuality.

Finally, the slowest and most comprehensive of the three pendular swings of the soul covers the totality of human evolution on earth and hence occurs only once. It belongs to the life of the collective psyche of humanity, to use C. G. Jung's expression. Here too we are dealing with the notion that the collective human soul, proceeding from a sleeplike state of diffusion in a spiritual cosmic world, enters a state of total corporeality that has grown to maturity during previous stages of cosmic evolution. In the course of primordial, pre-historic, and historic epochs, the soul gradually permeates this matter, and thereby comes to itself. This large-scale process of incarnation and the development of self-aware-ness culminates in the historical period beginning with the fifteenth and sixteenth centuries. But the counterprocess, by which the soul of mankind gradually releases itself and spreads out into the spaces of a spiritual cosmos, started al-ready at the beginning of this century. (We have seen a mate-rialistic caricature of this process in the technical conquest of space.) In this case, however, because it concerns a single swing, the soul will not lose the knowledge of itself that it acquired in its incarnate state, but rather will add the con-scious experience of the spiritual cosmos to its knowledge of itself. This is made possible by the spiritual fecundation of the soul of earthly mankind, caused by the appearance of Christ.

Since these three pendular swings of human soul-life oc-cur simultaneously on three different levels, and in different layers of it as well, they do not interfere, but only modify each other. Thus, for example, the fact that during prehis-toric and historic evolution the human soul was gradually entering the human body does not contradict the other fact that in all eras each human soul is incarnated and again dis-carnated at birth and death. Only in more ancient times, when the human soul was on its path toward incarnation, its way of being in the body was different from what it is now that we have reached the goal of that path. A similar change occurred in the rhythms of sleeping and waking throughout the various epochs of human evolution. However, one may well ask what these life events of the individual and human soul have to do with our theme.

They are of concern to us because there is a part of human life where they find specific expression: the experience and creation of music. If music, more than any utterance or activity of man, is correctly described as the "language of the soul," it is because these life processes of the soul find their creative expression in it.

The very fact that music is the art most closely linked to the element of time proves this connection; after all, these life processes of the soul all take place in greater or smaller temporal rhythms, and together they bring about a multi-faceted articulation of the element of time. Another indication of this relationship is the contrast between major and minor that permeates all our music. In major we are spiritually going outside ourselves, opening ourselves up to the world; in minor we are turning away from the world toward our inner being. The antithesis of high and low notes is also connected to this: the high ones lead us outward and transport us to the spiritual, the low ones lead us inward, binding us to the corporeal. This means that the character of major is best expressed by ascending sequences of notes, that of the minor by descending ones. In the light of the pendular movement in human history, moreover, one may say that in ancient, pre-Christian times musical experience and forms bore an overwhelmingly descending, minor character, whereas in the post-Christian era it is predominantly major.

These antipodal relationships lead to a third one: the contrast between large and small intervals. In the larger ones, the fifth, sixth, seventh, octave, etc., we experience ourselves to varying degrees outside of ourselves, transported into an outer, spiritual world, as demonstrated by the research of spiritual science. In the case of the fourth, third, second, and unison, we sense ourselves increasingly within our own inner being, anchored to the body.

2   Tone Systems and the Evolution of Consciousness

If all this is correct, it makes it possible to describe the soul-evolution of mankind musically by its inner rhythmic movement as it has unfolded since prehistoric times. For if the soul's state of surrender to the spiritual world is expressed in the large intervals and its corporeal being in itself in the smaller ones, then one can assume that in the older periods of human evolution, musical experience emphasized the larger intervals, since the soul was then on its way toward incarnation in the body; whereas in relatively recent times, as the human soul has bound itself more intimately with the body, this emphasis has shifted to the smaller intervals. In fact, this is precisely what spiritual scientific research shows. In addition, it even finds that over the various epochs of human evolution, musical experience has moved in regular stages through the different intervals from large to small. Rudolf Steiner[1] described this in detail in two lectures on "Mankind's Experience of Tone" (Stuttgart, March 7 and 8, 1923). This is the basis of our present essay on the changes in tone systems. One may assume, for instance, that if at various periods musical experience and creation have been totally dominated by certain specific intervals, these will also have determined the tone system in the corresponding epoch. If confirmed, this will provide the key to understand, from the very essence of music, the genesis and metamorphoses of the various tone systems that have appeared in the course of history. Among the riddles that music poses, we are dealing here with a central one that has remained an insoluble mystery for musicology, as evidenced by the following statements by Robert Lack in Adler's *Handbuch der Musikgeschichte* ("Handbook of Music History"), p. 8:

> In different lands, at different times, with different peoples and races, how does the human spirit succeed in constructing its musical configurations, that is, the sequence of pitches according to various given patterns and to systems of tonal crystallization, as it were, that are basically so different from one another, as is shown by the different scales and tone systems? The solution to this problem, the most complicated if not the major and fundamental problem facing musicology, is made even more complicated and difficult by the fact that this question

concerns psychology, ethnology, and sociology as well as comparative musicology.

We hope to be able to demonstrate that the results of spiritual scientific research not only clarify the construction and metamorphoses of past tone systems, but also open new perspectives on their further changes and future evolution.

3   Primordial Era

Let us begin by stating a fact that is actually one of the conclusions of our argument, but which at this point must stand as an assumption. Since the findings that we are presenting all mutually support one another, we have to state at the beginning what will truly become understandable only at the end. The fact is that the octave, regardless of whether we arrange it according to the sevenness of the diatonic scale or the twelveness of the chromatic scale, represents within the context of music the total range of man's being, from its lowest to its highest; in other words, from the outermost to the innermost principles of being.

On the basis of this fact, one can begin to understand what spiritual scientific research has revealed about mankind's most ancient musical experience. We must start at a very early period, namely that epoch of the earth and of man that spiritual science describes as the Lemurian Period. (In geology it corresponds to the Tertiary Era.) It was then that man actually became man, in that individual human souls began incarnating in earthly bodies. Of course the human soul also dwelled in those days unborn, as it were, in the womb of the spiritual world. But music is the oldest of arts: it arose at the end of that period in the shape of a wordless "primordial song." For at that time human spech had not yet been developed. In his lectures, Rudolf Steiner characterized the musical experience that was manifest in that primordial song as being defined by the experience of intervals larger than the octave: of ninths. "Man experienced the second above the next octave, and the third above the following one. He experienced a kind of objective third, and also the two thirds, major and minor; only what he experienced was naturally not a third in our sense." What we have said about the octave as the symbol of man's whole being must make it clear that this "Lemurian" music was not an expression of the human being, but rather of the superhuman, the divine. Anyone in those days who either heard or chanted this primordial song would have been transported into the spiritual cosmic world among the gods, there to learn of matters that the gods shared, as it were, among themselves. In that primordial chant, people did not yet sing themselves, in the sense of uttering something of their own, something that they themselves felt. Instead, the sound was an echo in man of that supersensible music that sounded in the spiritual worlds, as the gods revealed their joys and sufferings to one another in sounds of jubilation or songs of lamentation. As Steiner put it: "What we would have to characterize today as the inner experience of the major mode, Lemurian man perceived while transported out of his body as the gods' cosmic music of jubilation and as the expression of their joy at the creation of the world. What we experience today as the minor mode, he perceived as the frightful lament of the gods over the possibility that mankind could sink into what was to be depicted in the Bible as the Fall, the descent from the good, divine, spiritual powers."

4   Prehistory

In terms of music, we first enter the realm of man in that prehistoric epoch that corresponds approximately to the Paleolithic Era that preceded the Ice Age, described by spiritual science as the Atlantean Period. Its characteristic interval experience was that of the seventh. Steiner said: "If you were to return to the days of Atlantis you would find that everything there — it hardly resembles what we call music today — was actually tuned in successive sevenths." With the seventh, the threshold into the octave space was crossed; nevertheless, it still implied a supersensible experience occurring outside the body, and moreover one of an "intuitive" character in the spiritual scientific sense. Here intuition signifies the spiritual experience that comes from the highest or innermost powers of man. Through intuition man perceives himself both in these forces and in the world insofar as he is related to it. With regard to his innermost and highest nature, man may consider himself as both stemming from and related to the gods. In those days this nature, in its human aspect, had not yet entered its earthly corporeality; rather it had just begun germinating, as it were. It was already in the womb of the divine, spiritual world, but had not yet been born. During his musical experience, therefore, which amounted to an instinctive intuition, the Atlantean would still be transported into the spiritual world, though no longer directly among the gods themselves as the Lemurians were, but to the divine, spiritual core of his own being. Since this core was still enclosed by the maternal womb of the spiritual world, when experiencing music he found himself in another sense within the domain of the gods. Precisely because of these relationships, human speech was cultivated during Atlantis, and from there music transposed itself to a physical plane; from the wordless chant of the Lemurian Era, it became a spoken song whose melodic movement was strictly controlled by the Atlantean oracle centers.[2]

For the first period after Atlantean or Ice Age evolution, the seventh remained the interval that determined the musical experience. In the course of that same period, though, it gradually progressed through the sixth and into the fifth. The time periods during which this change took place, which constitute the first two post-Atlantean cultures, are described by spiritual research as the Ancient Indian and Ancient Persian epochs. They lasted from about the eighth to the fourth millenium B.C., and thus roughly correspond (for the Orient) to the Mesolithic and Neolithic eras. With the sixth, music is already experienced in the sphere designated by spiritual science as that of "inspiration." Certainly it is still in the divine, spiritual world, but no longer connected with the highest of its beings, as was the case with the intuition and the experience of the seventh; instead it is linked to the realm of a lower hierarchy of gods. This is the descent that occurred during the Ancient Indian and especially the Ancient Persian culture. For what is being witnessed during the gradual streaming of music from the heights of the divine world is, after all, as we mentioned in the description of Atlantean music, the essential spiritual-soul core of mankind. This core should be considered as an extract of the whole spiritual world, just as it has been regarded since time immemorial as a "Microcosm," i.e., the world in small. That was the core that dwelled in the divine womb during the Atlantean period, but that then followed the path down to the corporeal world through the spheres of the hierarchical beings during the post-Atlantean period.

It begins this road by traveling through a region that explicitly leads it to the experience of the extraterrestrial cosmos. For whereas the highest beings of the spiritual world, whom we depict for ourselves in the image of God the Father, comprehend both heavenly and earthly being, the realm of the next lower hierarchy is the extraterrestrial, namely the planetary cosmos. On its journey toward earthly corporeality the spiritual essence of mankind traversed this realm of the star gods mainly during the Ancient Persian era. This fact is most commonly expressed in the rise of the grandiose Persian cosmosophy, and in particular of the solar religion of Ormuzd, going back to the original Zoroaster of that era. It manifests itself musically in the experience of the sixth, which although it suggests a descent in relation to the seventh, implies a more decisive turn—or more onesided, if you will—toward the heavenly, spiritual world of the hierarchies than it had experienced earlier. Of course we have no tangible evidence for the music of that time in the physical world. In music, as in all other areas of life, nothing has been directly handed down from the two first post-Atlantean cultures. In their primordial form, Lemuria and Atlantis as well as the two first epochs of the post-Atlantean era, as it is described by spiritual science, are only traceable today through occult research. Whatever cultural monuments have come down to us from India and Persia belong to a far later era and include more recent forms of consciousness mixed with the older stages. Nevertheless we may assume that if in Atlantis, despite the highly spiritual and supersensible nature of musical experience, it had acquired a particular physical form in spoken song, now with the stronger turn toward the extraterrestrial spirit world this form must have become more limited again. Once again music was to a certain extent lifted far from the earth and completely amalgamated with the experience of the worlds of the star gods. Therefore the era of the sixth can hardly be conceived of as one that developed the future style of music within the physical world. Instead it seems to be simply a transitional phase between the two neighboring eras of seventh- and fifth-experience: a transitional phase that leaves no mark on the physical plane. (We have already met a similar transitional phase while crossing the octave-interval, and it will happen again in the case of the fourth.) We may then suppose that only a limited number of notes were physically sounded by the human voice or by instruments during the era of the sixth.[3] A scale system can only have existed in a fragmentary form, and as such (for reasons to be given later) could scarcely be experienced yet. Those few notes that man had at his physical disposal permitted a direct experience of the extraterrestrial world and its beings.

This homogeneity, even identity between the musical and spiritual experience of mankind in those days, is especially illuminating from the spiritual standpoint, for we have already characterized this experience for the Ancient Persian era as having been primarily "inspirational." Among the various forms of supersensible experience, inspiration is the specific trait of the musical nature. As we saw, even its content, which constitutes primarily the experience of the extraterrestrial, planetary world, has long been described as the "harmony of the spheres." Thus in a special sense the interval of the sixth may be assigned to this music of the spheres.[4] Consequently, the dominance of the sixth-experience during the ancient Oriental cultures implies that mankind possessed a spiritual experience that was essentially musical and expressible in musical terms; in other words, of the entire content of the world, that part which revealed itself through the harmony of the starry spheres was opened up in their soul.

People of those days could have expressed their experience in the introductory verses of the "Prologue in Heaven" from Goethe's *Faust*:

> *The sun-orb sings, in emulation,*
> *'Mid brother-spheres, his ancient sound:*
> *His path predestined through Creation*
> *He ends with step of thunder-sound.*
> *The angels from his visage splendid*
> *Draw power, whose measure none can say;*
> *The lofty works, uncomprehended,*
> *Are bright as on the ancient day.*

The fact that during the eras of the seventh and sixth musical experience reached out beyond the physical world, i.e., was identical to the supersensible experience that still existed then, can be grasped from another angle: if one sets out the twelve notes that form the basis of music separated by intervals of sevenths or sixths, one will exceed the range of seven octaves that approximately marks the limit of notes that can be distinguished by the ear.

5 First Historical Civilizations

Music first enters the domain of audibility with the rise to prominence of the next interval experience: that of the fifth. Rudolf Steiner suggests this as the decisive experience for the

next epoch of musical evolution, yet one that mainly occurred before Hellenic times. We may align this time period
largely with the third post-Atlantean cultural epoch, which
flourished mainly in Egypt and the Near East as well as in the
Far East (China), and made its influence felt over the rest of
the world from those centers. Once again there is a precise
harmony between the character generally adopted by human
consciousness at this time and the features of its musical
experience.

The experience of the fifth is one of the "imagination": the
instinctive imagination from which all other culture had
sprung. What is the nature of this imagination? Its name already indicates its pictorial character. In it pictures are in fact
seen, but although made up of elements drawn from the physical world, they are not experienced in a purely physical way
but rather as an expression or revelation of supersensible beings and facts. Imagination can best be described as a symbolic or sentient, supersensible experience. The facts of the
spiritual world no longer reveal themselves directly as such to
the Egypto-Chaldean; yet his worldview does not develop in
the form of abstract philosophical notions, but in the figures
of mythological pictures. The heavens no longer reveal themselves to him in purely supersensible experience, as a realm
of spiritual beings, nor do they present themselves to his sen-
sory eye as a plain world of twinkling dots; rather, they appear
to his imaginative gaze as a canvas of human and animal figures that tell him of different spiritual influences. He reads
these influences, as it were, in the celestial script of the zodiac's stellar images, the oldest portrayals of which have come
down to us precisely from Egypt and Babylon. And through
his many seasonal festivals he attempts to enter into those
that recur, one after another, in the cycle of the seasons.
These influences constitute the rising and falling processes
of life that operate between earth and its cosmic environment.

We mentioned above that at the stage of the fifth-experience, music attained the level of the audible. For the twelve

notes arranged in a sequence of fifths fill out exactly the seven octaves that make up this range. According to the indications offered by Rudolf Steiner, a member of that cultural epoch experienced the twelveness of the notes in this arrangement of fifths: "Let us take the seven [octave] scales from the lowest bass up to the notes marked by four primes, and now let us consider that the fifth occurs twelve times within these seven scales. Concealed at intervals of a fifth within the sequence of the seven musical scales, we have another twelve-note scale. What does this suggest in connection with the whole musical experience? It means that through the fifth-experience man with his *I* is still mobile outside his physical organization. In a way, he strides across the seven scales in twelve paces." Arranged in these intervals, however, these notes represent — if they are being experienced in a symbolic, imaginative way, rather than purely physically — the same twelve influences through which the life of the world passes, rising and falling, in the course of a year: a sequence also reflected in the journey of the sun through the twelve signs of the zodiac. We write out the notes as they appear naturally, putting the flat ones below and the sharp ones above:

$$A^b_{,,}\quad E^b_{,}\quad B^b_{,}\quad |\quad F\quad c\quad g\quad |\quad d'\quad |\quad a'\quad e''\quad b''\quad |\quad f\#'''\quad c\#''''\quad g\#''''$$

In the middle section, i.e., the notes of the diatonic series from F to b", we have the representatives of the bright, warm season (midyear) in which all those possibilities disposed toward life appear in physical view. In contrast, the low, flat notes on the left and the high, sharp ones on the right represent those darker and colder halves of the year—its beginning and end—into which life disappears into the unseen, or gradually reemerges from it. Therefore experiencing the notes in the sense expressed by their ordering into fifths, implies sensing them as an expression of cosmic-earthly life as it waxes and wanes in the annual course of the earth. The se-

quence of fifths is the symbol through which the life processes reveal themselves in sound. The organ used to read this
symbol is the imagination. This indicates an interconnec-
tion between the powers of the fifth experience, of the imagination, and of the perception of the life of the world as was
characteristic during the Egypto-Babylonian cultural epoch.

This era is the first for which we possess tangible records;
even those other ancient vestiges from peoples further to the
east do not predate this era, and even if in some respects they
do refer to a more distant past, they also contain the characteristics of their own time. In this third post-Atlantean period we encounter the first tangible evidence for music, as
well as for all the other usual domains of life. The following
question then arises: Does the fifth-experience, as depicted
above, affirm itself in the form that music then took on the
physical plane? Or, put differently: Can the shape that music then took be understood and based on the experience of
the fifth as we have characterized it?

This is indeed the case. Of course we have very little precise knowledge about the music of the Egyptians. Nevertheless we have traditions from many other peoples who either
represent or have remained at that stage of development, and
these justify our assumption that the musical experience of
the era was tuned to the order of the fifth. Thus, for example,
we have the tone system of ancient China, the so called "Lü
Scale," consisting of a twelvefold sequence of notes obtained
by successive fifths. (Naturally, for the sake of practical music making they are transposed into a narrower compass.)
Since each of the twelve Lü was assigned a month or a constellation of the zodiac, one must imagine this scale as a
circle of tones (see below). During a given month it was only
permitted to play music based on the pentatonic scale stemming from the corresponding Lü. In ancient China the musical system and the organization of the calendar were most
intimately connected, and the introduction of both is attributed to one of the mythical primordial rulers, the "Yellow
Emperor" Huang-ti.

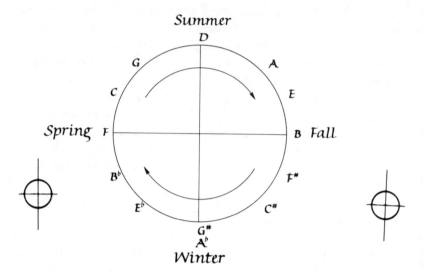

Those brought up on modern (post-Greek) concepts of the tone system may find a slight difficulty with this system of fifths, thinking that there are actually seven basic notes—those of the diatonic scale—and that the other five, as their accidentals show, are derived from these by adding sharps or flats. Looked at from another level, however, this is not so. Although the designation of the five tones as sharps or flats refers to the note names of the diatonic scale, those five steps are nevertheless entirely independent. Only they dwell on the darker, hidden side of the circle of life, and are named after the specific relationships they have to the notes on the light, revealed side. To regard them simply as derived would be equivalent to accepting only that phase of the yearly cycle of earth's life that goes from spring to fall, but not that which goes from fall to spring. A totality comes only from both phases together. The summer phase stands under the sign of evolution, of growth, of the externalization of life; the other one, winter, is that of its contraction, involution, and internalization. The turn of the year at mid-winter is a time both of looking backward to the old year and of looking forward to the coming one. Analogously, the tendency toward growth and rising appears on the upper right-hand side of the circle of fifths or of tones as shown above; on the lower left-hand side appears the tendency toward diminution and falling. The lowest point of the circle, the one equidistant in both directions from the upper, light half of the circle, thereby takes its name from both sides and appears in two forms, or pitch designations, depending on whether it is regarded as a beginning or endpoint of the circle. (But the endpoint of the twelfth fifth is not in perfect unison with the starting point of the first.)

The twelve notes can also be placed on a double circle or figure-of-eight (see below). The difference is now very clear between their sequence in fifths and another principle of arrangement about which we will speak later when treating Greek music, and which causes the modern difficulty in un-

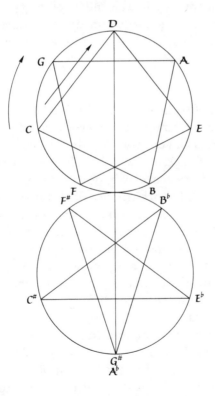

derstanding the old system of fifths: the scale in the strict sense of the word. If one proceeds from any note, a C for example, and steps to the next nearest note on the figure-of-eight, a series of fifths will emerge that leads one back to the point of departure after passing by all twelve notes. If, on the other hand, one proceeds from that same C but skips over the next nearest note each time, then a diatonic scale will emerge that will also lead one back to the C, but not via the lower half of the figure. In the first case these notes represent the forces of the zodiac, and in the second, as we shall see, those of the planets and hence their different intervals.

In today's tempered system, all the notes of the lower circle appear, admittedly, with two names: F#/G♭, B♭/A#, C#/D♭, G#/A♭, but each is only a single tone: the names are enharmonically equivalent. In the older, purer system, i.e., the tuning by fifths, this confusion did not exist, since only those unambiguous tones that appear on our circle of notes were known. G# and A♭, even if in a way they represent a single note within the system of the circle, were tuned to different pitches.

The system of fifths remained in this form not only in ancient China, but throughout the evolution of Western music until the sixteenth century. The flattest key used by Palestrina is E♭ (or C minor), which only goes as far as A♭; his sharpest does not exceed A major (or F# minor), which includes the G#. Only with the rise of chromaticism in the Venetian school of the sixteenth century, which we will come to later, was this G#-A♭ barrier first crossed and the number of sharps and flats increased. As long as one continues to add successive fifths, more and more double-named pitches arise. Only with the introduction of tempered tuning in the seventeenth century was the difference between the sharps and the flats equalized.

In our last remarks, we anticipated to a certain extent a later discussion. Yet they show how long the ancient fifth-experience, as expressed in the system of notes, survived in our own European musical evolution. Even today we live with the legacy of that period, for although the tuning of the notes by fifths has been discarded, the circle of fifths still reminds us of it. A further vestige of the system still endures in the interval of a fifth that separates the strings on our stringed instruments. The tendency to introduce the secondary theme in the key a fifth away from that of the primary theme, i.e., the dominant key, harks back to the ancient fifth experience.

The circle of fifths, however, is only one evidence of the fifth-experience of the third post-Atlantean Age. The other, equally significant for this era, is the dominance of the pentatonic or five-note scale, retained to this day among those peoples who have not gone through that inner phase of evolution that Hellenism implies for mankind, such as the Chinese in Asia, the Aztecs in America, the later Egyptians in Africa, the Celtic peoples of Europe (Scotland, Ireland) and the Hungarians (Transylvania). In practical music making only five of the twelve available notes were used: generally, D, E, G, A, B, but in China also the sequence C, D, F, G, A. It must be pointed out that this five-note "scale" is not a scale in the later strict sense, but is best considered as a forerunner. For the intervals from D to E and from E to G were not formed by taking first a major second, then a minor third; rather, with this row (and this applies to both series mentioned) we are dealing with five consecutive steps of the sequence of fifths that have been transposed within an octave. The gaps that we perceive in the pentatonic scale arise primarily from its compression into the space of an octave, but do not appear as such in the corresponding segment of the sequence of fifths. Since the notes of this "scale" originally formed no part at all of the octave space, but were placed there subsequently for practical purposes (and then, as we will presently see, in the most varied arrangements), no gaps at all were sensed between them. The notes were experienced as a defined, interdependent, self-enclosed segment from the sequence of fifths, i.e., the only interval governing them was the fifth; and this is why the tuning of instruments was also determined according to this interval.

It is not surprising that these five notes in particular were

incarnated from the twelve fifths by their use in the "scale."
After all, they lie on the upper arc of the circle of notes, on
the light, revealed side, in the phase of summer in the course
of the year, of earthly existence in the human life cycle. Previously, and especially in the preceding epoch, the musical
was experienced almost entirely in the realm of the supersensible; now during the epoch of the fifth the process of
musical incarnation has definitely begun, and we now follow its further progress through the evolution of the West.
Five out of the twelve notes have already acquired total phys-
icality. Obviously the first to do so will have been those that
belong on the side of the physical-sensible in the tone row.

Perhaps we should remind ourselves at this point that a
similar development was taking place in the visual realm.
Here too, the first colors representing the phase of incarnation to enter the field of sensual-spiritual experience were
the light, warm ones, yellow, orange, and red; whereas the
dark, cold hues related to excarnation, green, violet, blue,
only came later. Historically, the latter colors were not even
clearly differentiated for the soul experience in the Hellenic
era, but were placed under the general, unspecific category
of dark, sea colors.

If the pentatonic row shows itself through these properties
as a clear expression of the imaginative or fifth-determined
musical experience, it is also for another, inward reason. If
one wishes to perceive it as a scale, then it must be considered without a tonic or starting note. Since each of its notes
can take the tonic or lowest position, we find five different
variants of it in the pentatonic music known to us.[5] Thus
one should imagine the fiveness of these notes as a fivefold
metamorphosis capable of representing free-floating images
in musical space. The fact that in this system there are no
semitones or leading tones (i.e., those leading to a resolution) contributes considerably to its imprecise and weight-
less character. This floating, changing, and moving is once
again a principal mark of the imaginative experience, which
Rudolf Steiner characterized as transporting the soul into a
shoreless sea of flowing and billowing images.

6   Ancient Greece and the Middle Ages

In the imagination, the human experience attains the lower border of the spiritual, cosmic world, which is gradually entering into the realm of the physical, sensible world. Human consciousness during the Egypto-Chaldaean era had reached this border region, because at that time the human spirit-being, descending from cosmic heights, had arrived at the gates of corporeality. Its continued condensation, in which its prior state of diffusion through the cosmic spheres was superseded, made itself ever more evident. This process achieved its preliminary goal during the Graeco-Roman cultural epoch, the fourth one since the beginning of post-Atlantean evolution. The entrance of the human spirit into earthly corporeality occurred in Hellas. What had been for the Egyptians a definite approach is now fully accomplished in the Greek: he experiences himself as a closed, contained, self-oriented personality. This is easily documented by the fact that in Greece the individual human personality first became an historically formative factor, and its existence flourished in the emerging idea of the state. It found a special reflection in the birth of philosophy, i.e., in the conceptual thinking that now took the place of vanishing mythical experience. In the latter, the soul wandered outside the body, whereas in the former it operated within the body by means of the brain. Speaking figuratively, just as one can imagine the soul touching the skin that surrounds the body, philosophical thought as it first emerged in Greece did not yet reach into the depths of the body; it penetrated just beneath the surface of the skin and there, through the shell which now surrounded it, gently sensed the movement of the spiritual world outside. The other consequence of this stage of development was that the unfolding of thought toward the outside and the pure perception of the senses arose simultaneously. What in the imagination was a unified sensible-supersensible interior-exterior now divides into the duality of external sensible perception and inner spiritual thought. For the first time, the Greek looks into the physical world through his physical organs, in such a way that the spiritual world fades into its shadow. Yet if this world is no longer transparent to the spirit, it nevertheless still shines through, as it were. The veil of sense phenomena is still so thin that the spiritual operating behind it can still be felt.

The experience of the fourth represents this state of the soul precisely. And we are told by Rudolf Steiner that indeed in the Graeco-Roman era this meant a thoroughly felt interval experience. In the fourth, man experienced himself within his body, but not in its deeper regions, rather just beneath the surface of the skin.

One might ask whether this property of the fourth-experience can be explained by the musical function of the fourth. In order to answer this question one must first of all place all the notes at intervals of a fourth. What is the result? We find exactly the same sequence of notes as with the fifths, only in the opposite direction, and in addition the tonal material is more compressed. The sequence of fourths is a mirror image of the sequence of fifths, pressed into a smaller tonal space. The significance of this relationship between the two note series is twofold. On the one hand, the same sequence of notes appears twice. This means that if the arrangement of notes by fifths represents a particular world domain, as we have shown, then one would remain in the same domain with the arrangement by fourths, too. If the arrangement by fourths is an expression of the fourth-experience in the same sense and scope as the arrangement by fifths is for the fifth experience, then the era of the fourth would not have contributed anything new, at least not in content, to the previous tone. This is in fact the case: it does not stand beside that of the fifth as an independent musical epoch, but like the era of the sixth is merely a transitional phase to the era of the third. The Greek consciousness still takes an intimate part in the universal life and its cycles, which was musically symbolized by the arrangement of the notes into fifths and solidly embedded in the cultures of the Near East, though in a different, more inward way from that of the Egyptians or Chaldeans. The other aspect of this relationship between the sequences of the fourth and fifth points to the difference between the two: it is expressed in the fact that the one is the condensed mirror image of the other. One cannot help being reminded of how the retina of the eye carries a reduced and reversed image of the objects in the outside world. The fifth and fourth sequences contain a similar world domain— that of universal life—but in the first case it is spread out in its reality and in cosmic space, while in the second it is condensed in a mirror image. Of course, as with the perception of the eye, this condensation, internalization, and reflection only occurs here to a limited degree. Nevertheless, what is being expressed here is that strengthening of the human personality we described as characteristic of the Greek era.

Of course, this spiritual internalization reflected musically in the fourth and the fourth-experience did not find its most typical sound in a sequence of fourths, as we noted before by analogy to the arrangements by fifths and sixths. Instead it appears in a quite different element of musical life, the same as we saw emerging during the era of the fifth. We can learn about this clearly enough from the change that the tonal foundations of music underwent during the transition from Near Eastern to Greek culture. This will also answer, in the affirmative, the question of whether the fourth-experience can be deduced as the determining interval experience from the tone system as such, as handed down from the Greek era.

Seen from the outside, the progress from older to Greek music certainly appears to lie in the expansion of the pentatonic scale to a diatonic or heptatonic one by adding the notes F and C. The latter scale formed the tonal foundation of the musical art of Greece. Its difference from the pentatonic emerges in two ways. One can regard it as an expression of a further phase of the incarnation of music: seven of the twelve notes

are already totally incarnated, that is, the entire series of
notes that lies on the upper, revealed half of the tone circle.
Only those five notes that represent the hidden part of the life
cycle are still experienced in a more spiritual mode. Perhaps
the fact that now a majority of the notes has entered the physical world can be interpreted as follows: with the transition
from the pentatonic to the heptatonic system, a decisive midpoint in the total process of the descent from the spiritual
world into the physical has been crossed. With only the
smaller portion of the notes remaining in the super-sensible
region, experience of the latter seems to come to an end.
Heraclitus says, admittedly, that "The hidden harmony is
more powerful than the revealed." But whereas previously the
spiritual world was perceived as light and the physical as
dark, now day has risen on the latter and night fallen on the
former.

For the real understanding of the heptatonic system, however, it is far more important to consider a second perspective.
Here the heptatonic system is seen as the first pure actualiza-
tion of the idea of the "scale." This is a totally different principle of progression from that of the cycle of fifths or fourths.
Wherein lies the difference? In the sequence of fifths, the
notes appeared as contiguous spiritual-spatial entities, just as
their twelve corresponding constellations lie next to one another on the zodiac. If we traverse the annual time cycle of the
year in the order of these twelve influences, we will measure
off a certain amount of space. This is not yet independent and
genuine time, but rather the result of spatial changes, which
clearly suggests that the seasonal changes are caused by the
wandering of the sun across the firmament. We only enter
genuine, independent time, always associated with the moment of uniqueness, freedom, originality (or, if repetition occurs, with ever new planes) with historical human evolution
and all that is archetypally or reflectively related to it. Historical evolution achieved its first full expression during the
Graeco-Roman era; Hellas and Rome were the first to introduce a genuine historical writing to Europe precisely because
of the awakening of individual personalities that took place

then. (Judaism preceded them as a harbinger in the Near East.) But all human history has its archetype in cosmic evolution, as it runs through the seven planetary incarnations,[6] always known to esoteric cognition but described in many different ways. Just as everything spatial is linked to twelveness and the zodiac, all that is temporal is linked to sevenness and the planetary world. And this world of temporal historical progress, of unfolding soul-life, of changing states of consciousness, is the one in which we encounter the scalar principle. In coming to it from the arrangement of the notes by sixths or fifths, we once again accomplish the transition from the world of the zodiac to that of the planets. In order to avoid any misunderstanding, the following must be kept in mind: within the musical evolution depicted before we had to pursue a path descending from the highest divine sphere of being (the fixed stars), through the planetary and etheric-elemental, to the physical world. Yet until it reached the latter, the musical experience contained a hint of the supersensible even if it was continually becoming weaker, and hence was related in a deeper sense to the world of the fixed stars that is the most widespread representation of the divine-spiritual world. When in Greece the experience entered within the human soul, in this further sense it made the transition from the truly spiritual world of the fixed stars to the planetary world that is the cosmic representative and the ground of the human soul-life. Thus, at the turning point from the pre-Greek to the Greek era, music goes, generally speaking, from the world of the fixed stars to the spheres of the planets: from the representative of the spiritual or natural to that of the soul- or historical life.

This new world has very special characteristics. For the moment we shall name only one. (A second one will be mentioned further on because in the musical experience of mankind it does not appear during the Greek era; it comes when this same sphere is crossed, but from the opposite direction.) We mentioned that the planetary world is arranged according to the number 7. The number 7 is characterized by the fact that as an odd number it does not divide into two equal halves, but at best into 4 and 3. In fact, if we traverse the seven in the sense of its true nature, i.e., as it occurs in cosmic evolution, we attain a certain highpoint with the 4, at which the first phase of the evolution ends. But here we also find the point of departure for a second phase that then concludes with the 7. At this point the whole evolution disappears into invisibility, in order to reemerge in a new sevenfold development.

This inner constitution of the septenary reveals itself significantly in the structure of the scale. Its notes stand as representatives of the sevenness of the planetary phases of evolution (i.e., of time) and hence of the intervals, instead of the twelveness of the zodiac (a spatial structure). If we arrange the notes in a sequence of fifths, C G D A E B, etc., as we did in the earlier case, then they are separated by intervals of equal size—perfect fifths. But if we arrange them according to the second principle, so that they lie adjacent to each other in intervals of a second (C D E F G A B C), we notice that not all the intervals between them are of the same size. Major seconds (whole tones) alternate with minor seconds (semitones) in different but regularly recurring patterns. The semitones restrict the progressive movement and ultimately bring it to a resting point or a conclusion, thereby dividing it into periods. Rising upward from G, we reach a conclusion at C by virtue of the preceding semitone step. At the same time, though, this C may constitute the beginning of a new period that then comes to rest at F. And then we start again at G.

This gives rise to the same figure that we drew for cosmic evolution.

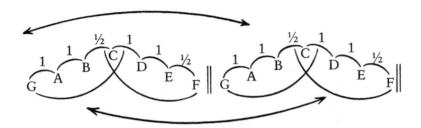

We see two things here: first, that the scale, by virtue of its objective structure, divides itself into two groups of four notes. Secondly, these may be constructed in two different ways, provided one maintains a single direction. Keeping the same example, one begins with G, whereupon the scale ends internally with the F and the G of the next octave is only attached to mark the beginning of the following scale. In this case, both groups of four notes share the middle note C: it simultaneously closes the first scale and opens the next. Alternatively, one can begin at C, and the two halves of the scale then have no common note but are separated from one another by a pause in their development (F-G). In such a case the C is not just attached to the scale, but forms its true conclusion, though it is still also the beginning of the new scale.

For reasons inherent in the position of his culture in the totality of human evolution, the Greek experienced the scale in such a way that the most important aspect for him was this double completion of a four-note group within an evolution through seven or eight steps. He did not experience the scale as a ready-made whole, but rather as a two-part structure, each part composed of a fourth, i.e., a fourfold group of notes. He named these fourfold groups "tetrachords," and from them he constructed all his scales. The tetrachord was the measure of all Greek scale formations. He was also aware that with the tetrachords he could construct a scale in the two fundamentally different ways that we mentioned above. In order to understand the multifaceted character of his scales, though, one must remember that he did not think of them, as we do, going from low to high, but rather as going from high to low. This reveals that he did not yet perceive evolution from the material side, but still from the spiritual one. If one contemplates it from below, one sees an ascent and a process of self-fulfill-ment of physical forms. Seen from above, however, one is aware of a descent and self-incarnation of spiritual forces. As the world process appeared to the whole of the Orient as descending from the divine to the human, so it still did to the Greek.

Next he developed tetrachords on different notes. In doing so, the interval between the first and last notes always remained the same: a fourth. As in the construction of tetrachords in general, the persistence of the perfect fourth as the distance between the limiting notes demonstrates the intensity of the Greek fourth experience. The sequence of interval steps could be radically altered, however, within the tetrachord by taking different starting notes. Three variations were possible.

The first tetrachord to be named was the one whose sequence of steps most clearly expressed a downward tonal movement. It is the one that contains first steps, then a semitone. The whole tones cause a rapid sinking into the depths that is slowed down and brought to rest by the semitone. This clearly must have been the most suitable tetrachord for the Greek musical experience, which after all sensed all scales as descending. It was named the Dorian, and it lent ancient Greek music much of its character because of the many scales that could be derived from it. In the series of the diatonic notes, this tetrachord appears twice:

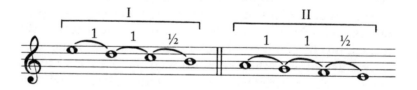

Following the two principles outlined above, both sequences could be either with the tetrachords not sharing a
common middle note, but divided by a whole tone step (that
is, the Dorian scale, as in the above example), or in such a way
that they overlap:

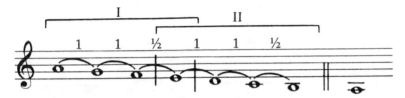

They then have a common middle note E, and a note has to be
added below. This scale is called the Hypodorian.

A second form of the tetrachord is produced when the semitone step is placed between the two whole tone steps. It is
called the Phrygian, and represents, as it were, an equilibrium
between forces pulling upward and downward. This sequence
of steps could also be presented in two ways.

As with the Dorian tetrachords, a twofold construction is
possible here: first, as shown above, a whole tone lies between
the two series of notes, making the Phrygian scale; secondly,
they share a middle note, and an additional note is placed at
the lower end, giving rise to the Hypophrygian scale:

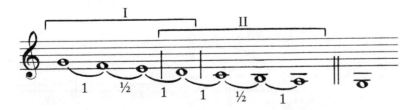

Finally, a third form of the tetrachord was constructed in which the semitone precedes the two whole tone steps. It was called Lydian and was the counterpart of the Dorian to a certain extent. In contrast to the severity and ponderousness of the latter, it was sensed as light, luxurious, and voluptuous. It consisted of the two groups:

Joined together as they are in this example, the two give rise to the Lydian scale. Connected in the alternative way, they result in the Hypolydian scale:

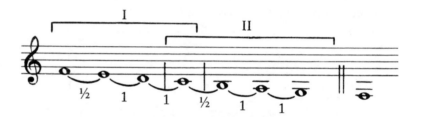

A seventh scale, the so-called Mixolydian, was ultimately derived from the Lydian tetrachord by removing the first note from the upper tetrachord of the Lydian scale, and placing another note below the lower tetrachord. Features from both principles of scale construction are combined in this scale, hence the name Mixolydian. It comprises the sequence of notes from B to B:

The system of the seven Greek modes outlined here shows that what characterized them for the Greeks was not so much whether they began or ended with certain notes, but rather that they traversed specific interval sequences. They were therefore not named after their first or last notes, but after the various peoples who preferred one over the other, depending on their character and temperament. In any case one cannot speak of "fundamentals" (tonics) with these scales, since, as already suggested, they were constructed from the top down, not from the bottom up. If one wished to specify the most important note in the Greek scale, it would be the middle one (mese), that is, the highest note of the lower tetrachord. The Pythagoreans compared its position to that of the sun amidst the planets. In his *Problems*, Aristotle says the following of it: "All good melodies make frequent use of the *mese*, and all good composers arrive at it often, and when they leave it, they return shortly afterward, but this is not the case with any other tone. . . . The *mese* is like a bond of the notes, especially of the best ones, because its tone is the most often heard." To a certain extent, therefore, it bore the same significance as the tonic. Apparently the rule for singers was to begin with it, for in the 33rd Problem it states: "Why is it more euphonious to go from the top down than from the bottom up? Perhaps because it is to start from the beginning? For the *mese* is the most highly placed leader of the tetrachord (i.e., the lower one). Otherwise it would mean starting not at the beginning, but at the end.[7]

This simple account of the scale system of the golden age of Greek musical development shows how it was explained until quite recently. But since the publication of Kathleen Schlesinger's *The Greek Aulos* (London, 1939), this presentation, at least of the genesis of these scales, can at best pass as an approximation of the true intervals. According to Schlesinger, the original intervals experienced an actual coarsening and modification in the course of Greek evolution. In the early Hellenic period the various scales (called *harmoniai* by the Greeks) had been distinguished from one another in a far more refined and differentiated fashion. There were as yet no semitones, only whole tone steps, but these were of seven different sizes. The two sizes of whole tones still occur today in the untempered system ("just" tuning), as characterized by the string ratios 8/9 and 9/10, while the ratio 15/16 corresponds to the semitone. But the early Greeks also employed the intervals represented by the string ratios 7/8, 10/11, 11/12, 12/13, 13/14. This was done precisely because scales were not constructed upward but downward.[8] The result was a series of progressively diminishing intervals. The largest, 7/8, was larger than today's major whole tone, and the smallest, 13/14, was already in the neighborhood of the semitone, while in the middle stood the 10/11 step.

7/8   8/9   9/10   10/11   11/12   12/13   13/14

From top to bottom then, the original Dorian scale was built as follows:

The upper tetrachord thus included the smaller intervals, those diminishing almost as far as the semitone, while the lower tetrachord comprised the greater intervals, also diminishing, and the largest step of all coincided with the gap between the two tetrachords. Consequently both tetrachords were striving downward toward the smallest interval.

In the Hypodorian scale:

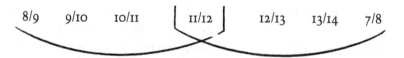

The upper tetrachord began with the second largest interval, passed over the middle one common to both upper and lower tetrachords, diminished continuously until the smallest, and concluded with the largest interval that leads to the last note appended at the bottom. The interval adjacent to the semitone step is here the penultimate one of the scale.

Similarly, the Phrygian and Hypophrygian scales began respectively with the intervals 12/13 and 9/10, the Lydian and Hypolydian with 13/14 and 10/11, and finally the Mixolydian with 7/8.

In these scales, then, no two intervals were the same; instead, the gap between tones changed seven times from one step to the next, diminishing continuously from top to bottom until the smallest was reached, then beginning once again with the largest, only in such a way that each scale started with a different-sized interval. Our first presentation of the scales, representing the development of later times with its differentiation into whole and semitone steps, implies, as we have already said, a coarsening of the original form since the finer differentiations are blurred. Kathleen Schlesinger explains that the scales she has rediscovered are specified in ancient Greek writings as stemming from the influences of the various planets. Originally, then, it was a matter of "planet-scales" (in the sense of the seven planets of the old cosmology), which confirms our assertion above that in the Greek era the musical crossed over from its original source into the planetary spheres, the representatives of soul- or historic life.

In sum, the following may be said about the musical experience of the Greeks: the fact that they constructed and used seven different scales for music making shows with what vigor and flexibility they lived in that element manifested by the progressions that take place within the scales. It is, as we have said, the intervallic element. Thus Greek music theory consisted mainly in a doctrine of intervals. The musical experience of the Greeks lay in their mutual relationships and tensions; it was no longer primarily in the tones themselves, as in the pre-Greek era. Furthermore, we have seen how it was the alternating sequences of different intervals that lent this whole world element its inner structure and gave a different soul-character and mood to each individual scale. This possibility of music reflecting various temperaments and soul-states arose for the first time in Greece. This was not the case for the musical experience determined by the fifth, since there the musical still occurred entirely in the spiritual, objective realm. Admittedly in Greece we see only an early phase of music being colored by the soul. We shall see a further step taken in this direction when the epoch of the third (major and minor) begins. By these early hints, however, the "fourth music" of the Greeks appears as a transitional phase between the epoch of the fifth and that of the third, and even as the dawning of the latter. At the same time, we can see that the epoch of the fifth still endured into the Greek era, from the fact that the precise pitches of the notes of the diatonic scale were determined by their relationship by fifths. As mentioned above, this Pythagorean or fifth-tuning persisted throughout the entire Middle Ages into early modern times.

As the continued presence and development of Platonic and Aristotelian philosophy in Scholasticism shows, the Middle Ages belong in a certain way to that same soul-related stage of evolution as Graeco-Roman antiquity, i.e., the fourth post-Atlantean cultural epoch. Yet at the same time it was the period in which the fifth post-Atlantean age, that is, our present one, was being prepared. Both traits of its historical position appear distinctly in the realm of music. On the one hand it manifests its dependence on the Graeco-Roman era by adopting the Greek modes as its "church modes" (albeit with certain notable changes), and does not go far beyond the diatonic system. On the other hand, during this period certain significant changes took place that gradually gave music the form it has in our fifth post-Atlantean Age. Briefly stated, this form is characterized by the fact that whereas music during the Fourth Age was still included, in a way, in poetry, in the Fifth Age it stands beside the latter as an individual, equal artistic genre. For the first time ever, at the beginning of our age, music became an independent art.

This process had already begun during the Middle Ages, in particular through two important events that are in fact connected. The first was the emergence of polyphony around the tenth and eleventh centuries. This caused the music to predominate over the words in vocal music, so that the sung notes, whose length had earlier been determined by the words, were now provided with their own durations based on musical considerations (mensural notation). The other event was the gradual breaking away of the melodic movement from its textual foundation. This began with melismata on the closing words of liturgical texts (Amen, Allelujah) and was then extended to more and more parts of the text. Ultimately it would lead to a totally different conception and manipulation of the scales. As long as the song was intimately bound to the word, it focused entirely on the content of the text with regard to its opening and closing notes. When it became autonomous, the song had to shape its beginning and end purely musically, i.e., make itself known as such. It happened with increasing frequency that one would start on a given note and return to it at the end. While singing one left the ground for a while, as it were, alighting once again at the end. The opening and closing note symbolized this ground. This is how the tendency to consider various scales as rising from specific starting notes considered as their fundamentals came about. Thus the earlier experience of the scales, which had its point of departure at the top or in the middle and progressed downward, was reversed to the point of being felt as unfolding upward from a fundamental. Of course this new feeling did not completely supersede the earlier one during the Middle Ages; rather the two were intertwined and achieved equilibrium. This was expressed in the distinction between the so-called "authentic" and the "plagal" church modes, which are formed, albeit in a somewhat altered way, on those dual principles of scale formation that were discussed in reference to the Greek scales. The tonic of the authentic modes was the fundamental: that of the plagal ones was, in a way, still in the middle, at the fourth step. Thus the system of church modes expresses the parallel existence of the upward and downward feeling of the scales. The upward feeling would assert itself as the victor only with the onset of the modern era.

7   Modern Era

All these changes are symptomatic of the complete birth of music as an independent art, a process that came to its conclusion in the sixteenth century. For the being experiencing it, "birth" means incarnation, or entrance into the earthly, physical world. Thus music's autonomy as an artistic genre is nothing less than an expression of its crossing over, in its whole being, into the sense world. This incarnation is now perhaps more comprehensible from the other side, since we have seen music in ancient Greece as still linked to the planetary world. This relationship was mirrored in human experience in that music was still heard, in part physically and in part supersensibly, as the expression of various objective soul-states by virtue of its various melodic movements, and in that it was cultivated principally as song, i.e., sounding through the human voice. In the modern age it is mainly produced through external instruments: instrumental music now reaches its full bloom. In tone painting it is often molded into a sound-picture of events in nature, while dance and marching music stimulate our emotions from the physical side. But the total immersion of music in the world of the senses was overwhelmingly evidenced in the changes that took place in its tonal foundations, particularly in the sixteenth century.

Sometime in the middle of the same century, the use of chromaticism gained acceptance, first in the works of the Venetian school (Willaert, etc.). It developed as the result of the need to transpose vocal parts to different pitches. The singers (and this is the period when opera arose) were no longer active as selfless servants of the church for the glory of God, as in the sacred choirs of the Middle Ages, but rather for their own reputation as self-conscious artists. For this purpose they required that their parts be in the most comfortable range. Hence many transpositions became necessary, and consequently the practice of sharpening and flattening every note of the diatonic scale became common. This chromaticism was at first designated as "musica falsa" or "ficta," i.e., false or artificial music, when considered from the standpoint of the old system of fifths that accepted as real and genuine only those twelve notes mentioned above. Nevertheless, it soon gained widespread recognition. Its appearance implied that now all the notes had come into the physical world. The series of notes on the sensible plane was complete. But how do all the notes appear now? In the ancient epoch of the fifth they still spread over the whole tonal realm in a sequence of fifths, to a lesser extent in the physical and to a greater extent in the supersensible (i.e., they were experienced as diffused over the whole celestial circle as the representation of its twelve influences). Now they are compressed, in the chromatic sequence, within the limits of an octave, and hence reveal the twelveness of man represented as the microcosm. As we stated at the beginning, the octave is man. Music appears now as thoroughly human, as flowing from man. But just as the twelve-toned circle of fifths is not a scale, so neither are the twelve chromatic steps. Rather, just as man as a microcosm is a counterpart or a compendium of the macrocosm, the chromatic "scale" is in the same sense a counterpart to the circle of fifths. Therefore we also still differentiate the actual scales from these chromatic note sequences.

With regard to the latter, however, at about the same time a new construct, long in the making, was finally completed. Of the various church modes, two gained prominence and were from then on the only ones used: the major and minor modes. The Italian music theorist Zarlino introduced them for the first time into the teaching of harmony in the mid-sixteenth century. The major scale corresponded to the Greek Lydian mode, the minor scale to the Hypodorian mode, which can also be considered a combination of the Dorian and Phrygian scales. Why did these two scales in particular evolve from the previous seven? Just as in ancient Greece, where the scales were formed downward, and the Dorian scale was the most common because it most strongly embodied the striving toward the depths, clearly in the modern era, when the scale is experienced as ascending, the one that has become most standard is the Lydian, in which the striving upward is most decisively expressed. It is, incidentally, the perfect mirror image of the Dorian. In the inversion of scale construction, this exchange between Dorian and Lydian modes seems already predestined. If we experience any scale in particular as climbing upward, it is the major scale. We sense its character as active and outward-looking. This is already inherent in rising scales as such. In contrast, in the minor mode we turn toward the inside, taking the world receptively into ourselves and surrendering to the forces of gravity. Although we construct it upward, its more natural direction is downward. Indeed, it is only during melodic descent (e.g., AGFE) that its characteristic "natural" form is heard, whereas during ascent we assimilate its upper half to the major mode (e.g., E F# G# A).

If we now construct these two scales from each of the twelve notes, we obtain twenty-four different scales and just as many keys. A more precise wording is required, however, since we still only have two scales, if we take them to be what they actually are: a specific sequence of interval steps. It is in fact the same sequence of intervals that we pass through in the "different" scales, only transposed to different starting notes. In spite of the number twelve or twenty-four that appears to contrast with the old number seven, we are dealing here in truth with an impoverishment from the old seven to the modern two scale types or modes. The case of the keys is different: they arise with their own characteristic numbers of sharps and flats, i.e., raisings or lowerings, when we construct these two scale types on each of the twelve notes. And the essence of these notes is thus revealed in a double manner. The essence of the twelve notes emerges from the twelve or twenty-four keys.[9] But in the diatonic system, all these keys have only a single pattern, that of C major/A minor; whereas despite all the differences between the ancient Greek *modes*, they all belonged to a single *key*. To summarize: in antiquity there was one key and seven modes; in modern times we have twelve keys and two modes.

We have already pointed out how the notes or the keys represent the sphere of the zodiac, whereas the scale is organized according to the planetary world. And thus we see confirmed from a new perspective that antiquity did not experience music in the tones, i.e., in connection with the world of the fixed stars, but rather in the intervals, i.e., in the planetary world, in that it knew several scales but only one key. (It resembles a key to us, although it was not used as such in those times.) Secondly, these facts show that along with the entrance of music into the world of the senses, the spiritual nature of notes has gained the possibility of revealing itself in a new fashion in the modern era. By virtue of the twelve double keys, we can in fact live in the individuality of the twelve notes. Admittedly, apart from the great creative musicians, average people of the modern era cannot make any good use of this possibility, for reasons we shall discuss later. One can see this from the fact that most musical people seem to have no distinct sense of the differences in character, mood, and coloring between the individual keys. One seldom encounters the feeling that a piece of music loses its original character and is imbued with a different one when transposed into another key. It can nevertheless be said that the spiritual, cosmic nature of notes reappears in a definite way in the musical experience of mankind as shaped during the modern era. On the other hand the shrinking from the former seven modes to the two of today undoubtedly implies an impoverishment, in particular with regard to the element manifested in the "scale": the intervallic and soul-quality. Instead of having the seven colors of the spectrum represented to a certain extent in the seven modes, we are left with the mere contrast of light and dark in the major and minor modes. Here again we see music's descent from the planetary world.

But to what point in this descent into the world of the senses has it actually sunk? In mentioning the chromatic scale we already hinted at the answer: entirely within earthly incarnate man. The music that is created by composers comes forth from the same soul that grows and changes through the totality of experiences and events of earthly existence. Stylistically, in terms of temperament and coloring, their creations are as different as the soul-lives of earthly men, through their individual and inherited dispositions, experiences, and destinies. And they contain much that is purely earthly and tied to the transient and corporeal. This personal soul-life intertwined in the corporeal is what is

musically represented by the interval of the third. It is thus
symptomatic that since the end of the Middle Ages the third,
which until then had been considered a dissonance, started to
be felt as a consonance, i.e., as a euphonious sound. One
symptom appeared in two-part harmony, where the earlier
use of parallel fifths and fourths was replaced by parallel
thirds and sixths (for the sixth can be considered an inversion
of the third). Furthermore, it appears significant that the major and minor modes distinguish themselves from one another specifically with regard to the third (and sixth) degree,
in that one uses the "major" third and the other the "minor"
third. In experiencing the contrast of major and minor, we
therefore move in the world of the third. Hence, as Rudolf
Steiner suggests, music from the modern era that is mainly
determined by this contrasting quality is governed by the
third-experience.

Just as the third and the sixth can be heard as inversions of
one another, and with an inner community similar to that between the fourth and the fifth, modern third-music can also
be considered a mirror image of the sixth-music as it was experienced in the very ancient past. In those times, both musical and supersensible experience were one and the same. The
latter still bore an inspired character by which it perceived
the harmony of the stellar spheres where the celestial hierarchies, the world soul-beings, revealed themselves to man. In
the epoch of the third, music has come to sound in the earthly
realm; once again it discloses a soul-quality, though no longer
the supersensible, cosmic soul-life of the gods, but the earth-
incarnate soul-life of man. A kind of mirror-image relationship nevertheless exists between these two. We shall examine
more carefully below how the third-experience has increasingly pervaded the formation of music over the course of the
last centuries. First, however, we must consider one more
phenomenon.

The entrance of music into the world of the senses is also
manifest in the development of modern instrument building,
which made it increasingly possible to sound the whole range
of physically distinguishable notes, from the highest to the

lowest. Besides the stringed, wind, and percussion instruments, in which certain functions of the human organism are either extended or replaced, and the organ, the instrument of sacred art, the piano came more and more into prominence: it is the only instrument that is not drawn from human nature but developed as a purely mechanical construct. Characteristically, it has become the prime representative of modern, earthly music. As had already been the case with the organ, certain difficulties arose out of the old tuning by fifths with the piano as well. In that tuning, the twelfth note of a series of fifths (the G# of the seventh octave, if one starts from low A♭) did not produce the exact pitch of the starting notes but one a little higher. In addition, the whole tone steps within the scale were not all of the same size: the first step was somewhat greater than the second and the fifth step greater than the sixth. Hence, for instance, the E, which is the third degree of the C scale, had a slightly lower pitch than the E that is the second degree of the D scale. Allowances could be made for these subtleties on stringed instruments, where the player pitches the note himself, or in singing. Not, however, on an instrument with fixed notes: in building these instruments, one would have to account for every note and its multiple pitches. There were many attempts in this direction, but they led to such a proliferation of notes on the keyboard as threatened to make the instrument unplayable. In the seventeenth century, in order to overcome these difficulties, so-called equal temperament was introduced. Whereas the old Pythagorean tuning was based on the fifth, this one was based on the octave, whose limiting notes are in the vibration ratio of 1:2. This octave space was now divided into twelve exactly equal intervals. Consequently all the notes were fixed, once and for all, and the differences between the sharp and flat notes were eliminated. This method provided greater flexibility and made composition in all twelve keys possible. Whereas with the pure or fifth tuning one could go directly from one key only into a closely related one, now by means of enharmonic modulation one could modulate directly into the most distant keys. This freedom of movement throughout the whole tonal system was what first made modern music possible with its mobility, its ability to modulate, and its expressiveness.

This advantage, however, is counterbalanced by a certain loss, which must be considered in order to see the full significance of this achievement. In the tempered tuning of the twelve notes, we actually no longer have the notes themselves before us in all their liveliness and variability, but rather a rigid, dead image of their twelveness. This signifies that when music became totally immersed in the sense-world, its actual reality did not follow; only its image appeared therein. The reality of music remains outside. Yet it is precisely this unreal, purely imagelike character that music bears in the sense-world that permits us to manipulate it so freely. The freedom and mobility of musical creation is paid for in that one no longer dwells within the reality of music.[10] This is why we cannot generally feel the essence of the twelve notes in all their liveliness, as they are revealed in the twelve keys. This revelation has been dulled by the tempering of the pitches, indeed its life has actually been killed. A kind of veil covers it.

This state of affairs in the realm of music is similar to the development of thinking during the modern era. In our epoch the element of thought has also moved completely into the physical body, whereas it was previously experienced and observed to a greater or lesser extent supersensibly, by way of the spiritual organs of the human constitution. Modern thinking takes place via the physical brain. On the one hand, therefore, the thought itself has lost its reality and life. It has faded into a dead image of reality. On the other hand, modern man has thereby gained the ability to manipulate his thoughts freely and to express his own being through them. What comes to expression in the worldview of modern thinkers is their personal stand vis-à-vis the world, and reflections of their individual characters. The independent life of music is similarly obscured for modern consciousness. At the same time modern man has achieved the freedom and gained the ability to express himself, his nature, his experience and suffering in music—an ability that reached its apex with Beethoven and

Wagner. On the whole it must be said that in the form adopted by music in the modern era, its cosmic nature certainly appears both in its sevenfold and its twelvefold ordering. However, instead of the true spirit or spiritual reality of the twelve notes or keys, we have before us only an unreal image of their nature. And the two scales into which the former seven have been condensed show that in place of the once protean mobility, rigidity and lameness have entered the very life and soul of music. We may conclude, then, that today we live neither completely in the notes nor in the intervals. So where do we actually live?

We live primarily in harmony, as it appears in the simultaneity of notes: in the chords. We can now turn to the final great achievement of modern music, which concerns its tonal foundations: Jean-Philippe Rameau's establishment of modern harmony in the eighteenth century. In his music theory Rameau began directly from chords and sought to understand single notes through their chords. He constructed his chords, as had already been done in the figured bass, upon fundamentals, whose original forms were triads of thirds. The other forms of the same chord were then derived as different inversions of these triads. He singled out those triads based on the tonic, the dominant, and the subdominant as the most important. The notes contained in these comprise all the steps of the scale. As a result, these notes are no longer experienced as the various steps of a scalar progression, but as the members of various triads, and principally in their third-relationships and kinships to one another. Here the loss of the scale-experience and the dominance of the third-feeling are finally expressed purely and completely.

We can see how melody has increasingly shifted from the principles of intervals and scales to those of chords and triads. Countless themes and motives could be cited, especially from the works of Beethoven and Schubert, that represent nothing more than a series of triads variously dissected or laid out. Even the melodic is totally immersed in the harmonic element.[11] In the latter, however, we can perceive the musical reflection of the human soul-life consolidated and incarnated in its earthly body. And thus, just as the contents of this soul-life are a kind of corpse in comparison to what it contained prior to its incarnation, while it was still spread over the spiritual world, vibrating freely to its life-rhythms, so, too, the freedom of movement within melodic intervals undergoes a kind of death and burial through harmonic chords.

As a music maker, modern man lives primarily in the harmonic dimension. Furthermore, he lives in the various compositional forms that have gradually developed since music became an independent art form: fugue, sonata form, Lied, and so on. As the whole earthly soul-life is expressed in harmony, so the construction of the various compositional forms expresses its midpoint: the human *I*. The stronger or weaker the composer's *I*, the more successful or limited he will prove in the mastery, formation, and rounding of these forms.

Toward the end of the nineteenth century, however, the classical forms of composition began dissolving, together with the harmony that moves within fixed keys. Particularly in the domain of program music, the forms became looser, less precise, and accommodated to poetic ideas brought in from outside. At the same time, the keys were broken up by the ever more prominent element of chromaticism. A milestone on this road was, of course, Wagner's *Tristan und Isolde*.

8   Present and Future

Since the beginning of the twentieth century, overcoming the existing tonal system appears to have become a necessity. The existing system is felt to be "worn out." The new ideal is atonality. In the twelve-tone system, the twelve notes of the chromatic scale are supposed to form a kind of tonality in which the contrast between major and minor has been eliminated. As a structural principle taking the place of the former scales, to a certain extent, Schoenberg based his twelve-tone compositions on specific melodic structures. Johann Mathias Hauer, the most important exponent of twelve-tone music after Schoenberg, used a system of "tropes" for his compositions. They are fundamental melodic structures formed from the twelve-tone row according to the principle of permutation.

As opposed to the seven-based principle of the scale, which first appeared at the time of the Greeks, the evolutionary necessities of our time undoubtedly require that the twelve-based principle of the tones be brought again into prominence. This was already evident in the structure adopted by the modern tone system in recent centuries, with the development of the twelve keys and the reduction of the scales or modes from seven to two. In the atonal music of today, this tendency has plunged into an extreme onesidedness, in that the seven-based principle has been totally rejected in favor of the twelve-based principle alone. But even if the music treats the twelve-tone system in a modern, polyphonic way, in the atonal form it nevertheless implies a certain return to the form of music governed by the twelve-based principle that we described earlier as prevailing during the pre-Greek, Oriental cultures of the third post-Atlantean culture epoch. The seven-based principle of the scale was still unknown, because human personality had not yet awoken to itself, and hence humanity's life had not completely adopted a historical character. Hauer still values the sevenfold principle of the scale, and therefore his "twelve-tone play" transports the listener into an "I-less" wandering in a cosmic-musical happening that appears timeless, allows of no development, but reflects certain secrets of cosmic life in its pitches: but man himself is lost in it. This attempt is the counterpart to the general return toward the spirituality of the ancient Orient that is taking place on a broad front in other regions of contemporary spiritual life, in answer to the need to escape the materialism and egotism of Western civilization. These efforts cannot truly further evolution, because they deny or abandon what made that evolution effective: the unfolding human *I* (individuality). Rather than extinguishing it, it would be better to develop it further, to enable it to conquer its entanglement with subjectivity and find in itself again the spiritual world from which it once emerged. In musical terms this means not rejecting the seven-based principle of the scales or modes, but rescuing it from the impoverishment and rigidity that it suffered during the progression from the Greek to the modern eras; it must be revitalized and enriched in itself, so that it may enter a fruitful dialectic with the newly strengthened twelve-based principle to the betterment of music as a whole. How can this be achieved?

It can only be accomplished if one consciously cultivates the evolution of that new interval experience whose emergence is making itself manifest amid all the searching and experimentation of our century, albeit chaotically and aimlessly, and thus in danger of manifold errors. Rudolf Steiner described this new interval experience in his music-historical lectures as the "second-experience." One can only speculate on the many directions in which, under its dominance, all musical experience and creation will be changed. At this point, in conclusion, we will develop a single train of thought about it, following what Rudolf Steiner presented concerning the character of the second or of the second-experience.

We experience modern music, ruled by the third, within the body. Yet, as already mentioned, what is reflected in it is the incarnated soul-life bound to the body. We associate music directly with our soul but not with our body. Indeed, we know basically nothing of the relationships that might exist between it and the inner constitution of our body. We know as little about it as we understand our soul-life in terms of its relationship to the body. We do know and feel that our soul-life is linked with, even dependent on the body. How this relationship is actually formed, however, is a mystery. During the modern era, psychological and physiological research has put forward a vast number of theories, yet none has been able to explain these relationships satisfactorily. For science, the body-soul problem has remained an unsolved riddle to this day. Neither can our ordinary consciousness penetrate these connections. Anthroposophical research cultivates higher forms of consciousness of which one form, for example, enables one to experience consciously (with an other than everyday awareness) what one normally experiences unconsciously in sleep as a soul-being. This research is thus able to show what in fact happens to the human soul during sleep. One can describe it by saying that in sleep the soul leaves the body to a certain degree, in order to return to the spiritual world which is its home; at the same time, though, working from that world and in conjunction with those forces, it regenerates the body, which is always worn down by the waking state. The difference between waking and sleeping states can therefore be understood in twofold fashion: seen from one point of view, the soul seems to work on the body in a destructive way while inside it in the waking state, whereas during sleep it performs a restoring function from the outside. The soul is capable of regenerating the body, because it did in fact build it during the embryonic and early childhood stages, in conjunction with the forces of the spiritual world. Its dwelling in the body during waking is only possible because it has formed it according to its own measure and image.

But music represents nothing less than the inner laws of the soul-spiritual nature in man. With the imbuing of the body's structure with these laws, the body itself is formed according to musical principles. When we observe this musical construction of the body with the higher form of consciousness mentioned above, one perceives it in those forces that form the body. In reference to this cognition, we should indicate here what Rudolf Steiner presented in his Stuttgart lectures, and more thoroughly in his "Tone-Eurythmy course": how the threefoldness in music corresponds to the threefoldness of the functional systems making up the human organism: the nervous system, the rhythmic system, and the limb system; how, furthermore, the human motor organs—arms and legs—acquire their structure from the forces of the intervals, so that if the distance from the collarbone to the upper arm is taken as the prime, the upper arm itself is the second, the lower arm (with ulna and radius) the major and minor third, the wrist the fourth, the palm of the hand the fifth, the fingers the sixth and seventh, while the octave lies outside man and must be received from the outside. Eurythmic gestures and movements were developed by Rudolf Steiner from these insights. The same could be said about the tones themselves. This opens the possibility of incorporating music into the body-experience, indeed of experiencing it with the whole being, including the body, i.e., through the formative forces of the body. Forces and elements are not then experienced as merely soul-subjective, but as spiritual-objective, as world forces. The experience of music here, in which it is discovered as a world of cosmic formative forces in the life-building forces of the soul, is the second-experience. We can therefore conclude that the musical revelations of Rudolf Steiner and the founding of tone eurythmy flowed directly from the second-experience. Furthermore, this art is the most powerful and effective means of bringing about the unfolding of the second-feeling. What is today primarily achieved by spiritual research as a cognitive experience, and can to a certain extent be cultivated as an ability through the art of eurythmy, will surely emerge increasingly in the future as an elemental, self-evident artistic feeling.

What are the other traits of the musical experience determined by the second-feeling? Through it we once again enter the intervallic-melodic from the chordal-harmonic; from standstill we enter motion; from the spatially juxtaposed (as occurs in the chord and the overtone row) we enter the chronologically sequential (as occurs in the melody). And finally we return from the *note* itself, i.e., from the physical sounds whose full range has appeared, completely filled out, in the modern era, to that which lies *between* the notes. We need not surrender any of the tonal material gained for the physical world, but we must learn to mold it differently. After having lost the desire even to listen to music, owing to the sheer strident noise of the era of extreme materialism, there is already felt today a strong desire for just such a spiritualization of the tonal that would make the inaudible once again palpable through the spiritual. But in that we go from standstill to motion, returning to temporal sequence and, in short, reentering the intervallic realm, where we also reacquire the feeling for the scalar progression that has atrophied in the last centuries. This implies a kind of rebirth at a higher stage of evolution of the Greek musical experience that was governed by the scalar principle, i.e., the intervallic. However, because it emerges at a higher level it is constituted somewhat differently from what it was in antiquity. It will draw still more from the world of the intervallic than the Greeks were able to create from it.

We suggested earlier how Greek antiquity, precisely because it was the age of the fourth-feeling, experienced primarily the cardinal meaning of the fourth within the scale; how it felt the self-defining and completion that occurs with the fourth, and how thereby the scale divided itself neatly into two tetrachords. This significance of the fourth is thoroughly based on the objective constitution of the scale, and therefore its importance must be appreciated in the future, too. It appears fully in the motions and gestures of tone eurythmy. And so this justifies a new kind of tetrachord construction. In the future, however, under the rule of the second-feeling, an additional experience of the scale will come forward. In spite of the octave's inner divisions—because we already live in the fifth post-Atlantean Age—we will experience it as a continuously unfolding whole. We will sense the stepping from note to note, from the prime up to the seventh or octave, as a single ascending set of steps; and we will discover there our own nature. We will traverse its organization step by step, and our consciousness will constantly undergo new metamorphoses from one step to the next. We shall thereby traverse a series of changes of consciousness. It will imply a far more inner experience of the scale than could have been possible in ancient Greece. Whereas man then observed the scale-event to a certain extent spiritually, surveying its architecture from the outside, he will now be internally part of it, as a gradual self-change takes place. The scale will become a path to an inner soul-experience, a path upon which we will be led first through ourselves, and then outside ourselves, in order finally (with the octave) to find ourselves again in the world in a new and higher way. This will imply experiencing the scale from the standpoint of the second. For after all, each one of its stages forms a second in relation to the note immediately preceding, even though each step forms a third, fourth, fifth, and so on with the fundamental. A scalar progression is always at the same time a progression of seconds. This again illuminates the inner connection of the second-experience with the scale-experience or the interval-experience. To a great extent the second is the most common, most basic form of the intervallic, from which all other similar structures can be felt as differentiating or unfolding. This is why Rudolf Steiner was able to offer for the first time a description of the inner nature of the individual intervals, i.e., of the various states of consciousness represented by them. That description also forms the basis of the present work. And the fact that these descriptions have made possible a more profound understanding than ever before of musical evolution, shows that a truly musical understanding of the historical evolution of music can only arise out of the second-experience, i.e., from the fully matured interval-experience.

Reentering the actual life of music in this fashion does not, however, imply rejecting the tempered tuning of the notes. We owe our musical freedom to tempering, and it should not be lost. What will be most important in the future musical experience will lie more in our struggle to penetrate music's lively spiritual reality by the activation of our inner experience, for example through tone eurythmy, while freeing ourselves from the unreality and pictoriality with which it comes to us from the outside. Nevertheless, it is perfectly conceivable that achieving this inner experience in such a manner can awaken the need to express creatively, even physically, this life of notes and intervals by varying them in a new manner: one through which each vibration of the whole tone interval also experiences a rebirth on a higher plane, as once characterized the early Greek planet scales. From this perspective one can see in such efforts as quarter- and sixth-tone music, where the intervals can be diminished or increased by small nuances, some initiatives from which possibilities may evolve toward incorporating the new experience in creative work.

In contrast to the spiritual dependence that governed the musical experience of the Greeks, an important aspect of the future experience that will have to be considered and affirmed will be the character of freedom. As a result of this state of freedom it appears perfectly conceivable that all the tone material present in the physical should be retained and used in the most multifaceted manner for the construction of scales or scalar structures. Thus those attempts at novel scale constructions that have appeared here and there (Busconi, Scriabin, etc.) may be considered as striving toward such possibilities.

Of course, under the dominance of the second-experience music theory and harmony in particular will be fundamentally transformed. The second-principle will in some way replace the third-principle. Alois Hába, for example, has already demonstrated in his *Harmony*[12] that it is perfectly possible to explain all consonances of notes in terms of seconds, if one only extends them to sevenths (and this is definitely the tendency in today's music), whether they be chords of thirds, fourths, or fifths: the seconds appear in their original form (close position), and the sevenths as their inversion (open position). Insofar as we have the scale itself as a chord in second- and seventh-based harmony, all chordal constructions stem from the scale as its open positions or inversions. This is why Hába concludes: "The principle of the scale forms the basis of all melodic and harmonic constructions. There are no separate constructive laws governing the formation of melody (the scale) and that of harmony (third, fourth, and other systems); instead the scale . . . is the common law for melody and harmony."

Once again, however, the soul-penetration and spiritualization of the musical experience, implied and effectuated by the second-feeling, must be considered in the final analysis only as a transition to what Rudolf Steiner described as the actual future goal of music: acquiring the feeling for the uni-

son, or the octave. And this will bring for the first time a profoundly new revelation of music into the physical realm.
Perhaps this justifies the view that with the feeling of the unison, that is, movement within one and the same tone, we
shall regain in a new form the tone as such, which in a different way was once the starting point for musical evolution.
Through the planetary world, then, we would rise in a new
way in musical experience through the second-feeling. Then
we would reach again the sphere of the zodiac in which the
tones are at home, and indeed from which music originally
descended. But whereas during the fifth- and sixth-experience, the tones only revealed themselves in a specific compass, now, under the rule of the unison, i.e., of the wandering
within oneself, each individual tone will directly reveal its
most personal and profound nature. Just as the spiritual nature of man once descended from celestial heights together
with music, it will be once again transported to that world in
the coming musical ascent, together with the free and independent humanity acquired on earth. However, since it will
reappear as an independent being in that region from which it
once took its leave, it will also rediscover itself there in a
most profound way. This coming to oneself in the return to
one's own primordial native world at a higher stage of development will constitute the octave-experience that will be
linked to the unison-experience or the experience of individual tones. However, in this reattainment of the original world
through the completion of the individual being's evolution
also lies the point of departure for a new evolution. Perhaps
this fact contains the key to understanding Rudolf Steiner's
assertion concerning the experience of the individual tone
and how this will then manifest, namely, that within the individual tone itself a melody will be perceived: a second tone
that refers to the past, and a third tone referring to the future.
In this melody that will spring forth from the single tone, it
will be revealed that at the height of this attainment man is
immersed in a world element in which simultaneously his
memory is connected to a past evolution, while his creative
urge is impelled toward a future evolution. Perhaps we can

perceive at least an inkling of this in Anton Webern's attempt to discover a "tone-melody" in the individual tone.

Let us now reiterate what we have said about the future experience of melody and the related changes in the whole musical experience, with a statement made by Rudolf Steiner during a question-and-answer session at the end of a course for teachers in the Goetheanum, Dornach, January 5, 1922: "For a variety of reasons I am of the opinion that music will experience a kind of evolution that I would like to call intensive melody. This intensive melody will consist in becoming accustomed to experiencing what we consider today a single tone as a kind of melody. One will then become used to a greater complexity of the single tone. And once this takes place, it will result in the modification of our scale, for the simple reason that the intervals will be fulfilled in a different way than has been done until now. And once again on this very path one will find access to certain elements of what I would like to call primordial music [Urmusik], of which I think I recognize a very important manifestation in the modes discovered by Miss Schlesinger. I believe there is certainly an opportunity there to enrich the musical experience and to arrive at certain things that will overcome that which has entered music through the more or less—I would say— accidental scales that we have."[13]

Whoever feels that the above explanation of the musical experience as characterized by the second- and unison- (or octave-) experience goes too far should also bear in mind what Rudolf Steiner said at the same time about the content that will be embodied in this future music. It will no longer consist of merely earthly concerns, as they now fill the soul in the body from birth to death and as have been fashioned overwhelmingly by the third-dominated music of recent centuries. It will rather consist of experiences such as those that occur on the inner path of evolution leading the soul outward to experience the extraterrestrial worlds, their spiritual beings, and their formative effects on the body. The object of the musical art—and the future of musical creation in particular above all the other arts—will be to represent the inner changes that the human soul has to undergo on the path of initiation. In the lecture, "Impulses Toward Transformation for the Artistic Evolution of Mankind,"[14] are the following words, with which we close: "If one day man could totally experience what can be portrayed with regard to the path of initiation in such a way that he experienced both exaltations and profound disappointments at seeing what the soul must go through, then his soul might be profoundly shaken: so shaken that in its participation in the destinies of all the beings that live an extra-human existence and in the events of the cosmos, it would feel within itself convulsions, deprivations, and redemptions that may come to expression in tone-relationships when the soul, stimulated by the experience of the depiction of the initiation path, feels compelled to do so . . . In the future there will be people who will feel the depiction of the initiation path. They will feel that an intense experience lies in what seems to be quite abstract for us, far more intense than would be the case for our external physical experience. For those natures who sense the truth of the things depicted on the path of initiation, a moment will come when they say to themselves: 'now I feel that what I am experiencing is bringing me in touch not with the nature within which I stand while on this earth, but with that which is interwoven and lived through in the cosmos. O, I cannot merely experience it all, but I can sing it, I can compose it.' "

Notes

1. These lectures are translated by Maria St. Goar in *The Inner Nature of Music and the Experience of Tone* (Spring Valley, N.Y., Anthroposophical Press, 1983). The first edition of Lauer's book (1935) began at this point. Ed.
2. See Rudolf Steiner, *Unsere atlantischen Vorfahren* (Berlin, 1920).
3. "If one tries to summarize the characteristic traits from which the picture of primitive music is put together, one could well say that the most prominent feature is this: as far as the tonal material is concerned, the use of one or a few tones, one tone or phrase recurring again and again with tiring monotony . . . It was the observation of this typical occur-

rence that already caused the English music historian John Frederic Rowbotham to assume different developmental epochs of primitive and archaic music, distinguished through the number of tones used: the first epoch used one or two, the next three or four, etc." (G. Adler, *Handbuch der Musikgeschichte*, Frankfurt a. M., 1924, p. 3).

4. Cf. the article of Heinrich Ziemann on "Polaritäten-Metamorphose in der Tonskalen-Bildung," in *Jahrbuch Gäa-Sophia* (Dresden, Emil Weises Buchhandlung), vol. 2 (1927), pp. 413 ff.

5. Examples of this are given by H. Helmholtz in his *Lehre von den Tonempfindungen*, 4th ed., 1877, pp. 429 ff. (English translation by A. J. Ellis, *On the Sensation of Tone*, N.Y., Dover, 1954, pp. 250 ff. Ed.)

6. See Rudolf Steiner, *Occult Science*, trans. H. B. Monges (London and New York, 1949, pp. 98 ff).

7. See Helmholtz, *op. cit.*, p. 396; Engl. ed., p. 241.

8. See Ernst Bindel, *Die Zahlengrundlagen der Musik im Wandel der Zeiten*, vol. 1 (Stuttgart, 1950), pp. 31 ff.

9. Cf. Hermann Beckh, *Das geistige Wesen der Tonarten* (Breslau, 1923).

10. For this interpretation of temperament I am grateful to Alois Hába of Prague.

11. See Hans Georg Burghardt, *Das Melodische im Stilwanderl deutscher Musik* (Breslau, 1934).

12. A. Hába, *Neue Harmonielehre* (Leipzig, 1927).

13. Published in the journal *Die Menschenschule*, 1950, no. 4/5.

14. Published as vol. I of the series *Kunst im Lichte der Mysterienweisheit*.

APPENDIX
AND
INDEX

JOHANNES KEPLER

In order to appreciate Rudolph Haase's articles on "Kepler's World Harmony and its Significance for Today" and "The Sequel to Kepler's World Harmony," it will be helpful for the reader to have at hand some of his original source material: Kepler's own writings on cosmic harmony. Extracts are given here from Kepler's *Mysterium Cosmographicum* (Tübingen, 1596) and *Harmonices Mundi Libri V* (Linz, 1619). The source for these translations from the Latin (for which the editor is responsible, as well as the explanatory notes) is: Johannes Kepler, *Gesammelte Werke*, ed. Max Caspar, vol. I (Munich, C. H. Beck, 1938), pp. 39–43, and vol. VI (1940), pp. 104–107, 317–323. Caspar's German translations were also consulted; *Mysterium Cosmographicum: Das Weltgeheimnis* (Augsburg, Filser, 1923), and *Harmonices Mundi: Weltharmonik* (Munich and Berlin, Oldenbourg, 1939). For a detailed commentary and evaluation of Kepler's and other theories of planetary music, see the editor's *Harmonies of Heaven and Earth* (London, Thames and Hudson; Rochester, Vt., Inner Traditions, 1987).

Mysterium Cosmographicum (1596)

CHAPTER 12 *The division of the Zodiac and the aspects*
Many people consider the division of the Zodiac into exactly twelve signs a human invention, unsupported by any natural phenomenon. They believe that these divisions do not differ in natural force or influence, but that they are merely made because the number is suitable for calculation. While I do not entirely disagree with them, in order not to reject something out of hand I would suggest, on the grounds of this division, a reason why the Creator may have disposed these qualities (if indeed they do have distinct ones).

We have seen above what the object of numbers is. To be sure, without quantity, or something that is like quantity and endowed with a certain power, nothing in the whole universe can be numbered except God, who is the Holy Trinity itself. Now, therefore, we have sectioned all bodies by means of the Zodiac. We shall see what the Zodiac itself has attained or suffered by this sectioning. By sectioning in the aforesaid way the cube and octahedron, a square will result; from the pyramid a triangle; and from the other two figures a decagon. 4 × 3 × 10 makes 120. Therefore when a square, a triangle, and a decagon are inscribed in a circle, starting from the same point, they will mark off various arcs on the circumference, all of which are measured by a portion no greater than the 120th part of the whole circle. Thus the natural division of the Zodiac into 120 arises from the regular placement of the solids between the orbits. Since three times this is 360, we see that this division is in no way irrational. Now if we inscribe a square and a triangle separately, starting from the same point, the smallest arc will be 1/12 of the circumference, namely one sign. And it is remarkable that both the monthly movement of the sun and moon and the great conjunctions of the outer planets[1] so nearly fit the arcs which are determined by the same solids through the triangle and the square.

Furthermore, you can see from another example how highly nature prizes this twelvefold division; for although the cause is not known, it gives occasion to learn more about these five figures. Take a string tuned to G. As many notes as are consonant with G between it and the higher octave (g), so many divisions can one make in the string in which the parts are consonant both with each other and with the whole. The ear will tell how many such notes there are. I will give them in notation and numbers:

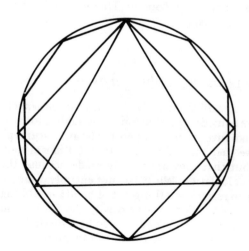

You will now see both those harmonies and the proportions of string lengths in numbers: the lower note represents the note of the entire string; the upper one, the shorter portion; the middle one, the longer portion. The largest number indicates in how many parts the string is to be divided; the others, the length of the portions.

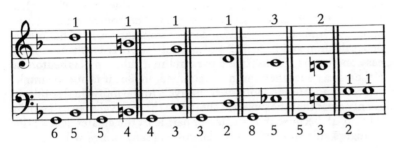

And these notes seem to me the only natural ones, because they have definite numbers. The other notes cannot be expressed in exact (*certa*) proportion to the ones already given. For the note F is different, depending on whether you reach it from C above or from B-flat below, although these both seem to be perfect fifths. But to resume: the first and second consonances are, as it were, neighbors: thus, too, the fifth and sixth. For they are all imperfect,[2] and so always unite in pairs—one major and one minor—as if to resemble the single and perfect ones. Their ratios are also not very different. For 1/6 and 1/5 are to one another as 5/30 and 6/30, differing by only 1/30. Similarly, 3/8 and 2/5 are to one another as 15/40 to 16/40, and therefore differ by only 1/40. And thus properly speaking we have only five consonances in music, the same as the number of solids.[3] Now if one seeks the lowest common multiple of 6, 5, 4, 3, 8, 5, 2, one will again find 120, as we did above when treating the division of the Zodiac; but the lowest multiple of the perfect consonances is again 12. It is just as though the perfect consonances came from the square and triangle of the cube, tetrahedron and octahedron, the imperfect from the decagon[4] of the other two solids. This is the second correspondence of the solids with the musical consonances. But since we do not know the causes of this correspondence, it is difficult to accommodate the individual intervals to individual solids.

We see, indeed, two orders of chords, three simple and perfect, and two duplex and imperfect; likewise three primary solids and two secondary ones. But since the rest does not agree, we must give up this relationship and try another. Just as the dodecahedron and icosahedron above increased the 12 to 120 through their decagon, so here the imperfect harmonies do likewise.

Let therefore the perfect consonances correspond with the cube, pyramid, and octahedron, and the imperfect to the dodecahedron and icosahedron. Then something else occurs which, to be sure, points a finger at the deeply hidden cause of these things (which we will discuss in the next chapter): for there are two treasures in geometry: one, the ratio of the hypotenuse to the side of a right-angled triangle; the other, the Golden Section. The construction of the cube, pyramid, and octahedron derives from the former, that of the dodecahedron and icosahedron from the latter. This is why it is so easy and regular to inscribe a pyramid in a cube, an octahedron in either, or a dodecahedron in an icosahedron. But it is not so simple to accommodate the individual intervals to the individual solids. It is only clear that the pyramid should be the interval they call a fifth (our no. 4), because in it the lesser part is 1/3 the greater, just as the triangle's side subtends 1/3 of the circle. Many things will confirm this when we treat the aspects below; but to understand it here we must imagine that the string is not a straight line but a circle. The said interval will therefore be given by a triangle whose angle opposes the side as the corner of a pyramid opposes the surface. For the cube and octahedron, then, the octave and fourth remain (our nos. 3 and 7). But which of them supports which interval? Or should we say that the secondary figures contain the intervals which lead to straight lines, the primary ones those which lead to figures? Then the cube would be the fourth. For if you make a circle of the string, and draw a line from one quarter to another until you return to the same point, you will make a square—which also arises from the cube. To the octahedron will correspond the octave, which is half the string. For if one divides the circle in two and joins the points of division, one will only have a line. So the dodecahedron will be the first double imperfect consonance. For if a circle is divided in five and six, the pentagon and hexagon will result. The icosahedron remains as the second double imperfect consonance, since only lines result when one joins points of 2/5 of the circle apart until one returns to the starting point. It is the same when joining points 3/8 of the circumference apart. Or would we rather give the octahedron the fourth, since its edges quarter the circle twelve times, as no cube's edge does? Thus the cube would be left for the octave, the most perfect interval, just as it is the most perfect solid. Perhaps it is also more accurate to give the icosahedron the first imperfect conso-

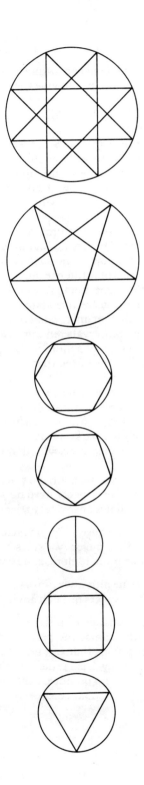

nance on account of the hexagon, which is closer to its triangular surfaces than the pentagon, but to give the dodecahedron the eight-fold division because of the cubic number 8, since the cube can be inscribed in the dodecahedron. All this is in the balance, until someone can find the causes.

Let us now look at the aspects.[5] Since we have already made a cir-cle of the string, it is easy to see how the three perfect consonances can be compared beautifully with the three perfect aspects; opposi-tion, trine and square. The first imperfect consonance, B-flat, is very close to the sextile, which is said to be the weakest aspect.

Thus we have a reason (such as Ptolemy did not give) why planets separated by one or five signs are not counted as being in aspect. For as we have seen, nature knows of no such concords in tones. Since in the other cases the ratios of influence and interval are the same, it is credible that it is the same here. Without a doubt both have the same cause, to be sought in the five solids: but I leave the seeking to others. Since, then, all four intervals concord with their aspects, while in fact three more intervals remain in music, I once suspected that in judging a nativity one should not neglect planets 72°, 144°, or 135° apart, especially since I see that one of the imperfect conso-nances has its aspect. It will soon be obvious to any observer of me-teorological phenomena whether these three rays contain any power, since constant experiments confirm the changes of the atmo-sphere   under   the   other   aspects.   The   causes which one may plausibly adduce for the fact that 3/8, 1/5, and 2/5 sound on the string but do not operate in the Zodiac may be as follows:[7]

1   One opposition, two squares, a trine plus a sextile each make a semicircle: but these three aspects have no kinship with this func-tion which music would not absolutely reject.[6]

2   The remaining aspects have a simple rational from the diameter, while the one subtending one or two sides of a pentagon or three of an octagon are one step more remote, and irrational.

3   Another cause: a trine plus a sextile, a square plus a square, make a right angle: the other aspects no such angle with any accepted line.

4   The imperfect consonance of B-flat is in a way perfect, since it possesses the same division as the perfect ones, and is half a fifth. Therefore it is not surprising that among the imperfect consonances it alone corresponds to any aspect, namely the sextile, which itself is half the trine. The others do not fit the twelvefold division, nor are parts of any perfect consonance.

5   Finally, six angles of a trine, four of a square, three of a sextile, and the space enclosed in two semicircles fill the whole area of the plane. But three angles of a pentagon are less than four right angles, while four are more. So it is also clear from this why neither the aspect of an octagon, nor that of a decagon, nor any other is efficacious.

And here I would separate the causes of aspects from those of harmony. Certainly a reason drawn from angles is true of aspects, since they work on account of the angle made on a point on the earth's surface at which they meet, not because of their configuration on the circle of the Zodiac, which exists rather in the imagination than in reality. Now the division of a string is not made on a circle, nor does it use angles, but is done on a plane with a straight line. Nevertheless, concords and aspects may have something in common, since, as we have said, they both have the same cause. I leave it to the industry of others to investigate them.[7]

Notes to Kepler, Mysterium Cosmographicum

1. Sun: one sign a month; Moon: whole Zodiac each month; conjunctions of Saturn and Jupiter: every fourth sign.
2. In the theoretical terms of Kepler's time, "perfect" consonances were the octave, fifth, and fourth; "imperfect" ones the thirds and sixths.
3. The five "Platonic" or regular solids: tetrahedron or "pyramid", cube, octahedron, icosahedron, and dodecahedron.
4. These are the plane figures needed to generate the respective solids geometrically.
5. The aspects and intervals under discussion are:

Opposition	180°	Octave 2:1	G - g
Quincunx	150°	no interval	
Biquintile	144°	Ma. sixth 5:3	G - e♮
Sesquiquadrate	135°	Mi. sixth 8:5	G - e♭
Trine	120°	Fifth 3:2	G - d
Square	90°	Fourth 4:3	G - c
Quintile	72°	Ma. third 5:4	G - B♮
Sextile	60°	Mi. third 6:5	G - B♭
Semisquare	45°	no interval	
Semisextile	30°	no interval	
Conjunction	0°	Unison 1:1	G - G

6. One cannot add intervals as one can aspects: two squares, or a trine plus a sextile, make an opposition; but two fourths do not make an octave,

neither do a fifth and a minor third. Herein lies the snag in trying to compare the arithmetically divided circle of the Zodiac with the logarithmically divided string. Kepler recognizes this, in a way, at the end of this chapter, and wisely leaves it to others to push the analogies to absurdity.

7. Marin Mersenne, in *Harmonie Universelle* (Paris, 1636), gave an even fuller table of possible interval-aspect correspondence, but rejected the one as explaining the other.

Harmonices Mundi (1619), Book V

CHAPTER 5   *In the proportions of the apparent planetary motions (as if for observers on the sun) are expressed the steps of the system of the notes of the musical scale, as well as the major and minor modes.*

Since therefore harmonic proportions exist between these twelve *termini* or motions of the six planets circling the sun upward and downward, (or at least intervals that approach these by an imperceptible difference), we have proved what was posited in numbers on the one hand by Astronomy, on the other by Harmonics. We first elicited in the third book the single harmonic proportions one by one in Chapter 1, then in Chapter 2 compiled every one of them into a common system or musical scale, or rather divided one of them, the octave, which embraces in its power the rest, into its degrees or steps by means of the others, so that a scale arose.[1] Now having formed the harmonies which God himself has incorporated into the world, we shall see whether they stand singular and separate, none having a relationship with the others, or whether in truth they all fit together. Certainly it is simple to conclude, without further investigation, that these harmonies are fitted one to another with the greatest ingenuity, as if they were parts of a single assemblage, so that none oppresses another. In all our manifold comparison of the same terms we see that harmonies never fail to arise. But unless all things were fitted together in one scale, it could easily happen (and here and there it necessarily has happened) that many dissonances should exist. If, for example, one were to put a major sixth between the first and second terms, and between the second and third a major third, without respect to the first, one would admit the dissonant and unmelodious interval of 12:25 between the first and the third.

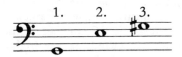

Let us see whether what we have now learned by reasoning is found in reality. We would, however, issue some cautions so as not to impede our progress. First, we must for the present ignore those excesses or defects which are smaller than a semitone: what their cause is, we shall see afterward.[2] Next, we shall reduce everything to the system of one octave by means of the doubling and halving of motions,[3] because of the identical nature of every octave.

The numbers which express all the steps or notes of the octave system are shown in a table in Book III, Chapter 8, folio 47:[4] these numbers are to be understood as lengths of two strings. Consequently the speeds of the motions will be in inverse proportion to one another.[5]

Let us now consider the movements of the planets in the fractions which arise after repeated halving. They are as follows:

[Diurnal] Motion

of Mercury at Perihelion	divided by	2^7 or	128	3′ 0″
of Mercury at Aphelion	″	″ 2^6 or	64	2′ 34″ −
of Venus at Perihelion	″	″ 2^5 or	32	3′ 3″ +
of Venus at Aphelion	″	″ 2^5 or	32	2′ 58″ −
of Earth at Perihelion	″	″ 2^5 or	32	1′ 55″ −
of Earth at Aphelion	″	″ 2^5 or	32	1′ 47″ −
of Mars at Perihelion	″	″ 2^4 or	16	2′ 23″ −
of Mars at Aphelion	″	″ 2^3 or	8	3′ 17″ −
of Jupiter at Perihelion	″	″ 2		2′ 45″
of Jupiter at Aphelion	″	″ 2		2′ 15″
of Saturn at Perihelion				2′ 15″
of Saturn at Aphelion				1′ 46″

Now let the slowest motion at the aphelion of the slowest planet, Saturn, represent the lowest note G of the system, within the number 1′ 46″. The same step will also represent the aphelion of Earth, only five octaves higher (for who would argue about 1″ difference from the motion of Saturn's aphelion? The difference would be no more than 106:107, which is less than a comma). If one adds to this 1′ 47″ a quarter, i.e., 27″, it makes 2′ 14″, while the perihelion of Saturn is 2′ 15″ and Jupiter's aphelion the same, but an octave higher. Therefore these two motions represent the note B, or a very little higher. If one takes from 1′ 47″ a third, i.e., 36″ −, and adds it to the whole, it will make 2′ 23″ − for the note C: and here is the perihelion of Mars, the same magnitude except four octaves higher. Add to the same 1′ 47″ its half, 54″ −, making 2′ 41″ − for the note D, and just here is the perihelion of Jupiter, only an octave higher: it is very close in value, namely 2′ 45″. If one adds two thirds, i.e., 1′ 11″ +, they make 2′ 58″ − :

and look, the aphelion of Venus is 2' 58" − . So this represents the step or note E, but five octaves higher; and the perihelion of Mercury is not much more, being 3' 0", but seven octaves higher. Lastly, divided twice 1' 47", i.e., 3' 34", by nine, and subtract one part of 24" from the whole, leaving 3' 10" + for the note F, which represents nearly the aphelion of Mars, 3' 17", but three octaves higher; this number is a little larger, approaching the note F#. For 1/16 of 3' 34", namely 13½", subtracted from 3' 34" leaves 3' 20½", which is very close to 3' 17". In fact in music the note F# is often used in place of F, as one can see everywhere.

Thus all the notes of the major mode are represented within one octave (except for the note A, which was also not represented by harmonic divisions in Book III, Ch. 2)[6] by all the extreme motions of the planets except for the perihelions of Venus and Earth and the aphelion of Mercury, whose value of 2' 34" approaches the note C#. For taking from D, whose number is 2' 41", the sixteenth part, 10" + , there remain 2' 30", the note C#: therefore only the perihelions of Venus and Earth are absent from this scale, as can be seen in this table.

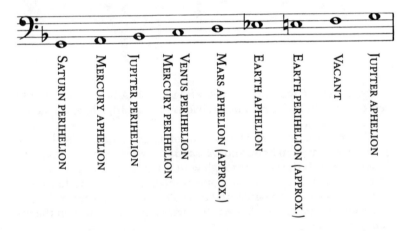

If, on the other hand, one begins the scale with the motion of Saturn at perihelion, 2' 15", and makes that represent the note G, then the note A will be 2' 32", which closely approaches the aphelion of Mercury; the note B-flat will be 2' 42", which is very nearly the perihelion of Jupiter, following the equivalency of octaves; the note C will be 3' 0", nearly the perihelion of Mercury and Venus; the note D will be 3' 23"− which is only a little deeper than the aphelion of Mars, i.e., 3' 18", so that its number here is as much less than its note as it was formerly more than it. The note E♭ will be 3′ 36″, which approaches closely the aphelion of Earth; the note E will be 3′ 50″, while the perihelion of Earth is 3′ 49″. Jupiter in aphelion takes G again.

In this way all the notes within one octave of the minor mode, except F, are expressed by most of the planetary motions in aphelion and perihelion, especially those which were formerly left out, as can be seen in this table.

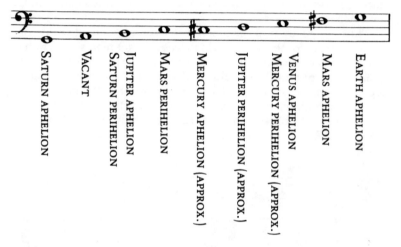

Previously F# was specified, A left out. Now A is specified, but F# left out; and in the harmonic divisions of Book III, Ch. 2, the note F was also left out.

The musical scale or the system of a single octave is thus expressed in heaven in a twofold way, and as it were in the two melodic modes, with all the steps through which a natural [diatonic] melody moves in music. There is only one difference: that in our harmonic divisions both ways begin with one and the same G, whereas here in the planetary motions what was formerly B now becomes, in the minor mode, G.

IN THE HEAVENLY MOTIONS:

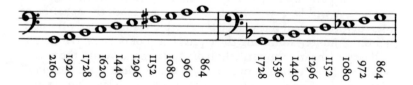

THROUGH HARMONIC DIVISIONS:

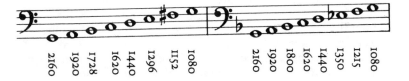

For just as in music 2160 is to 1800 as 6 to 5, even so in the system which represents the heavens 1728 is to 1440 as 6 to 5, and so with many others:

$$2160 \text{ to } 1800 : 1620 : 1440 : 1350 : 1080$$
$$\text{as } 1728 \text{ to } 1440 : 1296 : 1152 : 1080 : 1864$$

Now one will no longer be surprised that man has formed this most excellent order of notes or steps into the musical system or scale, since one can see that in this matter he acts as nothing but the ape of God the Creator, playing, as it were, a drama about the order of celestial motions.

There remains one other way in which we can understand the twofold musical scale in the heavens.[7] The system here is the same, but the tuning is conceived as double: one to the motions of Venus at aphelion, the other at perihelion. For the motions of this planet vary the least, being contained within a diesis, the smallest of intervals. And the tuning at aphelion, as above, has the aphelion motions of Saturn, Earth, Venus, and Jupiter (approximately) as G, E, and B; the perihelion of Mars and Saturn (approximately) and, as appears at first sight, also Mercury, as C, E, and B. The perihelion tuning, on the other hand, gives the aphelions of Mars, Mercury, and Jupiter (approximately), the perihelions of Jupiter, Venus, and Saturn (approximately); in a certain respect also the Earth's, and doubtless Mercury's too. For now that it is not the aphelion of Venus but its perihelion of 3′ 3″ that occupies the step of E, the perihelion of Mercury at 3′ 0″ approaches it most closely, two octaves away, as was observed toward the end of chapter 4. And subtracting from this perihelion of Venus, 3′ 3″, a tenth, 18″, we are left with 2′ 45″, the perihelion of Jupiter, providing the step D. And adding a fifteenth, 12″, makes 3′ 15″, nearly the aphelion of Mars, providing the step F. Similarly, at the step B of this tuning there follow nearly the movements of Saturn in perihelion and of Jupiter in aphelion. But if one subtracts an eighth, 23″, five times, it gives 1′ 55″ which is the perihelion of Earth. Admittedly, this does not square with the previous ones in the same scale (since this does not contain the intervals 5:8 below E and 24:25 above G). But if, outside this order, one gives the perihelion of Venus and also the aphelion of Mercury the step E^b instead of E, then this perihelion of Earth will take the step G. The aphelion movement of Mercury will also agree with this, since a third of 3′ 3″, 1′ 1″, multiplied by five, makes 5′ 5″, whose half, 2′ 32″ +, comes very close to the aphelion of Mercury, which in this extraordinary arrangement will take the step C. Thus all these motions relate within one and the same tuning. But the perihelion of Venus divides the scale in another way; the first three (or five) are in the same mode as in the aphelion tuning, i.e., in the major, but with the last two motions it divides the scale in another way, not into different intervals but into a different order of intervals: one proper to the minor mode.

This chapter has sufficed to make the matter in question visible. But the reasons why everything has been made thus, and what are the causes not only of so much agreement but also of disagreement in details, will appear with the clearest proof in chapter 9.[8]

CHAPTER 6   *The musical modes or tones are somehow expressed in the extreme planetary motions.*

This follows from the above, and requires few words. The individual planets in a way represent, by their movement at perihelion,[9] the individual steps of the system, in that it is given to each one to traverse a certain interval in the musical scale, lying between certain notes or steps of the system. Each begins from the note or step which in the previous chapter was assigned to its aphelion motion: Saturn and Earth had G, Jupiter B, which may be transposed higher to G, Mars F#, Venus E, Mercury A in a higher system. (See the individual planets in the usual notation.) They do not form the intermediate steps which one sees here filled out as notes in an articulate way, like the extremes, for they move from one extreme to the other not by leaps or intervals but by a continuous rising or falling, touching on all the intermediate notes, potentially infinite in number.[10] I could express this in no other way than by a continuous series of intermediate notes. Venus remains almost in unison, since the range of its rising is not equal even to the smallest of melodic intervals.[11]

Now the specification of two of the common system of notes, and the formation of an octave framework by setting up a certain harmonic interval, is in a way the first means of distinguishing scales or modes. Thus the modes of music are distributed among the planets. (I know of course that more things are required for the formation and

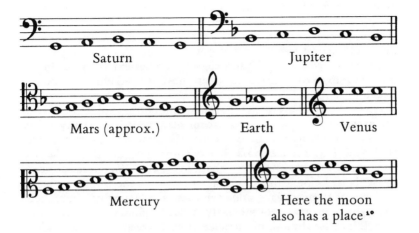

Saturn   Jupiter

Mars (approx.)   Earth   Venus

Mercury   Here the moon
                          also has a place [10]

definition of the different modes, such as are proper for human melodies proceeding by intervals; hence I used the term "in a way.")

The harmonist will be free to form his own opinion as to which planet best expresses which mode by the extremes here assigned to it. Of the modes commonly used I would assign Saturn the 7th or 8th, because if one puts G as its keynote, its motion at perihelion rises to B; Jupiter the 1st or 2nd, because if its motion at aphelion is aligned with G, its perihelion reaches B-flat;[12] Mars the 5th or 6th, not only because it covers about a fifth (for this interval is common to all the modes) but mainly because when reduced to a uniform system with all the others its motion at perihelion reaches C, at aphelion approaches F, the keynote of the 5th and 6th tone or mode. To Earth I would give the 3rd or 4th, since its movement oscillates within a semitone, and the first interval of these modes is a semitone. Nearly all the tones and modes would suit Mercury equally, because of the width of its interval; Venus, because of the narrowness of its interval, would suit none, unless it were the 3rd and 4th of the common system, because in respect to the other planets it occupies the step E. (The Earth sings Mi-Fa-Mi, from which syllables you can infer that MIsery and FAmine obtain in this our home.)

CHAPTER 7   *There are universal harmonies of all six planets, similar to common four-part counterpart.*

Now, Urania, let it sound louder, as I ascend to the heights by the harmonic scale of the celestial motions, where the tones and secret archetype of the world's making are preserved. Follow me, you musicians of today, and judge the matter by your arts, unknown to antiquity. In these last centuries, after two thousand years in the womb, ever-prodigal nature has finally produced you to give the first true image of the universe.[13] Through your counterpoints of many voices and through your ears she has suggested what exists in her innermost bosom to the human intellect, most beloved child of God the Creator.

I have shown above which harmonic proportions obtain between the extreme motions of two adjacent planets. It is certainly a very rare thing for two of them, especially the slowest ones, to coincide with their extreme intervals. The conjunctions [apsides] of Saturn and Jupiter, for example, occur about 81° apart.[14] Therefore 800 years must elapse before this aspect has run through the whole Zodiac in its leaps of twenty years; and even then, the leap which concludes the eighth century is not precisely on the original point of conjunction. If it misses by a short distance, it will take another 800 years to see if a happier leap is to be expected from one's reckoning; and this will be repeated so many times that the quantity of aberration will amount to half a leap in length. Similar periods, though not so long, also occur in the various other planet pairs. In the meantime, however, other harmonies have occurred between the two planets: not between their extreme motions but with one or both of them in intermediate position, as if in different tunings. For Saturn is tuned from G to B and a little higher, and Jupiter from B to D and a little more: so between Saturn and Jupiter there can occur both kinds of thirds and a fourth (all plus an octave). The thirds can each be sounded over a range equal to the other,[15] but the fourth only over a whole tone, i.e., from the G of Saturn and the C of Jupiter to the A of Saturn to the D of Jupiter, and in between at all pitches from G to A and from C to D. But the octave and the fifth only occur at the extreme points. Mars, whose own interval is higher, has the property of making an octave with the higher planets within a certain tuning range. Mercury has received such a wide interval that in one of its revolutions, lasting no more than three months, it usually makes all the harmonies with all of the others. Earth, on the other hand, and Venus even more so, have narrow intervals which restrict them in their harmonies not only with the other planets but especially with each other, to a remarkably limited degree.[16]

If three planets are to coincide with the same harmony, one must wait for many revolutions. These harmonies, however, are very numerous, and occur all the more easily as one follows closely on its neighbor. It seems, too, that three-part harmonies occur somewhat more often between Mars, Earth, and Mercury. Four-part harmonies of the planets already begin to be scattered over centuries; five-part

ones over myriads of years. The cases of all six harmonizing are separated by immensely long periods. I even think it may be impossible
for this to have occurred twice by precise evolution: such a harmony
may rather indicate the beginning of time, from which the whole
age of the world proceeds.

If there were only a single six-part harmony, or one outstanding
among others, we could doubtless regard it as the constellation of
the Creation. The question is, therefore, how many ways the motions of all six planets can be reduced to a single mutual harmony.[17]

Notes to Kepler, Harmonices Mundi

1. He refers to the exposition of the harmonic division of strings, and the
    way in which the possible harmonic divisions within the octave form
    an almost complete scale. The term "harmonic division" is taken not in
    its strict mathematical sense, but to mean the division already used in
    our extract from *Mysterium Cosmographicum* in which the two result-
    ing parts of the string are consonant both with the whole string and
    with each other. Such divisions are those into 1 + 1, 2 + 1, 3 + 1, 4 + 1, 5 + 1,
    3 + 2, and 5 + 3, giving (with the whole string tuned to G) the "scale" G,
    B♭, B , C, D, E♭, E , G.
2. He refers to the forthcoming discussion in his chapter 7–9 (not trans-
    lated here) of the possible harmonies between two and more planets, in
    which intervals too small for melodic use become important in order to
    make pure tunings of one kind and another.
3. An important principle of harmonics, which assumes that because of
    octave equivalences any number representing a tone can be halved or
    doubled any number of times for purposes of comparison. Therefore
    every note/number whatsoever can theoretically be brought within a
    single octave space.
4.

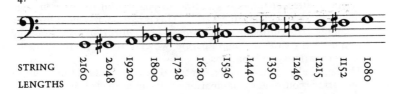

| STRING | 2160 | 2048 | 1920 | 1800 | 1728 | 1620 | 1536 | 1440 | 1350 | 1246 | 1215 | 1152 | 1080 |
| LENGTHS | | | | | | | | | | | | | |

5. I.e., the slowest motion, that of Saturn at aphelion, will correspond to
    the longest string length, that of low G.
6. See note 1. The harmonic division of a string tuned to G at A, giving the
    proportions 8 + 1, produces discords. So does the division at F (see be-
    low). There is nothing surprising in this: A and F are each a dissonant
    whole tone away from G. But Kepler was struck by the coincidence
    when he came to construct his planetary scales.

7. Just as he had given two different scales starting from the two extreme positions of Saturn, now he shows how the two scales tuned from Venus' extreme positions each involve consonances with different planets.

8. This is the chapter in which the exact intervals between planets are calculated at length.

9. "From aphelion to perihelion" would be more accurate, since it is now not the extreme motions/notes that are in question but the differences between them.

10. Kepler is describing what is now called a glissando.

11. The moon does not enter into the planetary harmony. Its music is presumably calculated from the point of view of the Earth, not from that of the sun, as the others are.

12. The 7th and 8th modes have their final on G and begin with a major third, G A B: the 1st and 2nd have their final on D and begin with a minor third, D E F. Hence their assignment to the planets which cover respectively a major and minor third. But on this basis Saturn could just as well be given the 5th and 6th (F G A, etc.) and Jupiter the 3rd and 4th (E F G, etc.)

13. Kepler is referring to the invention, unknown to the ancients, of polyphonic music which best reflects the situation in the heavens.

14. If Saturn and Jupiter both start from 1° Aries, they will not coincide again until they meet at about 9° Capricorn, approximately twenty years later, when Saturn has gone most of the way round the Zodiac once, Jupiter nearly twice. The intervals between successive grand conjunctions (as these conjunctions between the two slowest Chaldean planets are called) are what Kepler describes as "leaps." 800 years, i.e., 40 leaps, are needed for the 81° separating conjunctions and the 360° of the Zodiac to reach a common multiple ($81 \times 40 = 360 \times 9 = 3240$). But 81° is an average, not an invariable or exact distance, so the eventuality very seldom occurs with theoretical tidiness.

15. The minor third can occur anywhere between G, B-flat and B, D; the major between G, B and B-flat, D.

16. Later in the chapter Kepler describes the relationship of Earth and Venus in picturesque terms as a marital one, oscillating from the "masculine" G# – E to the "feminine" G – E. This is particularly audible on the recording *The Harmony of the World"—A Realization for the Ear* (LP 1571) by Willie Ruff and John Rodgers, which synthesizes these planet songs in various combinations.

17. The remainder of this chapter, not translated here, sets out in columns the various consonant combinations that can be made from the whole range of pitches available to each planet, e.g., Saturn—G, Jupiter – B, Mars – G, Earth – G, Venus – E, Mercury – E. Kepler finds four possible six-part chords, each in various spacings, and four other five-part ones if Venus is omitted.

INDEX